EXTRA-PLANETARY
EXPERIENCES

"Through his thorough analysis of 'extra-planetary experiences,' Thomas Streicher successfully prepares the ground for deeper questioning: Are they merely significant as subjective experiences, or are they also objectively real? This book shows that we should not dismiss these experiential reports."

JÜRGEN W. KREMER, PH.D.,
EXECUTIVE EDITOR OF *REVISION:*
JOURNAL OF CONSCIOUSNESS AND TRANSFORMATION

"Employing academic scholarship, detailed documentation, human curiosity, and humane compassion, Thomas Streicher provides the results of his investigations of persons who describe their encounters with extraterrestrials and their experiences on other planetary civilizations."

R. LEO SPRINKLE, PH.D.,
COUNSELING PSYCHOLOGIST AND
PROFESSOR EMERITUS AT THE
UNIVERSITY OF WYOMING

EXTRA-PLANETARY EXPERIENCES

EXPERIENCES

Alien-Human Contact
and the
Expansion of Consciousness

THOMAS JAMES STREICHER, PH.D.

Bear & Company
Rochester, Vermont • Toronto, Canada

Bear & Company
One Park Street
Rochester, Vermont 05767
www.BearandCompanyBooks.com

Text stock is SFI certified

Bear & Company is a division of Inner Traditions International

Library of Congress Cataloging-in-Publication Data
Streicher, Thomas James.
  Extra-planetary experiences : alien-human contact and the expansion of
consciousness / Thomas James Streicher.
      p. cm.
  Summary: "A rigorous scientific investigation into the veracity of accounts of
travel to other planets, moons, and stars"— Provided by publisher.
  Includes bibliographical references and index.
  ISBN 978-1-59143-136-7 (pbk.) — ISBN 978-1-59143-894-6 (e-book)
  1. Human-alien encounters. 2. Alien abduction. 3. Extraterrestrial beings.
4. Consciousness. I. Title.
  BF2050.S756 2012
  001.942—dc23

                                                                    2011047998

Printed and bound in the United States by Lake Book Manufacturing
The text stock is SFI certified. The Sustainable Forestry Initiative® program
promotes sustainable forest management.

10 9 8 7 6 5 4 3 2 1

Text design by Jon Desautels
Text layout by Virginia Scott Bowman
This book was typeset in Garamond Premier Pro and Gill Sans with Bank Gothic
and Gill Sans used as display typefaces

To send correspondence to the author of this book, mail a first-class letter to the
author c/o Inner Traditions • Bear & Company, One Park Street, Rochester, VT
05767, and we will forward the communication, or contact the author directly at
www.thomasstreicher.com or **tomasstreicher@hotmail.com**.

▼

I dedicate this book to the participants of this study. I acknowledge the pain and suffering they often have endured along with their lifelong devotion to their inner journeys, commitment to UFO/ET phenomena, and realization that they live in a cosmic encompassing spiritual reality. Accounts of unexplained phenomena are typically strange to someone who has not had similar experiences, and as a result many experiencers have not dared speak openly. Centuries ago, when people reported stones falling from the sky, scientific experts at the time claimed that this was impossible. Only after years of resistance was the existence of meteorites accepted. It is through the sacrifices of such pioneers—sometimes in the face of ostracism, ridicule, total disrespect, and even death—that we may envision a new reality.

CONTENTS

PART 1
Exploring the Context of Extra-Planetary Experiences

PART 2
Interviews with Extra-Planetary Explorers

PART 3

Where the Evidence Leads Us

FOREWORD
Stanley Krippner, Ph.D.

Human beings need to explain puzzling events in their lives, thus becoming myth-makers at many levels—cultural, ethnic, familial, and individual. The human brain searches for beliefs and it looks for facts. The resulting personal myths often collide with the prevailing opinion embedded in cultural myths. It is within this framework that I approach the controversy over unidentified flying objects (UFOs). I have discussed UFOs with such celebrated investigators as J. Allen Hynek, John Mack, and Michael Persinger, and I have heard lectures on the topic by Carl Sagan and Philip J. Klass. I have spoken to dozens of people who claim to have seen UFOs, sometimes at close quarters. I have even met a few individuals who claim to have had personal interactions with the inhabitants of UFOs, including "abductions," close scrutiny of their bodily parts, and the implantation of foreign objects in their bodies.

With this orientation, I had an unusual experience in February 1991. The Institute of Noetic Sciences (an organization founded by the astronaut Edgar Mitchell) had asked me to take a group of its members to Brazil in order to visit spiritual communities and folk healers. On February 22, we stayed at a rustic country hotel near Ouro Preto, a historic mining town in the state of Minas Gerais. During our evening meal, a member of our group asked me if I had ever seen a UFO, and I replied negatively. I mentioned that, several years earlier, two friends and I had visited the Valley of the Dawn, a Brazilian spiritual community. During an outdoor meditation session the three of us were sitting in different parts of the auditorium. Immediately after the session, one of my friends—Rolf—came up to me and told me that he had just seen a UFO. He described it as blue, disc-like, with flashing lights on the bottom. He said it was visible for about thirty seconds and then disappeared. A few minutes later, my other friend—Alberto—rushed over to me, asking if I had seen a UFO. I immediately separated him from Rolf, so that he could not hear Rolf's account, and asked for details. Alberto's description was exactly the same as Rolf's, except that his time estimate of the "sighting" was less than ten seconds. Residents of the Valley of the Dawn then told us that they often see UFOs during the afternoon meditation session, especially when music is played.

After relating this account to the group in Ouro Preto and offering several alternative explanations (a collision of space debris, optical illusions, hallucinations, cloud formations), I retired for the night. Within the hour, Shirley, a member of our group, telephoned my room requesting me to step outside to see a UFO. In my haste, I neglected to put on my shoes, and my slippers were scant protection against the rocky terrain as I followed Shirley up a hill where the object could be seen to advantage. By this time, a dozen members of our group had assembled, their attention focused on a distant circular formation of red, yellow, and green lights situated quite high above the horizon. During the hour that it remained visible, it moved neither closer nor farther from us. Its angle above the horizon appeared to remain constant as well. Its size was difficult to estimate, because it was so far away; however, it appeared to be at least four times the usual size of a planet viewed in the evening sky.

Every five or ten minutes, one of the lights would dart from the sphere, pause for a short period of time, and then rejoin the other lights. All the members of our group reported the same details, indicating that, if the sighting was hallucinatory, it must have been a group hallucination.

One by one, I began to eliminate ordinary explanations. It could not be an airplane or weather balloon because its position was stationary. The same characteristic ruled out the possibility of its being a comet, meteor, or earth satellite. The nocturnal timing of its appearance ruled out cloud formations, sun pillars, or ice crystals. Its geographical location eliminated the possibility of the aurora borealis. Ball lightning was unlikely, because the lights twinkled rather than pulsed. The fact that there were several lights counterindicated a planet or a star formation. The stationary nature of the formation did not suggest a group of airplanes; the occasional breaking of the formation by one light was not what one would expect if the circular system had been triggered by temperature inversion or a reflection of ground lights. The formation was too far away to consist of fireflies, birds, or other earthbound organisms, although it was impossible to accurately estimate its distance without additional visual cues.

Some writers influenced by Carl Jung have posited that UFOs might not be actual objects but "mandalas" visualized by people yearning for harmony and equilibrium. However, nobody had told me exactly what I should expect—the UFO had not been described to me before I saw it—and my account tallied with those of people who came outside before and after I had arrived. I cannot deny that all of us would be delighted if there were more harmony in our lives and more equilibrium in the world, but our accounts of this "mandala" seemed to describe exactly the same form.

The circular formation was too far away and too dim to be recorded photographically. But I recall the experience quite clearly, and I continue to discuss it with individuals from time to time, still being willing to entertain ordinary explanations. In the meantime, has this anomalous sighting affected my personal mythology? If anything, it has strengthened three of my personal myths: (1) Science has not provided us with explanations for all of our puzzling experiences. (2) When in doubt, the proper attitude toward an enigmatic situation is open-minded skepticism. (3) It is wise to be tolerant of other people's attempts to make sense out of mysterious events. If their personal myths are not blatantly harmful or malevolent, they can be regarded as viable stories, as attempts to understand perplexing situations. In addition, it is not impossible that one or more of these castings-about in personal myth-making might produce a clue that could eventually explain such an anomaly. Creative products have often reflected an individual vision that later became an ingrained part of the mainstream culture.

Even if these accounts and experiences do not provide evidence of extraterrestrial life forms, they take us deeper into the mysteries of human memory, emotion, and symbol-making—and help us chart the undiscovered realms of our inner worlds.

▼

Stanley Krippner is past president of the Association for Humanistic Psychology and coauthor of the watershed book *Dream Telepathy: Experiments in Nocturnal Extrasensory Perception.* An Alan Watts Professor of Psychology at Saybrook University in San Francisco, Krippner is internationally known for his pioneering work in the investigation of human consciousness, parapsychological phenomena, and altered states of consciousness. He has written hundreds of articles and numerous books including *The Mythic Path, Becoming Psychic,* and *Healing States: A Journey into the World of Spiritual Healing and Shamanism.* Krippner has conducted workshops and seminars worldwide on dreams, hypnosis, and personal mythology. See www.stanleykrippner.weebly.com.

This text was adapted from Stanley Krippner's chapter "An Anomalous Sighting" that appeared in *Zen in the Art of Close Encounters: Crazy Wisdom and UFOs,* edited by Paul David Pursglove.

ACKNOWLEDGMENTS

This work may be considered controversial and one that defies the worldview of certain mainstream authorities and their theories. We should keep in mind that even long-held theories can crumble under the weight of disconfirming evidence. I thank Dr. John Mack, along with Dr. Leo Sprinkle and Dr. Stanley Krippner, for their devotion in helping me complete this task and for launching me into the academic and public worlds.

The publishing of this book brings me to the close of a personal lifelong journey. Like most journeys, it started with the first step. At the time I had no idea in what direction it would take me. The length and difficulty of this journey have been compounded by the actions and stances of adherents of a relentless consensus reality predisposed to pathologize the very core of my being. Although I spent considerable time in agony and despair, I also experienced moments of pure joy obtained through my inner knowing. This discovery acknowledges and honors what I consider to be the benevolent extraterrestrial beings involved in my life journey who have guided me to this end. Sometimes I would like to separate myself from this personal belief, but perhaps it has been helpful in setting up a safe atmosphere in which my research participants felt they could tell me their stories.

PREFACE

As a child, I did not believe in the Bible or the biblical "God." Although my parents wanted me to, I just couldn't relate to it. Obviously a great narrative, the Bible ended up being stored in the fiction section of my bookcase. How could one story be everybody's reality? What about my story and those of others? My parents sent me to parochial schools and even had me live with a priest during one of my summer vacations, hoping that someday I might join the Jesuit order and be saved. But by the age of twelve, although neither an agnostic nor an atheist, I had already gone astray. At that time, I saw and felt what many people might consider to be the "heavenly realms." And the creation story of the Bible just didn't line up with what I was experiencing. The Church was proselytizing that life originated on Earth, that Earth was the center of the universe, and that there were no such thing as extraterrestrials. I was interacting with beings from other worlds who seemed much more advanced than anything here in this world, but I kept it a secret for fear of being criticized and ostracized from society.

Now that I am an adult and could not care less about what other people think of me, I have more to contribute to the world than I did when I was younger. There is absolutely no reason not to assume that highly intelligent life forms from other planets exist, with an intellect far superior to that of humans, and that those life-forms are with us today. No matter how fiercely both dogmatic religion and science want to convince us of who we are, we ourselves are the only ones who can truly answer this question. As we stare out into the abyss of the evening sky, the abyss stares back, reminding us that Earth is really not so special or so ancient as many would have us believe. Earth, in fact, is a relatively new planet in comparison to the ageless universe. We no longer have to rely on the dogmas of religion and science to answer the question of who we are. We just sometimes need to be reminded that we are a significant part of everything. We are all connected. This connection offers us the ability to tap into the limitless mind or consciousness of the universe to find the answers.

I do not believe in a lifeless universe, although many of my teachers wanted me to make that assumption. I have always maintained an innate sense of there being other intelligent life in the universe. Even when SETI (Search for Extraterrestrial Intelligence) concluded its program with the announcement of "no contact," I thought how ridiculous it was to assume that, simply because ETs have not answered our radio transmissions, we are truly alone, even though some would prefer it that way. I no longer supported what the scientific establishment had to offer in this area, for I thought they had sold out to consensus reality. Also, I do not believe in the big bang theory, where something supposedly came out of nothing, or in Darwinian evolutionary theory, where we supposedly evolved out of the organic soup brewing on the Earth's surface, though I support the theory of evolution. Of course, ETs could have evolved elsewhere. Call me a bad student . . . or maybe a good student with bad teachers? Most of my teachers were persuaded to accept consensus reality, or whatever dominant worldview teachings had to offer, in exchange for a good paycheck. There is plenty of financial gain in supporting the status quo. My view is different, because my experiences are different, and I will not be swayed into adopting popular opinion, not even for social approval or financial gain.

I do not believe that life originated here on this planet and that we are the superior beings of the universe, although many of my teachers tried to convince me so. Just think of how convenient it is to consider ourselves the "masters of the universe," where we can take anything at will! This is a problem today, as we continue to kill our own species and everything else on the planet. How could life have originated here with what we now know of planet formation? Scientists tell us that Earth is 4.6 billion years old, but the universe is older than old, with no conceivable age or boundaries; moreover, it includes a limitless number of other planets, suns, moons, and stars. I believe that life is everywhere, even though sometimes we can't see it, not only on this planet but on others that are much older than our own. Also, I am not suggesting that I am the only one who knows what is going on.

Clearly, we are continually being told by authority figures who we are supposed to be, to the point where we are forced to question our own antiquity and our place in the universe. Nonetheless, I am the expert concerning my own life. As we eventually acknowledge the existence of life beyond Earth, we must also acknowledge that our science, religions, belief systems, and entire worldview are no longer adequate or acceptable. This is reason enough to cause panic in the masses. I think the process will unfold slowly and will proceed for those who are ready and available to see it. As we acknowledge extraterrestrial life, we are really answering the ageless questions about ourselves and who we are in the deepest sense of the cosmos. If extraterrestrial life were demonstrated tomorrow, do you think most people's self-image would change?

INTRODUCTION

Many Tibetans share a story of an old frog who had lived all his life in a dank well. One day a frog from the great ocean paid him a visit.

"Where do you come from?" asked the frog in the well.

"From the great ocean," he replied.

"How big is your ocean?"

"It's gigantic."

"You mean about a quarter the size of my well here?"

"Bigger."

"Bigger? You mean half as big?"

"No, even bigger."

"Is it . . . as big as this well?"

"There's no comparison."

"That's impossible! I've got to see this for myself."

They set off together. When the frog from the well saw the ocean, it was such a shock that his head just exploded into pieces.

SOGYAL RINPOCHE, *THE TIBETAN BOOK OF LIVING AND DYING*

What is it like to experience another planet, moon, or star system? There are those among us who claim to have done so and have been courageous enough to share their experiences with others. The centerpiece of this book is a detailed examination of the reports of several people who believe that they have indeed had experiences on other planets, moons, or star systems. This possibility may at first sound improbable, but we may do well to remember that many people doubted the first moon walk in 1969, even after astronauts Neil Armstrong and Buzz Aldrin collected and returned to Earth with 21.7 kilograms of soil and rock samples[1] and even though their historic visit to the moon certainly changed many other peoples' minds concerning the possibility of space travel.

I interviewed individuals about their purported adventures on other planets, moons, or stars in order to explore the psychological implications of their experiences. My primary interest in this research can be put in the form of a question: Do people who report having experiences on other planets, moons, or stars describe important life changes as a consequence?

The answers given by the people I have interviewed are consistent with reports from astronauts and cosmonauts with space travel experiences, who have acknowledged the incredible personal transformations they have experienced, including changed states of consciousness such as ecstasy, connectedness, and bliss. In 1998 former astronaut Edgar Mitchell remarked:

> When you see the Earth like this, and the cosmos like this, and ten times more stars, ten times as bright because of no intervening atmosphere, in the full 180-degree view, if you put your face to the windows, it's magnificent, it's overwhelming. . . . What happened was a sudden recognition of heart. . . . It made me realize that the answers to the ancient questions, "Who are we? How did we get here? Where are we going?" within science were certainly incomplete and perhaps flawed. This feeling of unity and connectedness was an ecstatic, blissful experience. When I came back, I knew my life had changed. I knew that I had to go find out what was this experience I had had.[2]

Experiences of travel to other planets and stars are often linked with both UFOs and extraterrestrial beings, as the means of travel and as travel guides. The question of whether there is extraterrestrial intelligent life has intrigued philosophers, religious scholars, and scientists. According to Joe Lewels, Ph.D., author of *The God Hypothesis,* "Every religion in the world is based on the interaction of humans with extraterrestrials, either in human form or through mental communication."[3] For example, consider the roots of Christianity and the so-called "Immaculate Conception" of the Virgin Mary (Matthew 1:18), during which pregnancy was induced through nonterrestrial agency. According to Patrick Harpur, an English author, "All traditional cultures believe that they are descendents from gods, god-like humans, such as the ancestors or divine animals—many of whom came from the sky."[4]

Throughout history and in all cultures, human beings have reported seeing and having contact with strange beings and crafts from the sky. Studies of these reports generally fall under the rubric of such fields as cryptozoology, astrobiology, and folklore studies. Contemporary reports have been classified as delusional, pathological, mythical, visionary, imaginary, or the results of hysteria. However, many investigations provide evidence of psychological well-being in most experiencers. These findings have been published in mainstream journals in the social and behavioral sciences.

A 1997 *Time*/CNN poll revealed that 22 percent of the American public believes that Earth has been visited by extraterrestrial beings.[5] In 2000 Richard Dolan, one of the world's most prominent UFO researchers, stated that "a number of prominent military and scientific personnel have believed that aliens are here."[6] And in 2005 Stanton Friedman, a professional Ufologist, remarked:

> I am positively convinced that alien UFOs exist, that they are visiting earth, and that our government knows this. I do not base this on wishful thinking, nor am I some apocalyptic philosopher concerned about the coming of the millennia. My conviction comes from a scientific analysis of facts that I and other researchers have gathered over the years. This growing body (I might say mountain) of data overwhelmingly supports the idea that other civilizations, probably from nearby in our own galaxy, are checking us out from close range.[7]

But the tendency of the orthodox scientific community is to ignore or dismiss such reports.[8] Very few professional scientists are willing to consider evidence that upsets mainstream views. The people who are brave enough to report experiences on other planets or with entities from other planets are held to be extraordinary at best, and deviant at worst, from our culture's dominant worldview. Such experiences do not fit easily into consensus reality, which is far too often supported by conventional science. Yet a great deal of scientific "fact" has actually been based on dogma and faith.[9] According to astrophysicist Halton Arp:

> The tradition of "peer review" of articles published in professional journals has degenerated into almost total censorship. Originally, a reviewer could help an author improve his article by pointing out errors in calculation, references, clarity, etc., but scientists, in their fervid attachment to their own theories, have now mostly used their selection as a referee to reject publication of any result that could be unfavorable to their own personal commitment. . . . The press, of course, only reports news from established academic centers that have a strong financial and prestige interest in glorifying the status quo. The result is that real investigative science is mostly now an underground activity.[10]

This quotation from the *Journal of Scientific Exploration* illustrates that, even today in our modern world, many ideas and results of studies that challenge the dominant worldview simply are not published in conventional journals. As a result, many scientists are unaware of the evidence that has accumulated concerning such topics as UFO experiences or remote viewing. It is common knowledge that there are many reasons why scientists do not conduct experiments on these unorthodox topics. Foremost among these reasons is the risk that they may lose their funding or put their careers in jeopardy.

Many professional people have neglected the UFO field since its inception over fifty years ago, claiming that investigators sympathetic to this area of study deserve little beyond mockery. However, other perspectives are being voiced. According to Dean Radin, a researcher and author in the field of parapsychology:

One hopes our leaders will have the courage to break the UFO taboo that has intimidated mainstream scientific interest in these and related phenomena. With sufficient long-term funding and access to the immensely powerful (and mostly military) technologies, already in place for detecting flying objects that are virtually anywhere in the world, we would gain a much better chance to more fully understand these potentially paradigm-shattering phenomena. But as long as the UFO remains an outcast from the halls of science and scholarship, the taboo will persist. Of course, some may prefer it that way.[11]

A study of such claims, however unusual, may permit us to look at the formation and perception of reality, and into human consciousness itself. Clearly, the act of reporting experiences on other planets, moons, or stars is central to the individuals' perception of reality. Gaining insight into how and why certain persons are able to form peculiar beliefs and hold them despite criticism from conventional science or popular opinion may serve to further our present understanding of how individual consciousness relates to the perceivable universe.

In the mid-twentieth century Carl Jung became deeply interested in studying the psychological aspects of these types of experiences. In his book *Flying Saucers: A Modern Myth of Things Seen in the Skies,* he commented on the UFO phenomenon.

So far as I know it remains as established fact, supported by numerous observations, that UFOs have not only been seen visually but have also been picked up on the radar screen and have left traces on the photographic plate. . . . It boils down to nothing less than this: that either psychic projections throw back a radar echo, or else the appearance of real objects affords an opportunity for mythological projections.[12]

Jung was fascinated by alleged UFO phenomena and found extraterrestrial beings to be his new all-consuming interest in the later portion of his life.[13] Jung had begun to collect data on unidentified flying objects as early as 1946 and was both fascinated and puzzled by UFO phenomenon. In 1959 he ruled out a purely psychological explanation of UFOs, because the large numbers of observations indicated that they were a natural phenomenon. He hypothesized that "if these things are real and by all human standards it hardly seems possible to doubt this any longer then we are left with only two hypotheses: that of their weightlessness on the one hand and of their *psychic nature* on the other."[14]

I find it fascinating that, in the epilogue of Jung's saucer book, he explicitly cited the extraterrestrial journey experiences found in Orfeo M. Angelucci's book, *The Secret of the Saucers* (1955). I will be discussing Angelucci's reported experience along with seven other published accounts of experiences on other planets in chapter 4. Angelucci claimed that his experience of life on another planet helped him to realize how disconnected with the universe he had been, writing that "Man here on this tiny planet is cut off from contact with those other worlds and fully content to vision himself grandiosely as the highest intelligence in the universe."[15] In his book Jung commented on how this story related to the mystic experience associated with a UFO vision: "It could even be regarded as a unique document that sheds a great deal of light on the genesis and assimilation of UFO mythology."[16]

Jung also commented on what an actual extraterrestrial reality would mean for us.

> Naturally, the first thing to be consigned to the rubbish heap would be our science and technology. What the moral effects of such a catastrophe would be can be seen from the pitiful decay of primitive cultures taking place before our eyes. That the construction of such machines would be evidence of a scientific technology immensely superior to ours admits of no two opinions. Just as the Pax Britannica put an end to tribal warfare in Africa, so our world could roll up its Iron Curtain and use it as so much scrap along with the billions of tons of armaments, warships, and munitions. That wouldn't be such a bad thing, but we would have been "discovered" and colonized—reason enough for universal panic.[17]

More recently, John Mack, a psychiatrist, professor at Harvard Medical School, and Pulitzer Prize–winning author, studied hundreds of cases of alien encounters, which experiencers claimed had actually occurred in their lives, even though these cases were improbable in terms of mainstream society's consensual reality. In 2004 he stated that some of the conflict and misunderstanding may be due to a type of resistance.

> Usually the resistance to a topic of this nature has to do with the concern that people's reports of having been in spacecraft, visiting other planets and the like, are being accepted simply as literal truths, and, of course, no evidence that would pass mainstream scientific scrutiny can be provided to that effect. What tends to be missed in this is the extraordinary interest that attaches to the fact that so many people of sound mind are reporting complex and fairly consistent narratives of such "encounters" or "journeys" in the absence of anything about their psyches or personalities that sheds light on the matter. At the very least this is a psychosocial or cultural phenomenon of remarkable significance. Furthermore, if we are to restrict science to what can be materially "proven," then that, in effect, would cause us to dismiss out of hand the evidence or meaning of all human testimony that concerns matters not already accepted as part of a culture's consensus reality.[18]

The way people understand themselves may have a profound impact on how they conceptualize the universe. Many informed people allow the possibility of there being other intelligent life in the universe, whereas others feel that we are alone in the universe and that we are the dominant masters of the cosmos. According to Mack:

> For we may be led to realize that not only are we not physically at the center of the universe, transcending other life forms and rational masters of our psyches—we are not even the preeminent or dominant intelligence in the cosmos, in control of our psychological and physical existence.[19]

Mack evaluated the reports of over two hundred UFO experiencers, many of whom reported what is often called an "alien abduction experience," in which the experiencer is taken from Earth by aliens and transported elsewhere. Mack was interested in the meaning these experiences had for the so-called abductees and what the related phenomena could tell us about ourselves. He elaborated as follows:

> Perhaps these individuals, who seem to have spiritual leadership qualities, have a different consciousness, are more fearless—or willing to be out of control and move through their terror—than other abductees. It is a question that deserves further study.[20]

Mack also had a special passion for working with clients and experiencers of paranormal incidents, such as encounters with beings not accepted as real in their everyday world. To try to reach the truth of the reports given him by his clients and experiencers, Mack used what he called *witnessing*. Witnessing is something more than observing or perceiving; it includes recognition of *truth telling*. When witnesses speak their truth, there is a sense of a pattern running so true that listeners may feel and recognize that they too have been in other realms; at the very least they recognize the sincerity of the speakers. This level of exchange between witness and listener is called *resonance*. Resonance is a key to effective witnessing, and it can also be referred to as *sympathetic resonance,* in which the experiencer's emotions must resonate as true to the listener. When resonance occurs the experiencer has truly been heard, and the sincerity resonates between experiencer and listener like the resonance between two tuning forks. In his essay "Why Worldviews Matter," Mack explains that the use of witnessing is based on open-mindedness, intuition, sympathetic resonance, and a "knowing of the heart."[21] This method of witnessing was used in the interviews presented in part 2 of this book.

In order to enhance our capacity to gain insights from these interviews, they are presented here in a broad context. Part 1 thus discusses classical spiritual texts describing visitations of otherworldly beings to Earth, ancient religious perspectives, modern scientific views, and historical accounts of experiences on other planets. Also included is a review of other experiences that may be related, such as near-death experiences (NDEs), exceptional human experiences (EHEs), and particularly alien abduction experiences (AAEs), along with an overview of the psychological issues surrounding individuals claiming that they have experienced contact with extraterrestrial intelligent life. Perhaps we can learn something about human perception and cognition from them.

Reports of experiences on other planets may be challenging for many people. Rather than staking out a position either for or against the possibility of visiting other planets or stars, or the existence of aliens or UFOs, both contentious propositions, the goal of this study was to analyze the common themes and descriptions of these experiences on other planets and the profound life changes apparently resulting from them. These experiences were not only of great importance to the individuals concerned, but they may also contribute to our understanding of the world we live in.

Part 2 begins with a description of my study design and related concerns. Of course, any reported experiences are purely subjective in nature. With this in mind I did not feel it necessary to investigate the truthfulness of the individual reports I collected. The reason is that with such type of reports it is not possible to tell if participants are telling the truth; there is no way to know for a fact whether they are reporting fantasies (earnest or deliberately fabricated) or are completely deluded. Rather, I examined the processes of obtaining and maintaining such beliefs despite the incredulousness of society in general, which tends to regard such claims as absurd, or as hoaxes, frauds, or symptoms of mental illness. I can say that all of those who shared their experiences with me seemed to be sincere and that they were willing to answer all of the questions put to them.

Part 3 of the book presents my findings, particularly in relation to common themes that emerged from the interviews, themes such as: the participants' ability to articulate a meaningful narrative concerning their experiences; a belief that other intelligent life forms exist in our universe, and that they are presently visiting the Earth; detailed observations such as of spacecraft and landscapes; the transformational effects evoked by those experiences, which were mostly positive; a change in consciousness to be more oriented to the greater good, linked to an enhanced connection to humanity.

In addition, in chapter 14, the information received from study participants is compared with the alternative explanations of alien experiences that are presented in chapter 2.

I conclude with considerations of the value of such research for us all.

The book also includes a glossary, in which the definitions of significant terms are provided, and two appendices: the first is a copy of the questionnaire that was used to gather demographic information such as age, health status, and descriptive information concerning participants' alleged planetary travel; the second is a description of a self-report measure of psychopathology used with the interviewees and a summary of the results.

Finally, I wish to notify the reader at the outset that I am not seeking to prove the physical or material reality of the phenomenon of extra-planetary experiences, such as people's reports of being taken to other planets, suns, or moons by spacecraft piloted by extraterrestrial beings. Rather, I am interested in and concerned with the meaning of these experiences for the experiencer. In this sense, this book is not just about extra-planetary visitations but has to do with what these experiences can tell us about ourselves and the cosmos in which we live. I ask readers, first, to be open-minded and, second, to immerse themselves in the mysteries of human experience. We must all try to accept and understand that human beings may undergo many experiences for which there is little if any corroborative physical evidence.

PART 1

Exploring the Context of Extra-Planetary Experiences

1

ANCIENT TRADITIONS AND MODERN SCIENCE

The discovery of life beyond Earth would transform not only our science but also our religions, our belief systems and our entire world view. For in a sense, the search for extraterrestrial life is really a search for ourselves—who we are and what our place is in the grand sweep of the cosmos.

PAUL DAVIES, *THE HARMONY OF THE SPHERES*

ACCOUNTS IN CLASSIC TEXTS

Since time immemorial there have been reports of visitations to planet Earth by angels and others who come and go with and without the use of machines.[1] Myths and legends tell of beings that came from the heavens to create and teach humankind.

Sumerian

The Sumerian texts were written about six thousand years ago and reveal a culture established in Sumer (present-day Iraq). According to Kramer:

> In Sumer, a good millennium before the Hebrews wrote down their Bible and the Greeks their Iliad and Odyssey, there was

a rich and mature literature consisting of myths and epic tales, hymns and lamentations, and numerous collections of proverbs, fables, and essays.[2]

These texts, originally written on tens of thousands of clay tablets, are among the oldest inscriptions unearthed to date. The Sumerians are said to have gained their knowledge of the stars, the calendar, and a worldview linking the Earth with the heavens from the Anunnaki ("Those who came from heaven to earth"), space-traveling peoples who not only flew in spherical and winged air ships but also, according to Sumerian calendars, first arrived on this planet almost five hundred thousand years ago. For more than three thousand years the gods of Sumer were worshipped by Sumerians and Semites alike, and for more than three thousand years the religious ideas promoted by the Sumerians played an extraordinary part in the public and private life of the Mesopotamians, providing models for their institutions and coloring their works of art and literature.[3]

These same gods, the Anunnaki, claimed credit for creating the Earth, the heavens, and the stars. However, the Sumerians did not view the Anunnaki as ethereal beings but rather as beings similar to humans. According to the Sumerians, the Anunnaki came to Earth in spacecraft from another planet.[4]

Vedic

Ancient experiences on other planets are described in the Vedic literature of India, including the Bhagavad Gita and the Srimad Bhagavatam. These ancient Sanskrit texts describe many strange events involving aerial phenomena. Vedic literatures include descriptions of spacecraft called *vimanas*. In his commentary on the Bhagavad Gita—the best known and most frequently translated of Vedic religious texts—A. C. B. Prabhupada, founder of the International Society for Krishna Consciousness, also known as the Hare Krishna movement, speaks of interplanetary travel being obtainable in *subtle* body form:

> The living entities are traveling from one planet to another, not by mechanical arrangement but by a spiritual process. This is also

mentioned: no mechanical arrangement is necessary if we want interplanetary travel. The *Gita* instructs: The moon, the sun and higher planets are called *svargaloka*. There are three different statuses of planets: higher, middle and lower planetary systems. The earth belongs to the middle planetary system. *Bhagavad-Gita* informs us how to travel to the higher planetary systems (*devalaka*) with a very simple formula: *Yanti deva-vrata devan*. One need only worship the particular demigod of that particular planet and in that way go to the moon, the sun or any of the higher planetary systems. Yet *Bhagavad-Gita* does not advise us to go to any of the planets in this material world because even if we go to Brahmaloka, the highest planet, through some sort of mechanical contrivance by maybe traveling for forty thousand years (and who would live that long?), we will still find the material inconveniences of birth, death, disease, and old age.[5]

The Srimad Bhagavatam—another classical philosophical and literary text inspired by and derived from the Vedas—is considered to be "the ripened fruit of the tree of Vedic literature,"[6] meaning that it is the most complete and authoritative exposition of Vedic knowledge. There is speculation regarding the accuracy of the interpolated and translated literature that has developed from the original oral traditions of the Vedas, so one must use discernment, just as with any literary text. There are many verses in the Bhagavatam that describe traveling through outer space from one planet to another. There is a description of how yogis (or practitioners of yoga) and devas (benevolent supernatural beings) can travel between planets in the universe without using spacecraft through the utilization of mystical powers. The Bhagavatam also describes spaceships of different categories called *ka-pota-vaya,* which are similar to spaceships known on this planet. A transcendental spaceship is described in verse 4.12.27 of the Bhagavatam. According to this text, traveling from one planet to another is easy for the perfect yogi who has attained spiritual enlightenment and success in the method of leaving his body in perfect consciousness. It is important to understand that the Bhagavatam describes the physical body as just a covering of the spiritual soul.

In Vedic literature, the proposal is made that our innermost self (described as *Atman*) is identical to the entire universe (described as *Brahman*). The Vedic texts exemplify the concepts of how *going within* and finding *inner truth* become matters of individual states of consciousness and reality. Consciousness, as we experience it, is individual and personal. In the Bhagavad Gita, Lord Krishna personally teaches the highest techniques of yoga to his disciples. Yogic meditations were the foundation of the spiritual life, or the deeper practice of going within and into the inner stillness and perceiving God manifested within.

Egyptian

The ancient pyramid texts of Egypt, which are among the oldest surviving religious writings in the world, dating back to 3100 BCE, present teachings that purport to describe the nature of the universe, consciousness, and life after death. These funerary inscriptions also contain astronomical material that reveals a detailed and sophisticated understanding of the movement of heavenly bodies. Much of this information is believed to have come from ancient extraterrestrial Egyptian gods who will soon return to Earth.[7] For example, one prayer is "Here I am, O Ra (Sun-God), I am your son, I am a soul . . . a star of gold."[8]

Tibetan

In classic Tibetan texts, there are references to human beings seeing and having contact with strange beings from the sky and their craft. A Tibetan book titled *Kantyana,* meaning "the translated word of Buddha," described the flying "pearls in the sky" and transparent spheres containing gods who come to visit humans.

The *Royal Pedigree of Tibetan Kings,* which is a Tibetan document dating back to the seventh century, states that the first seven Tibetan kings came from the stars, to which they eventually returned.[9]

Biblical

There are many written accounts in the Jewish Bible (the Christian Old Testament) that seem to describe events with UFOs. Repeated references are made, for example, to "messengers of God" and "flying wheels." Ezekiel described his first vision of God (40:1) as follows:

> I looked, and I saw a windstorm coming out of the north, an immense cloud with flashing lightning and surrounded by brilliant light. The center of the fire looked like glowing metal and in the fire was what looked like four living creatures. In appearance their form was like a man but each of them had four faces and four wings. . . . As I looked at the living creatures, I saw a wheel on the ground beside each creature with its four faces. This was the appearance and structure of the wheels; they sparkled like chrysolite and all four looked alike. Each appeared to be made like a wheel intersecting a wheel. As they moved, they would go in any of the four directions the creatures faced; the wheels did not turn about as the creatures went. Their rims were high and awesome, and all four rims were full of eyes all around. When the living creatures moved, the wheels beside them moved, and when the living creatures rose from the ground, the wheels also rose. . . . Above the expanse over their heads was what looked like a throne of sapphire, and high above on the throne was a figure like that of a man.

Presbyterian minister Barry Downing has concluded that UFOs and the beings that flew them were responsible for many of the beliefs of humankind. According to Downing (1997):

> My theory is that UFOs come from another dimension, a parallel universe in the midst of us as Jesus said (Luke 17:21). According to the Bible, God is invisible, but his angels can become visible if they need to, and this accounts for the reports of visible angels in the Bible.[10]

Another book in the Bible advises, "Do not neglect to show hospitality to strangers, for thereby some have entertained angels unaware" (Hebrews 13:2).

SHAMANISM

Much shamanic work, from ancient times until today, is said to be devoted to developing a relationship with the spirit world and being of service to members of the shaman's community. Shamans have provided information gained from dreams, visions, and intuitions. Krippner writes that shamanism can be described as a group of techniques by which its followers claim to enter the spirit world and obtain information that is used to help and to heal members of their social group.[11] Ken Wilber, a psychologist and writer on mysticism and transpersonal consciousness, noted that shamans were the first practitioners to access higher states of consciousness.[12]

Shamanism, which is a worldwide spiritual phenomenon, is also described as a technique of ecstasy.[13] However, as Harpur writes, shamanic ecstasy "does not always involve an otherworld journey. It may be a straightforward communication with, or possession by, a spirit or spirits who speak directly through the shaman."[14] Shaman travel does not always refer to extraterrestrial relationships, although early accounts of the origins of Mongolian shamanism describe how the sky spirits living in the Pleiades and the moon placed and looked after humans on Earth.[15]

INDIGENOUS RELIGIONS

The oldest religions on our planet were developed by the native peoples of the Americas, Africa, Europe, Australia, Polynesia, and Asia.[16] Each one of these religions posits some sort of extraterrestrial tenet as a foundation of its belief system. Many members of the Lakota Sioux tribe of North America, for example, believe that the spirit separates from the body at death, returning to its original home among the stars.[17] Wallace Black Elk, an esteemed Lakota elder and shaman, wrote as follows:

> We don't need a piece of paper to contact the spirits. We send a voice to the Creator—Yo-Ho—and somebody responds and comes in. Someone might say Yo-Ho, I'm lost. I need help. Then a spirit comes and takes me some place. They'll fly you there. They'll take you any

place. If you want to visit the moon, they'll take you up there. They'll put you in one of those little flying saucers, and they'll zoom you up there in no time. Then, they'll bring you back.[18]

The Hopi claim they were taught by spiritlike beings from other planets called Kachinas, who helped shape Hopi culture.[19] The ancient Dogon tribe of Africa possesses complex knowledge about the Sirius binary star system, suggesting extraterrestrial intervention as a possible explanation.[20] According to French astronomers Daniel Benest and J. L. Duvent (1995), the Dogon do not claim a superior technology but believe they received their star knowledge from extraterrestrials visiting the Earth long ago.[21] The Dogon have also long known that planets orbit the sun. According to Scranton (2006):

> The clear implication of the Dogon myths and their apparent relationship to science is that, at some point prior to 3400 B.C., mankind was the beneficiary of deliberate civilizing instruction presented (if the Dogon account is to be believed) by careful, well-meaning, knowledgeable teachers.[22]

PANSPERMIA

The theory of panspermia is based on the premise that life may be abundant throughout the cosmos. It suggests that only life can create life and proposes that life on Earth came from elsewhere in the cosmos, possibly in the form of microorganisms such as bacteria and viruses. When life first began is unknown, but panspermia proposes that living creatures may indeed have arrived on Earth in the form of encased microorganisms carried by comets, asteroids, and planetary debris, possibly in remnants of planets shattered by a supernova.

The term *panspermia* has an ancient history along with extensive research; such writers as Hoyle and Wickramasinghe (2000), for example, have identified comets and cosmic dust as a likely delivery source.[23] Panspermia has limited life to the form of microorganisms, because there is no conclusive evidence that would pass mainstream scientific scrutiny for the existence of intelligent extraterrestrial life. Yet modern scientists such as Joseph et al. (2010) have stated that

> there are trillions upon trillions of ancient galaxies consisting of a trillion trillion trillion trillion aged solar systems that are likely ringed with planets—many probably quite like our own. And, just as Life "evolved" on this world, it could be predicted that Life has emerged on at least a few of these planetary archipelagoes and this would include creatures who long ago "evolved" in a fashion similar to woman and man.[24]

This is definitely an area worthy of further research.

ASTROBIOLOGY

Astrobiology is concerned with the origin, distribution, evolution, and destiny of life in the universe. Rhawn Joseph, a neuroscientist, writes that we are "immigrants from the stars. Our ancestors, and their DNA, came from other planets."[25] Joseph also claims that the history of science is more like a history of scientific revolutions where disconfirming evidence can no longer be suppressed. Astrobiologist Richard B. Hoover (1998) explains the impact of astromaterial and the life within as follows:

> Life on earth has been traced back 3.8 billion years to the era of heavy bombardment by comets, asteroids, and meteorites. These giant impacts probably brought water and organic chemicals (biogenic materials essential for life) to prebiotic Earth while simultaneously battering the crust with lethal energy, ejecting terrestrial debris back into space. These processes may strongly affect the distribution of life in the Cosmos. The rocks and astromaterials may help determine whether there are properties or characteristics of life that are universal and measurable. The development of definite biosignatures (biomarkers) is profoundly important to the search for evidence of ancient life on earth, other planets, comets, and astromaterials.[26]

According to most astrobiologists, cosmic collisions are commonplace between planets and even galaxies. Earth has been repeatedly pummeled by meteorites, which are debris sheared from the surface of other planets. Twenty thousand meteorites have, in fact, been recovered from the Antarctic continent alone. Among these finds is a particular Martian meteorite, ALHA 84001, which holds evidence of microfossils that may be present within certain carbonate structures found in the meteorite.[27] Research has shown that forms of bacteria traveling like cosmic hitchhikers on meteorites that have landed on Earth are ideally suited for gene transfer and can easily withstand a journey through interstellar space. According to Joseph, these bacteria harbor volumes of genetic libraries, possibly including human genes. He writes, "Our ancient ancestors arrived on Earth from other planets."[28]

Many modern scientists now agree that there may be an infinite number of ancient galaxies and solar systems composed of many planets similar to Earth. We can also assume that life probably has evolved on these other planets, not unlike how life on Earth has evolved. At the same time, the life that has evolved on planets billions of years older than Earth may be much more advanced, due to this longer time span. Furthermore, there is absolutely no reason not to assume that highly intelligent beings with an intellect far superior to that of humans are with us today.

2

ALIEN ABDUCTION EXPERIENCES

WHAT ARE ALIEN ABDUCTION EXPERIENCES?

Alien abduction experiences (AAEs) are described by people who say they were taken aboard spacecraft or to other planets secretly or against their will by entities that are apparently nonhuman. Aliens lure (or kidnap) these people to board alien spacecraft or unidentified flying objects (UFOs). Once aboard, these people may be subjected to complex physical and psychological tests and procedures. Many of them have reported having sexual intercourse with aliens, and some women report having borne offspring who were kept by the aliens and possibly became part of an alien-human hybrid reproductive program. In addition, many abductees appear to undergo profound personal growth and transformation. Most appear to come out of their experience concerned about the fate of the Earth and the continuation of human and other life forms. In the course of a decade, Dr. John Edward Mack worked with over two hundred "experiencer participants" who reported encounters with alien beings. Virtually *all* the abductees with whom he worked closely purportedly demonstrated a commitment to a changing relationship with the Earth, of living more gently on it or in greater harmony with the other creatures that live here. Each seemed to be devoted to transforming his or her relationships with other people, to expressing love more openly, and to transcending aggressive impulses.[1]

Mack asserts:

> We may learn from further research a great deal about the nature of the human psyche and expand our notions of psychological and physical reality. The phenomenon may deliver to us a kind of fourth blow to our collective egoism, following those of Copernicus, Darwin and Freud.[2]

Budd Hopkins, a painter and sculptor, David Jacobs, a historian, and Ron Westrum, a sociologist, investigated hundreds of alien abduction experiences (1992). They noted that AAEs are associated with waking up paralyzed, with a sense of a strange figure or figures present, with periods of time that are unaccounted for, with seeing unusual balls of light in one's room, and with the sudden appearance of body scars.[3] Ted Bloecher, founder of CSI or Civilian Saucer Intelligence, Aphrodite Clamar, a clinical psychologist, and Hopkins (1985), along with UFO researchers June Parnell and R. Leo Sprinkle (1990), presented research indicating that the mental-health measures of claimants are not significantly different from those of the general population.[4] However, Mack (1994) suggested that ontological shock from the paradigm shift of the alien abduction encounter may be experienced by some UFO/AAE claimants, who later may be diagnosed with post-traumatic stress disorder.[5]

ALTERNATIVE EXPLANATIONS OF AAES

AAEs may be actual events. Or these experiences may be attributed to factors such as fantasy proneness, escape from self, sleep anomalies, hypnosis, psychopathology, hoaxes, electromagnetic effects, visions, and so forth. It is worth taking a closer look at these and other alternative explanations for the AAE phenomenon.

1. **Fantasy proneness.** The fantasy-prone individual often has difficulty distinguishing between fantasy and reality. Psychologists

Cheryl Wilson and Theodore Barber (1983) calculated that most fantasy-prone individuals spend half or more of their working day fantasizing.[6] In a survey of psychiatric illness in abductees and contactees, psychologists Robert E. Bartholomew, Keith Basterfield, and George S. Howard (1991) found no apparent evidence of mental illness, although the study did conclude that 87 percent had histories that met one or more of the characteristics of the fantasy prone profile.[7] Psychologists Kenneth Ring and Christopher Rosing (1990) reported that encounter participants were more likely to report childhood experiences of purported paranormal phenomena and were generally fantasy prone.[8] Professor of psychology Nicholas P. Spanos and fellow authors Patricia A. Cross, Kirby Dickson, and Susan C. DuBreuil (1993) found that UFO/ET experiencers did not score more fantasy prone or suggestible than control groups,[9] as measured by Wilson and Barber's (1983) Inventory of Childhood Memories and Imaginings (with a range from 0 to 52).[10] Sincerity about one's subjective experiences is independent of whether the experiences are fantasy. Delusional people tend to be just as sincere as nondelusional people because subjective experience is the only direct contact they have with their world, delusional or not. This does not rule out the possibility of malingering (deliberate lying) in some cases.

2. **Escape from self.** Memories of alien abduction experiences can be created and maintained through the desire to escape from self-awareness. Psychology professors Leonard Newman and Roy Baumeister (1996) reported that their research on accounts by experiencers of abduction could not be explained through conscious fabrication. They concluded, "People are sometimes mistaken in their beliefs about what they have experienced. Those mistakes usually do not involve capture and abuse at the hands of extraterrestrial tormentors."[11] This study also became the catalyst for the possibility of masochistic fantasy as an explanation for AAEs. Researchers Caroline McLeod, Barbara Corbisier, and John E. Mack (1996), however, disagreed with the proposition

that reports of abduction experiences represent the reporters'
attempts to psychologically "escape from self." To summarize,
"We present elements of subjective human experience that support the notion that some kind of extraordinary, traumatic event
has occurred."[12]

3. **Sleep anomalies.** Sleep anomalies, such as sleep paralysis,
nightmares, sudden awakenings, and dreams of aliens, might
also explain reports of alien abduction experiences. However,
McLeod et al. reported that attempts to find significant asso-
ciations between abduction experiences and abnormal neurol-
ogy such as sleep paralysis have been unsuccessful,[13] and Spanos
et al. found no direct link between sleep anomalies and UFO
experiencers.[14] These researchers also found that 60 percent of
UFO experiencers involved in intense alien encounters occurring at night often have sleep-related experiences such as sudden
awakenings. It is worth noting that some of these experiences
were simply nighttime dreams that involved UFOs and aliens.

4. **Hypnosis.** Can hypnosis create false memories? Hypnosis can
play a major role in producing alien abduction experiences in
people with dissociative identity disorders (formerly known as
multiple personality disorders).[15] However, Spanos et al. (1993),
using the Carleton University Responsiveness to Suggestion
Scale, found that abduction experiencers were no different
from the general population with regard to hypnotic suggestion
responses.[16]

5. **Psychopathology.** Is reported contact with aliens evidence of
psychopathology? Previously cited researchers Bloecher et al.
(1985), Mack (1994), Parnell (1988), Parnell and Sprinkle (1990),
and Ring and Rosing (1990) directly examined abductees with
tests such as the Minnesota Multiphasic Personality Inventory
(MMPI), the Rorschach inkblot test, and the Wechsler Adult
Intelligence Scale (WAIS). They found no evidence for psy-
chotic disturbances.[17] Spanos et al. (1993) found no support for
turning to psychopathology to explain UFO/ET experiences.[18]
Mark Rodeghier, president and scientific director of the J. Allen

Hynek Center for UFO Studies since 1986, reported in 1994 that psychological testing of experiencers did not result in pathological profiles, based on the *Diagnostic and Statistical Manual of Mental Disorders* (APA, 1994).[19] However, intelligence, high functioning, and even good articulation and social skills are independent of some forms of psychopathology.

6. **Hoaxes.** This explanation suggests that reports of alien abductions are often deliberate attempts to deceive. The rewards for this type of behavior are usually monetary or psychosocial, but these rewards do not characterize the life stories of the majority of experiencers, who prefer anonymity. Professor Troy A. Zimmer (1985) tested the cultural rejection hypothesis that UFO believers are social marginals and cultural outsiders who express their alienation by adopting deviant beliefs. His methodology included an anonymous questionnaire obtained from 475 college undergraduates that questioned their belief in UFOs and cultural rejection. Questions included "Want to live in another time?" "Want to live on a remote island?" and "Want to start society over?" Data presented did not confirm the cultural rejection theories.[20]

7. **Temporal lobe involvement.** Spanos et al. (1993) assessed temporal lobe lability in forty-nine experiencers with the two-item temporal lobe subscale of the Personal Philosophy Inventory. In general, people with high lability have very "unstable" temporal lobes with frequent bursts of electrical activity that can be seen on an EEG (electroencephalograph). Some researchers have found that such people tend to be anxious and judgmental as well as artistic. People with low lability, by contrast, rarely show bursts of activity in their temporal lobes and are much less imaginative. Spanos et al., however, found no differences between control participants and abduction experiencers.[21]

8. **Traumatic birth experience effects.** Although McLeod et al. (1996) and Newman and Baumeister (1996) concluded that abduction reports cannot be dismissed as traumatic birth experience memories,[22] Lawson (1984) suggested that alien abduction

memories result from people recalling and re-experiencing their own birth.[23] The birth trauma explanation has received considerable attention, but unfortunately it assumes that a fetus in the womb can perceive itself and store this image in its memory, an assumption that is at odds with fetal development patterns.

9. **Attention-seeking behaviors.** Mack (1994), Jacobs (1998), Vallee (1988), and Hopkins (1987) found that their experiencers were not seeking attention, special status, or financial gain. They were generally ordinary people who seem to have had extraordinary experiences.[24] Westrum (1977) stated that only 13 percent of UFO/ET experiencers actually reported their experience.[25] Newman and Baumeister described *mendacity* as "simple lies told by people seeking attention and notoriety," but their research concluded that deliberate fabrication did not explain most abduction accounts.[26]

10. **Low-intelligence effect.** Spanos et al. concluded that a sample of forty-nine UFO experiencers was not less intelligent than a community comparison group or a student comparison group.[27] Participants were administered the Shipley Inventory of Living as a measure of intelligence. This is a scale widely used to assess general intellectual functioning, with a forty-item vocabulary test and a twenty-item test of abstract thinking.[28]

11. **False memories.** Many individuals who remembered, believed, and reported being taken by aliens in distant spaceships, sexually experimented on, and finally returned to their beds on Earth may have created false memories. Because many scientists would be willing to declare that these are false memories based on other experiences,[29] this possibility needs to be seriously considered.[30]

In her pioneering work, researcher and author Elizabeth Loftus discovered that many people, when told to imagine abusive childhood memories, actually believed these memories were real when interviewed at a later date.[31] Not only is memory vulnerable to suggestion, but there is also the propensity for traumatized people to repeat their trauma, thus reinforcing their memory. This notion is supported through the work of Bessel Van der Kolk, who has stated that many traumatized people expose themselves, seemingly compulsively, to situations reminiscent of the original trauma.[32]

It seems that no one single explanation that fits within consensual Western reality can account for all alien abduction experiences. McLeod et al. (1996) suggested that a more direct approach in accounting for experiencers' reports on alien abductions would be to accept that the claimed events actually occurred, at least in some instances.[33] If nothing else, the alien abduction experience is rich in cognitive, physical, psychological, perceptual, spiritual, and other qualities. The spiritual implications regarding alien abductions are further suggested by Mack (1994):

> I am often asked how experiences that are so traumatic, and even appear cruel at times, can also be spiritually transformative. To me there is no inconsistency here, unless one reserves spirituality for realms of the sublime that are free of pain and struggle. Sometimes our most spiritual learning and our growth comes at the hands of rough teachers who have little respect for conceits, psychological defenses, or established points of view. Zen Buddhist teaching is notorious for its shock treatment methods. One might even go further and argue that genuine spiritual growth is inevitably disturbing, as the boundaries of consciousness are breached and we are opened to new domains of existence.[34]

In a book published by the American Psychological Association, researchers Stuart Appelle, Steven Jay Lynn, and Leonard Newman (2000) wrote a chapter on alien abduction experiences that ended with these final remarks:

> The available theories of AAEs should be regarded as provisional and necessarily incomplete. It may be asking too much for any theory or even any combination of variables identified to date to

account for the detail, richness, and idiosyncratic aspects of any individual's AAE. At the same time, not all hypotheses remain as viable as others, or as strongly supported by empirical evidence. For example, our review finds only minimal support for certain hypotheses such as the boundary-deficit personality and the link between AAEs and psychopathology. . . . This notwithstanding, we might do well to keep in mind Meacham's definition of "wisdom" (cited in Seppa, 1997, p. 9) and "hold the attitude that knowledge is fallible and strive for a balance between knowing and doubting." In this respect, the study of AAEs might make us all a little wiser.[35]

3

OTHER REALITY-
EXPANDING
EXPERIENCES

In addition to references in numerous written texts, non-Western religions, and scientific and cosmological observations that relate to life beyond the terrestrial region of our planet, there are several other related experiences that should be mentioned in the context of expanded consciousness and a wider view of physical and spiritual reality.

NEAR-DEATH EXPERIENCES

Throughout history and in most cultures, people in situations of intense physical or emotional danger have had near-death experiences (NDEs) in which they came close to dying or were actually pronounced dead and then resuscitated. NDEs are defined by psychologist and medical doctor Raymond Moody and author Paul Perry as "profound spiritual events that happen, uninvited, to some individuals at the point of death."[1] *The American Psychological Association Dictionary of Psychology* offers a fuller definition of the NDE:

> An image, perception, event, interaction, or feeling (or a combination of any of these) reported by some people after a life threatening

episode. Typical features include a sense of separation from the body, often accompanied by the ability to look down on the situation; a peaceful and pleasant state of mind; and an entering into the light, sometimes following an interaction with a spiritual being. There is continuing controversy regarding the cause and nature of NDEs. Spiritual, biomedical, and contextual lines of explanation are still in play, and there is no solid evidence to support the proposition that NDEs prove survival of death. Term coined in 1975 by US parapsychologist Raymond A. Moody (1944–) in his book *Life After Life* (p. 612).[2]

Raymond Moody, a pioneer in NDE research, identified nineteen elements that recur in most NDE reports (1975, 1977). Some of these common elements are: ineffability, feelings of peace and quiet, being *out of the body,* meeting spiritual beings, experiencing cities of light, and eliminating fear of death. These elements include a transcendence of personal ego and union with something greater than oneself. According to many investigators, the most promising aspect of NDE research is the profound personal transformation created by the experience. Most NDE experiences are eventually regarded as positive events after the experiencer gradually adjusts from a paradigm shift.

Kenneth Ring, a former professor of psychology and investigator of near-death experiences, provided empirical research based on his many years of study concerning the NDE phenomenon. Ring's research, like that of Moody, revealed that NDE experiencers often reported a greater appreciation for life, a renewed sense of purpose, a greater confidence and flexibility in coping with life's problems, increased value of love and service and decreased concern with personal status and material possessions, a greater compassion for others, a heightened sense of spiritual purpose, and a reduced fear of death.[3]

Could the NDE experience be like a UFO experience? Research has indicated startling similarities between the NDE and the AAE.[4] Many aspects of experiencers' childhoods and lives before their encounters show some similarity, along with the changes reported after the experience. Ring also introduced the existence of "an encounter prone personality," where the experiencer has a tendency to be more open to further unusual experiences. Other researchers, like Mack, found no evidence associating personality types with alien abductions: "Cause and effect in the relationship of abduction to building of personality are thus virtually impossible to sort out."[5]

More importantly, are NDEs and UFO encounters alternate pathways to the same type of psychospiritual transformation? Could these experiences be leading us to a new truth concerning the survival of our species and our planet? The NDE holds a special significance in relation to shifts of consciousness and an expanded sense of reality. It reinforces the notion that if these thoughts and feelings have meaning and value to the people who have them, they may not be so swayed by popular opinion or current scientific theories.

REMOTE VIEWING OF OTHER PLANETS

*Without going outside, you may know the whole world.
Without looking through the window, you may see the
ways of heaven.*

LAO TSU (SIXTH CENTURY BCE)

Remote viewing is a term used to indicate the alleged human capability to detect and produce information regarding a person, place, object, or event while being completely isolated from that target. Other purported abilities such as clairvoyance, extrasensory perception, astral traveling, and psychic functioning while having an out-of-body experience (OBE) may also be considered forms of remote viewing in the context of complete blindness to the target. The OBE is often reported in conjunction with near-death experiences (NDEs) in which individuals report seeing their physical body from outside themselves.

The term *remote viewing* was first used in 1972 by physicists Russell Targ and Harold Puthoff in the context of hundreds of remote viewing experiments that were carried out at the Stanford Research Institute (later termed SRI International) from 1972 to 1986. The purpose of some of these trials was to elucidate the physical and psychological properties of *psi* abilities, while others were conducted to provide information for their CIA sponsor about events in far-off places.[6]

Targ and Puthoff credited their discovery of and success with remote viewing to two psychic claimants, namely, Ingo Swann and Pat Price. Ingo Swann was especially interested in remote viewing of outer space. In 1973 he reported that he had remotely viewed the planets Jupiter and Mercury.[7] Later, the Mercury Mariner spacecraft verified several pieces of data that he recorded.[8] Swann also claims to have remotely viewed the dark side of the Earth's moon, presenting information in his (1998) book, *Penetration: The Question of Extraterrestrial and Human Telepathy*.[9] In this book, Swann wrote about his involvement with a secret government agency that had requested his services. Among other things, he revealed that he saw human forms digging, plus extensive buildings and roads. Earlier, he had observed, "Perhaps we have seen human evolution come back full circle whereby exploration of outer space and inner space come together."[10]

Another remote viewer is Courtney Brown, associate professor of political science, Transcendental Meditation practitioner, and author of *Cosmic Voyage* (1996). Brown's interest in remote viewing escalated as a means of studying extraterrestrial societies. These experiences shattered his reality and worldview.

> I found that my experiences shook me to the core of my being. In only two years, all of the beliefs that I structured my view of the world on collapsed. I learned that we were not alone in the universe, and that non-physical beings shared this dimensional reality with me. I learned that ET civilizations rose and fell in my own planetary neighborhood, and that some traveled through time with the ease with which I walk across the street. I had to reformulate my understanding of God and all religion. It is impossible to relate to you how much I had to adapt and grow in order to confront the realities that were opening to me.[11]

EXCEPTIONAL HUMAN EXPERIENCES

Rhea White, parapsychologist, bibliographer, and founder of the Exceptional Human Experience Network (1995), coined the term *exceptional human experiences* (EHEs) in 1990, defining it as "an umbrella term for anonymous experiences that transform the individual who has them so that they are engaged in a process of realizing their full potential, which makes the experience an exceptional human one."[12] White studied more than two hundred different types of anomalous experiences that usually involved alleged psychic, mystical, healing, death-related, encounter, desolation/nadir, and peak experiences.

White believes that EHEs are spontaneous transitional experiences that the experiencer finds unforgettable, opening, connecting, transcending, and potentially life-changing. EHEs can help individuals realize their own potential. White proposes that most EHEs awaken the individual's consciousness of feeling united with humanity. The bottom line is that these experiences are important and often change people's lives. White emphasizes that through these experiences we find ourselves moving in the direction of *the More*. The More is an understanding of who we are, interconnected with everything else, both without and within. Some extraordinary dreams fall into the category of what White calls "potentially exceptional human experiences." These dreams call attention to themselves because of their unusual or anomalous quality. If they impact the dreamer's life, White would call the dream an "exceptional human experience."[13]

The self-reports of people who believe that they have had experiences on other planets, moons, or stars are rare, extraordinary, and usually unarticulated. This may explain why White did not receive reports from her respondents of experiences on other worlds. In most of the cases that other investigators have recorded, people who said they traveled to other planets reported aftereffects similar to those revealed by other EHE experiencers, with a few possible additions such as an opening to a new kind of awareness and to new concepts, along with perceived connections to extraterrestrial forms of life.

EXTRATERRESTRIAL DREAMS

Sigmund Freud and Carl Jung both looked at dreams as vital keys to unlocking the unconscious.[14] Both believed that dreaming offers the dreamers an opportunity to look deeper into their own realities. When asleep, people are no longer preoccupied with the external environment, but they scan their internal environment through the use of imagery and symbols. From ancient times, dreams have contributed considerable value, inspiration, and mystery to the dreamer's waking life. There is little wonder why dreams remain a vital source of the evolution of our thoughts and beliefs. The psychologist and parapsychologist Charles T. Tart, for one, wrote, "Dreams can tell us things about ourselves and our attitudes that we did not consciously know before."[15] The importance of integrating the unconscious and altered states of consciousness into the conscious mind is vitally important for the understanding of the mind itself.

Probably no one believed more in the value of unconscious material emerging from dreams, active imagination, and visions than Carl Jung. To Jung, this inner work was all part of his analysis or of his learning to read the symbolic language of the soul, which includes dreams, imagination, and visions. According to Jung, the symbolic imagery of the unconscious is the creative source of the human spirit. Jung believed that the unconscious communicates to our conscious mind through dreams.[16] He had a UFO dream that he found to be especially meaningful: "We always think that the UFOs are projections of ours. Now it turns out that we are their projections. I am projected by the magic lantern as C. G. Jung. But who manipulates the apparatus?"[17] He would certainly agree with researchers Stanley Krippner, Fariba Bogzaran, and André Percia de Carvalho (2002), who wrote that "extraordinary dreams . . . are filled with potential meaning and direction that can be as valuable as waking life experience."[18]

Many people who report alien abduction experiences also frequently refer to early memories of an apparently unusual or extraterrestrial dream.[19] This extraterrestrial dream phenomenon is not limited to alien abductees under hypnosis. Many other people have reported experiencing initial contact with extraterrestrial beings through an unusual dream without the use of hypnotism.[20] Alleged extraterrestrial contactees such as Orfeo Angelucci, George Adamski, Claude Vorilhon, and Woodrow Derenberger—whose accounts are shared in the next chapter—reported dreams where extraterrestrials communicated with them without the use of hypnosis.[21] This may be a topic for further exploration and research that might uncover wish-fulfillment fantasies or perhaps make everyone a bit wiser concerning the UFO/ET phenomenon.

4

HISTORICAL REPORTS OF EXPERIENCES ON OTHER PLANETS

As part of my exploration of whether people who report having experiences on other planets, moons, or stars also describe subsequent important life changes, I have selected eight reports from published accounts for review. Including these reports herein does not in and of itself substantiate the claim that these individuals actually set foot on other planets or moons, nor that these accounts are literally true. None of the eight was confirmed by physical evidence. All eight have been criticized as hoaxes, lies, and imaginary stories. Henceforth, I have considered factors that relate to the "alternative explanations for the AAE phenomenon" described in chapter 2 in numerous occasions in this chapter. Nonetheless, the experiences detailed in these accounts had deep meaning for the experiencers. Summarized below, therefore, are the accounts of Angelucci, Adamski, Hubbard, Vorilhon, Klarer, Rampa, Desmarquet, and Meier.

ORFEO M. ANGELUCCI (1912–1993)

According to Angelucci (1955), his first UFO sighting was on August 4, 1946, at the age of thirty-four. At that time he had no interest in the UFO phenomenon. He had just sent up mold cultures attached to weather balloons to test the impact of high altitude upon them. Through a mishap, the balloons broke loose and carried the molds far away, leaving Angelucci without the means to recover them. Gazing into the sky, tracking the ascending molds and balloons, Angelucci and other witnesses claimed that they saw a UFO, glistening in the sunshine, which they described as round and without wings.[1]

Angelucci's second experience reportedly came six years later on May 24, 1952. As he was driving home from work, he saw a red-glowing, oval-shaped object hovering over the horizon. This object released two balls of green fire from which a man's voice said, "Don't be afraid, Orfeo. We are friends." The voice bade him to get out of his car, which he did. He then claimed to witness two pulsating disks hovering in front of him that said he was in direct communication with friends from another world. The voice also asked if he remembered his experience on August 4, 1946. Suddenly, from the two disks appeared a man and woman of "ultimate perfection," who spoke with Angelucci thus:

> We see the individuals of Earth as each one really is, Orfeo, and not as perceived by the limited senses of man. The people of your planet have been under observation for centuries, but have only recently been re-surveyed. Every point of progress in your society is registered with us. We know you as you do not know yourselves. Every man, woman, and child is recorded in vital statistics by means of our recording crystal disks. Each of you is infinitely more important to us than to your fellow Earthlings because you are not aware of the true mystery of your being. . . . We feel a deep sense of brotherhood toward Earth's inhabitants because of an ancient kinship of our planet with Earth. In you we can look far back in time and recreate certain aspects of our former world. With deep compassion and understanding we have watched your world going through its "growing pains." We ask that you look upon us simply as older brothers.[2]

After these revelations Angelucci felt exalted and strengthened. It was "as though momentarily I had transcended mortality and was somehow related to these superior beings."[3] Two months later, on July 23, a third experience occurred. This time Angelucci entered the saucer and journeyed into space. The interior of the saucer was iridescent, and he felt as if he were in a dream state. A voice entertained him with explanations of how inhabitants of other planets were trying to help humans on Earth. They also wanted to clarify that Jesus Christ is an "infinite entity of the Sun" and not of earthly origin.

On August 2, Angelucci and eight other witnesses saw an ordinary UFO, which disappeared after a short time. Soon after, Angelucci made contact with an extraterrestrial named Neptune who gave him more information concerning the Earth, the reasons for its lamentable conditions, and its coming redemption. Then Neptune vanished.

During the first week of September 1953, Angelucci reported an experience on another world via spacecraft piloted by extraterrestrial beings.

> What a glorious world I looked upon! A dream world, beyond the wildest flight of imagination. Ethereal, scintillating color everywhere. Fantastically beautiful buildings constructed of a kind of crystal-plastic substance that quivered with continuously changing color hues. As I watched, windows, doors, balconies and stairs appeared and just as miraculously disappeared in the shining facades of the buildings. The grass, trees and flowers sparkled with living colors that seemed almost to glow with a light of their own.[4]

Angelucci concluded with the realization of how disconnected with the universe he had been, commenting that "man here on his tiny planet is cut off from contact with those other worlds and fully content to vision himself grandiosely as the highest intelligence in the universe."[5] Angelucci lived the rest of his life contemplating and sharing his experiences about the saucers and extraterrestrials that he allegedly contacted. Jung provided a brief profile description of Angelucci.

The author is self-taught and describes himself as a nervous individual suffering from "constitutional inadequacy." After working at various jobs he was employed as a mechanic in 1952 at the Lockheed Aircraft Corporation at Burbank, California. He seems to lack any kind of humanistic culture, but appears to have a knowledge of science that exceeds what would be expected of a person in his circumstances. He is an Americanized Italian, naïve and—if appearances do not deceive us—serious and idealistic. He makes his living now by preaching the gospel revealed to him by the Saucers. That is the reason why I mention his book.[6]

Even though Angelucci publicly offered to take a polygraph test concerning his experiences, he was eventually dismissed by the larger community, which required more concrete physical evidence. Angelucci eventually faded into obscurity. He repeatedly stated how he suffered from poor health and extreme anxiety for most of his life. He was terrified of thunderstorms and moved to California to avoid them. These issues can be regarded as major concerns regarding his overall mental and physical health and ability to rationalize and articulate his actual experience. If his medical records and the medications used were available to researchers, it would be helpful in discerning other possible detriments, such as hallucinations.

GEORGE ADAMSKI (1891–1965)

Adamski was nearly forty years old before he devoted time to teaching what he called the Universal Law. He claimed to have had contact with extraterrestrial brothers from Venus, Mars, Saturn, Jupiter, Neptune, and Uranus. He also maintained that all the planets in our solar system were inhabited to some varying degree. He also claimed that temperatures on certain locations of all the planets were temperate and reported traveling to other planets by spacecraft piloted by extraterrestrial beings.[7]

On October 9, 1946, during a meteor shower, Adamski and others claimed they saw a large cigar-shaped mother ship. In 1947, Adamski photographed this ship crossing in front of the moon over Palomar Gardens, California. On May 29, 1950, he claimed to have photographed six UFOs flying in formation. On November 20, 1952, he and six friends witnessed a large submarine-shaped UFO hovering in the sky near Desert Center, California. He claimed to have left his friends to make contact with the UFO, which he thought was looking for him. Shortly afterward, Adamski said he made contact with a translucent metal scout ship and its pilot, who claimed to be a Venusian named Orthon, who had come to warn humankind of the dangers of nuclear energy and pollution. Twenty-three days later Orthon's spacecraft allegedly flew over Adamski's home at Palomar Gardens, California, enabling clear photos to be taken by observers.[8]

Over the next few years, Adamski reported many other UFO sightings and contact with extraterrestrial beings from other worlds. He became a world-famous extraterrestrial contactee and was invited to speak about his alleged experiences throughout the United States and Europe. Adamski allegedly was given a Vatican medal during a visit with Pope John XXIII in May 1963. Carl Jung's cousin, Lou Zinsstag, followed the Adamski story, met with him on several occasions, and wrote a book on his behalf, *George Adamski: The Untold Story*. Zinsstag commented:

> To my knowledge, it is still the only contact case witnessed by six other people and legally attested by them. After more than 25 years, everyone interested in the subject knows that many similar claims have been made, but Adamski's case is unusually well-certified.[9]

In March 1962, Adamski reported that the (alien) brothers, as he sometimes called them, took him to one of their planets.

> On March the 26th, I left on a spacecraft for the journey. The ship had come in on the 24th to one of our U.S. Air Bases where a high official of the U.S. government had a conference with the crew. After the conference, the craft was returning to its home planet Saturn. The trip took nine hours, at a speed greater than 200 million m.p.h.[10]

The following Christmas letter written by Adamski was received by all his friends to help clarify his alleged trip to Saturn.

The trip to Saturn took longer than it should, for we were in a new kind of ship. But we could indeed have arrived in a twink-of-an-eye as I stated in the Report. So, what I am about to explain is not spirit traveling, materialization, dematerialization, or a trance method of any kind. This method is practically new to our knowledge, although it has been mentioned now for some time in scientific circles. The name for this is TELEPORTATION. And they have stated that once this is developed, a ten thousand man army with tanks and equipment could be transported to a great distance in a moment of time. It is most exhilarating and the mind is in a very high state of alertness, this law operates on an extremely high frequency. Yet it is not high enough to separate the molecules to the extent of dissolving the body, or any form. Now let me explain what I meant with a twink-of-an-eye. Had the law that governs teleportation been used by 100%, we would have reached our destination in a split second. And the ship would not have been necessary, for only the special instrument would have been needed to transport us from Earth to Saturn. But had this been done, the forms of the passengers would have been totally dissolved and only their consciousness would have been in operation. But the law was used with 5% less than 100%, thus conditioning all forms for such a speed, but keeping them intact. The ship was the controlling factor, not only of its passengers but itself, similar to a high-speed aircraft or a capsule with an astronaut in it. So because of this 5%, it took nine hours to make the journey.[11]

The Adamski case contains considerable documentation. Witnesses who filed affidavits along with photos and movies of alleged extraterrestrial spacecraft are available.* Adamski stated he received official

---

*The affidavits are pictured in Adamski's book *Flying Saucers Have Landed,* on pages 192 and 193, along with photos.

recognition for some of his claims, citing letters from varying government officials that are reproduced in Zinsstag and Good.[12] But there are critics who claim that his pictures of Venusian ships were models created from hats and hubcaps and that Adamski was a victim of hoaxes set up by human tricksters or even by the UFO entities themselves. There were other concerns that Adamski abused alcohol. Here again, if anyone were interested in verifying his claims, there is an opportunity for rigorous research into Adamski's medical records and evaluations by doctors, friends, and others that may exist.

ELIZABETH KLARER (1910–1994)

Klarer (1980) claimed to have had her first UFO sighting at the age of seven with her sister as a witness.

> We both saw it at the same time. An enormous silvery disk swooped down towards us moving with a changing brightness out of the clear expanse of sky—a globe of light as clear as a pearl.[13]

This experience changed her life. Through the years she would think back and hope for another opportunity to connect with the UFO and its occupants. Her hope became reality in later years as she experienced another episode with a UFO while copiloting a plane alongside her husband. Klarer commented:

> I tapped my husband on the back of his neck. He looked around and saw the enormous craft slow its speed, changing color to a brassy yellow as it leveled out and paced our plane. Fascinated, I observed every detail as I pressed my nose against the starboard window, seeing the bright hazy outline of the great circular ship as she paced alongside. Three portholes, shedding a softer glow, looked out from the side of a dome which sloped up from a vast hull.[14]

Klarer also claimed that her female intuition told her this was an alien ship from the far reaches of outer space. At this point, she attempted to initiate telepathic communication with the occupants of this craft. As the telepathy continued, she felt a deep and everlasting love for the man in the spaceship. She knew this man would return. Months later, she claimed that she saw the silver spaceship resting on the ground near her home. The pilot was a tall man named Akon who said that he was a scientist from another world. He explained that they rarely mate with Earth women and when they do they keep the off-spring to strengthen their race and infuse new blood. Klarer was then taken for a journey into space to visit the larger mother ship. Akon explained to Klarer the fundamentals of creating a spaceship.

> A spaceship is created from pure energy into physical substance, and we do this in space. The material of the spaceship's outer skin is completely smooth without rivets; the material is created in one piece in a continuously circular shape. The radius of the curvature transforms the total mass of the spaceship's outer skin into a combi-nation of matter and anti-matter, as the atomic creation of the outer skin is conductive to energizing in alternate pulses.[15]

As the dialogue continued, Akon reportedly continued to teach Klarer a variety of other-world innovations. He explained that his civi-lization is the guardian of the holy secrets of nature and that they must not be misused. He also explained that his civilization has full aware-ness of their cosmic origin and affinity with nature. Akon explained why humans do not share this awareness.

> Man's inhumanity to man must cease before these holy secrets of nature can be revealed for the benefit of all humanity on the sur-face of this planet, for the benefit of all fauna and flora and for the destiny of all nations and peoples, to attain wholeness and har-mony with the Universe, and to become one with the great inter-stellar human family. But expansion of thought will only come in the wavelength of time when the insight of mankind has reached a deeper and more spiritual level.[16]

Akon commented that their home system in Alpha Centauri consisted of seven planets, all inhabited by their civilization. He also explained that the key to their control and freedom throughout the galaxy was their science that enabled them to use cosmic energy and generate electricity from the atmospheres of planets. Their propulsion system for spaceships is their escape route to the stars, and they guard these secrets with their lives against misuse by other civilizations. Klarer ended her first journey into outer space with a soft touchdown back on Earth and was escorted back onto her family ground.

Klarer became fascinated with her new extraterrestrial friends and the knowledge she seemed to be gaining from these experiences. Public interest in her experiences was mounting. Flying saucer enthusiasts questioned and clamored for more information about her fantastic story once it had been reported in the press. But, as she explains, she was also harassed and threatened by UFO research societies: "I was threatened with abduction if I refused to hand over scientific details of the flying saucer and its propulsion systems."[17]

Nonetheless, Klarer claimed to continue telepathic communication with Akon. This relationship was intensifying, as Akon's spacecraft now landed to take Klarer on another journey into space. This time the journey was accompanied by lovemaking and the eventual impregnation of Klarer. When she was returned back to Earth, Akon said, "I shall be back to fetch you and claim my son who is one of us, and not of Earth . . . my beloved, my life."[18] Akon soon returned and they spent the next four months on Akon's home planet, Meton, in the Alpha Centauri star system, where Klarer gave birth to their son, Ayling. Klarer commented on the living conditions of planet Meton.

There were no cities or skyscrapers as Earth people know them anywhere on Meton. Homes were scattered in park-like grounds with flowering shrubs and beds of brilliant flowers and smooth green lawns that needed no cutting or trimming as the grass covered the ground like a springy moss. There was an abundance of all things needed by civilization—food, water and all materials for building, an unlimited supply of energy on tap from the atmosphere and the Universe, no shortages of any kind and no monetary system at all.[19]

Because of problems concerning environmental adjustments, Klarer was returned to Earth to live out her remaining years. She came back with a mission to bring the truth of the universe to the people, to help expand their cosmic consciousness, and to create greater awareness of their existence and their life purpose. Akon departed with these words:

> We all achieve spiritual advancement only through dire experience and deprivation. But remember always, my love will be with you forever and our telepathic link remains always on the alpha rhythm between our brains. And our son Ayling will come to fetch you home again. This physical parting is only temporary. Now, you must go back to care for your Earth family.[20]

At the end of this story, twenty-one years had passed since Akon had landed his spacecraft in Klarer's vicinity. Their son, Ayling, was nineteen years old. Although Akon had returned to greet Klarer several times, she was not permitted to go back to Meton. Klarer reported viewing a light ray projected in a three-dimensional image of Akon and Ayling reassuring her of their constant love and thoughts. Klarer ended her book with a message saying:

> The nucleus of our galaxy emits a stream of energy . . . the light we are all made out of. . . . The release of microatoms of light from oxygen is the source of all life. Microatoms are equal to atoms. All of creation is light.[21]

The Klarer case is poorly substantiated and has only a couple of witnesses, such as her sister and former husband, who attested to the UFO sightings. Alleged UFO photographs of spacecraft from the planet Meton taken by Klarer are included in her book. Although Klarer persisted in saying that her experiences were genuine, it is not known if her pregnancy was ever documented, and there are no witnesses available.

This inconclusive evidence seems to be a major issue relating to her claims. Could she have been a fantasy-prone individual who merely imagined most of her experiences? Or did something happen to Klarer that affected her life in a most profound way?

CLAUDE VORILHON (1946–)

Vorilhon's career as a prophet and eventual religious leader began with his purported sighting of a UFO on December 13, 1973. At the time he had no interest in the phenomenon, as his main passion was sports car racing. According to Vorilhon (1978), he was hiking in a volcanic crater area in France when

> all of a sudden, through the fog, I noticed a flashing red light and a kind of helicopter coming down towards me. But a helicopter makes noise whereas I could hear absolutely nothing, not even the slightest whistle. A balloon? The object was at about 20 meters of altitude and had a flat shape. A flying saucer![22]

Vorilhon then allegedly made contact with an extraterrestrial being that invited him into its flying saucer, where they communicated and scheduled another meeting for the next day. The following day, they conducted a meeting where Vorilhon took notes and listened to his new extraterrestrial mentor. His meetings with the human-like extraterrestrial lasted for six consecutive days, one hour each day; Vorilhon was instructed to pass the information on to the people of Earth. Vorilhon claimed that he was given the mission of informing the world of humanity's true origins. He claimed that certain mysteries were explained to him based on new interpretations of sacred texts such as the Bible.

His second encounter was on October 7, 1975. This time Vorilhon was taken aboard the extraterrestrial craft and congratulated for the work he had done during the past two years. He then claimed to have been taken to another planet where all the people were harmonious and peaceful beings who were free of money, sickness, and war. There he met Buddha, Moses, Jesus, and Muhammad. He described this other planet as a marvelous scenery, paradisiac, and I can't find the words to describe the enchantment of seeing those huge flowers, each more beautiful than the next, among which were walking some unimaginable animals, birds with multicolored feathers, pink and blue squirrels with bear cub heads climbing up on branches bearing enormous fruits and gigantic flowers. At about thirty meters from the craft, a small group of Elohim were waiting for us, and behind the trees, I saw constructions which harmonized perfectly with the vegetation and resembled sea shells of vivid colors. The temperature was very mild, and the air was perfumed by thousands of scents of exotic flowers. We walked towards the top of a hill, and the scenery which I was discovering was wonderful. Numerous streams were winding through the luxurious vegetation and at a distance an azure ocean was gleaming in the sun.[23]

Vorilhon seems to have assimilated his experience by becoming a prophet with deep devotion to the teachings given to him by the alleged extraterrestrials. Soon after his experience on another planet, he changed his name to Rael and started his own religion, called Raelism. For some thirty years, he has traveled the world promoting his books and religion. There seems to be no physical evidence available to verify any of his accounts.

WOODROW DERENBERGER (1943–)

Derenberger described his extraterrestrial experiences in a book authored by L. Ron Hubbard, titled *Visitors from Lanulos*. In this book, Derenberger described his first UFO and extraterrestrial contact experience, allegedly on November 2, 1966. According to Hubbard:

This ship, as I have come to call it, came up beside my truck, and at first, I thought it to be another car. Then I noticed it had no lights. I then turned my head and glanced at it and saw that it was something that I had never seen before. . . . I received a message to roll my window down on the opposite side of my truck.[24]

After coming to a halt, the extraterrestrial introduced himself as Mr. Cold and asked Derenberger why he was so frightened. They talked for about ten minutes, and Mr. Cold said that they would meet again soon. The second contact, which was completely arranged through mental telepathy, came two days later on November 4. Mr. Cold informed Derenberger that he was from a planet called Lanulos, close to the galaxy of Ganymede, and explained that his planet was practically the same as ours, with woods, fields and streams, and oceans, but that their time was different. He said their people had a life expectancy of 125 to 175 of our years. He also explained that his first name was Indrid.[25]

On May 11, 1967, Derenberger was invited on a trip to visit the planet Lanulos. He wrote that, although he did not have a watch, the entire trip from Earth to Lanulos did not take more than thirty minutes of our time, and that they went directly to the mother ship, which took them to Lanulos. According to Hubbard:

> We were watching Lanulos come up to meet us, and I have never in all my life seen anything look so beautiful as the rolling hills and vast plains, the oceans and rivers of Lanulos. I saw one place that was called *Kumyala* or the "mountains of sand." This place looked like nothing but pure sand for hundreds of miles. There were huge mountains, bigger than any that are recorded on Earth, and of pure sand. Indrid said nothing lived in this place but small reptiles, or lizards, as we would call them.[26]

Derenberger was invited to Indrid's home on the planet Lanulos to meet his family. They communicated through telepathy and the Lanulesian language. They did not understand and had no concept for our word *hate*. The people on this planet used air cars that traveled ten to twelve inches above the ground. Derenberger commented that he was never frightened while on Lanulos and that he had only the highest regard for all the people there, who were mostly happy, living a completely different life from ours. He said that much of their happiness was based on their ability to understand one another through telepathy.[27]

MICHEL DESMARQUET (1931–)

Desmarquet reported being benevolently abducted from his Australian home by an extraterrestrial named Thao on June 26, 1987, and taken for nine days to Thao's home planet Thiaoouba. Desmarquet (1993) described his initial contact thus:

> I had walked only a few steps when, quite suddenly, the color of the philodendrons changed. The wall of the house too, and pandanus— all were bathed in a kind of bluish light. The lawn seemed to undulate beneath my feet and the ground beneath the pandanus waved also. The philodendrons distorted and the wall of the house resembled a sheet floating in the wind. Beginning to believe that I was not well, I decided to return to the house when, at that precise moment, I felt myself lifted quite gently from the ground. I rose slowly at first, above the philodendrons, and then quicker, until I saw the house becoming smaller and smaller below me.[28]

Following this episode, Desmarquet was taken aboard a spherical UFO, which headed toward Thao's home planet, Thiaoouba. Upon reaching this planet, Desmarquet explained:

> I feel frustrated that my attempts to describe the colors I saw on Thiaoouba are so inadequate—I feel I need a whole new lexicon, as my language fails me. I had the constant impression that the colors came from within the objects I looked at, and the color was more than I had known it to be. On earth, we know perhaps 15 shades of red; here there must have been over a hundred.[29]

For the next nine days, Desmarquet was escorted around the planet and shown how the people live, work, and relax. Thiaoouba was described as about twice the size of Earth with many similar features, such as people, oceans, forests, birds, animals, and dolphinlike mammals. Desmarquet made friends with a number of different people on Thiaoouba and also met with seven masters who informed him that the main problem with Earth people is their continual seeking of money and materialism, which is extremely harmful to the cultivation of the mind. The masters also informed him that human beings are definitely not descended from apes or any other animals but moved to Earth from other planets. Thao explained that sects and religions are a curse on Earth and their misuse of money is a good example. He also suggested that the money could be available to help countries suffering from famine. Other revelations concerned the true identity of Jesus Christ, and Thao also corrected points related to the Bible.[30]

Desmarquet claimed to have returned to his home exactly nine days after leaving it, following an experience he would never forget. There are no other details available regarding this account.

T. LOBSANG RAMPA (1910–1981)

Rampa was a controversial figure whose original name was Cyril Hoskin, though he claimed that his body was occupied by the spirit of a Tibetan adept, Lobsang Rampa. He described a group sighting of a UFO in Tibet and the communication with the beings within.

> We looked at each other, wondering who was speaking, because a gentle but insistent thought kept coming into our minds. "Brothers, brothers, come this way for we are waiting." Hesitantly, one after the other, we got to our feet and looked about us. There was no one in sight, but again came the insistent command, "Brothers, this way, we are waiting." So we followed our intuition and made our way to the bustling camp where the machines from other worlds lay, where Beings of many other worlds swarmed about doing multitudinous tasks. As we approached one of the larger ships a man, the Broad One, descended from it, and came to meet us with his hand upon his heart in a gesture of peace and of greeting. "Ah, brothers, so you have come at last. We have been calling you for the past hour. We thought perhaps that your brains slept." We bowed humbly before him, bowed to the Superior Being from outer space; he turned and led the way to the vessel.[31]

Rampa and the four other "brothers" entered the vessel from outer space and made themselves comfortable. The five brothers were told by the extraterrestrials that the brothers had endured much and that they would be taken to visit the planet Venus and shown civilizations beyond anything that was known on Earth. Rampa (1966) described his view of Venus.

As we sank lower and lower we saw fairy cities reaching up into the sky, immense structures, ethereal, almost unbelievable in the delicate tracing of their buildings. Tall spires and bulbous cupolas, and from tower to tower stretched bridges like spider's webs and like spider's webs they gleamed with living colors, reds and blues, mauves and purples, and gold, and yet what a curious thought, there was no sunlight. This whole world was covered in cloud. I looked about me as we flashed over city after city, and it seemed to me that the whole atmosphere was luminous, everything in the sky gave light, there was no shadow, but also there was no central point of light. It seemed as if the whole cloud structure radiated light evenly, unobtrusively, and the light of such a quality as I had never believed existed. It was pure and clean.[32]

The five brothers were escorted to a building called the Hall of Knowledge where they commenced telepathic communication with a group of men called the Lords of Venus. The brothers were shown the past, present, and future of Earth. The extraterrestrials explained that they guard the Earth, for if human folly is allowed to go unchecked terrible things will happen to humanity. Rampa described the people of Venus as desiring only peace. The five brothers were soon returned to Tibet with a desire to learn more of this new cosmic consciousness.

Rampa remains an enigmatic figure. His book, *My Visit to Venus* (1966), is only fifty-eight pages long and lacks sufficient detail in the descriptions of his experiences to be persuasive to most critical readers. According to Brauen (2004), Cyril Henry Hoskins "had hallucinations—possibly the result of a minor accident in Summer 1949—and he seems to have been at odds with life. . . . From time to time, according to his wife, he would fall into a trance and speak in an unknown language."[33] All of this happened before Rampa "took him over." Brauen's account traces Hoskins' disillusionment with England and his move to Canada. But it also notes that most people who wrote letters to him "were enthusiastic about him and found through his books hope, consolation, and new courage."[34]

EDUARDO ALBERT "BILLY" MEIER (1937–)

One of the best-known cases of purported experience on another planet is of extraterrestrial contactee Eduardo Albert "Billy" Meier.[35] Meier claims his first contact with extraterrestrials was in 1942 when he was five and still continues. He has written thirty-one books about his experiences with extraterrestrials.[36] He also wrote about his experiences on the planet Erra, which according to Meier is approximately five hundred light-years away from Earth, or eighty light-years beyond our constellation of the Pleiades. Meier described the planet Erra as being very similar to Earth with four seasons, blue sky, vegetation, animal life, and a single government, but without war, criminality, or disease. He has reported traveling there via spacecraft piloted by extraterrestrial beings and most recently by teleportation. He claims that these experiences have changed his life, inspiring him to be of service to others by providing information he has obtained from the Pleiadians. Meier has extrapolated about his experiences with extraterrestrials and traveling to other planets.

> You should study our writings, contact reports and books. Then you will see and know that extraterrestrial life is no nonsense, but it is reality, namely, such as daily life is occurring—without so-called doings of the channelers or otherwise schizophrenic impulse attacks; and without the idiocy of any kidnapping by extraterrestrials! My contacts are reality and not just pulled out of the air, also it is no imagination and I have innumerable witnesses to prove it and also other evidence of materials, photographs, etc.[37]

Meier and an ex-Greek-Orthodox priest named Isa Rashid claimed to have discovered an ancient Aramaic text called the *Talmud Jmmanuel* outside of Jerusalem in 1963. According to Meier, Isa Rashid kept the manuscript and sent Meier the translation around 1970. Meier claims that the *Talmud of Jmmanuel* does indicate extraterrestrials were strongly involved in the writings of the New Testament. This purported text supposedly bears considerable resemblance to the biblical scriptures, especially the Gospel of Matthew. Research professor James Deardorf claims that there is evidence that the writer of the Gospel of Matthew omitted part of the *Talmud of Jmmanuel* to suit his theology.[38] One alteration was omitting the extraterrestrial connections to Jesus and his father. The *Talmud of Jmmanuel* (1:88, 28:59) states:

> Behold, god and his followers came from out of the depths of space,
> Delivering themselves from a strong bondage, and creating a new race
> And home with the early women of this earth. God and his celestial sons
> Are other human races that have come from the far distances of the universe
> in their machines made of metal.[39]

Photos of UFOs flying in the Swiss countryside make up some of the most important evidence for supporters of Meier's claims. These photos have become very controversial. Some critics say they were models,[40] while others argue the photos actually presented sizable objects about twenty-two feet in diameter.[41]

The events detailed in these accounts had deep meaning for the experiencers. The reports of people who believe that they have had experiences on other planets are rare, complex, and often poorly articulated. The problem in articulation may result from the ways these experiences diverge from the viewpoint of Western culture's dominant worldview. One of the purposes of mentioning these previous accounts of people who have allegedly spent time on other planets was to determine if there are common themes in these reports. All eight people reported traveling to other planets in spacecraft piloted by extraterrestrial beings. Other themes identified include: 1) visual experience of an unidentified flying object (UFO); 2) communication initiated and sustained with occupants of UFO; 3) a meeting between experiencer and UFO occupant; 4) UFO occupants identified as extraterrestrial; 5) extraterrestrials are friendly with messages for humankind; 6) extraterrestrials acknowledge that there are many inhabited planets in the universe; 7) a reciprocated relationship is formed with the extraterrestrials; 8) experiencer is shown another inhabited planet; 9) extraterrestrials reveal their cosmic knowledge and technology; and 10) experiencers attain a new attitude about themselves and the world they live in.

▼

PART 2

INTERVIEWS WITH
EXTRA-PLANETARY
EXPLORERS

5

LIFTING
THE CURTAIN

We now have reason to believe that billions of such
planets must exist and that they hold the promise of
expanding not only the scope of human knowledge but
also the richness of the human imagination. . . . The
curtain is going up on new worlds with stories to tell.

TIMOTHY FERRIS, *SEEKING NEW EARTHS*

The preceeding chapters have helped build a foundation for the discussions ahead. The previous eight published accounts of people who reported experiences on other planets can assist in further research as anecdotal evidence. Now, I want to initiate new reports from people who claim to have experiences on other planets, moons, and stars. Within these interviews more details of extra-planetary visits emerge, as well as consistencies in particular themes and features, which I analyze further in part 3.

GENERAL DESIGN OF THE STUDY

This study consisted of self-reports and demographic data, collected through participant questionnaires and responses to probing, open-ended interviews. Qualitative interviewing requires intense listening, a respect for and a curiosity about people's experiences, as well as a systematic effort to really hear and understand what people have to say. That is why, if you really want to know how people understand their world and their life, you have to talk with them. The form used here is a semistructured interview, often referred to as a patterned interview, where certain specific questions are asked; at the same time, it allows the interviewer the flexibility to change the sequence of questions. These questions were developed from the original questionnaire. The purpose of the questionnaire is to provide a general structure and understanding of the study to each possible participant. The questionnaire also gave me the opportunity to screen for the best possible candidates based on their articulation skills and lack of confounding variables.

Interviews and summaries of themes derived through thematic content analysis of the interviews and questionnaire materials were obtained. Such methods are fruitful in obtaining descriptions of extraordinary experiences and offer a broad interpretation of the contexts in which they appear. They do not represent proof and generalization but rather discovery and appreciation.[1]

In qualitative research, the researcher is the most important instrument available for data collection.[2] While the researcher provided the means to explore participants' experiences, every effort was made to encourage them to speak for themselves. In utilizing paranormal witnessing techniques developed by Dr. John Mack, there are certain steps that require attention. First, consciousness turns outward and requires a keen and sensitive listener. Second, resonance becomes the key between speaker and listener. Third, love is required to allow witness and listener to resonate with one another. Fourth, the witness often feels compelled to specific actions by the event. Often this comes in the form of giving their testimony to key people in their lives who will listen, followed by a sense of feeling incomplete and needing to make changes that will give them a better sense of fulfillment. Sometimes this means working in an entirely different field for little or no money and perhaps no social prominence. Others may satisfy this compulsion by pursuing artistic endeavors that speak specifically to issues that were uncovered by the experience. Fifth, this type of exchange is considered sacred, or set apart from ordinary human affairs.

A copy of the questionnaire that was used to screen participants for the interview process is provided as appendix A. The questionnaire was also used to gather demographic information such as age, health status, use of medications and other drugs (none of my participants reported abuse of drugs or medications), and descriptive information concerning participants' alleged planetary travel. The questionnaire also gathered descriptions regarding participants' reported experiences on another planet, moon, or star and what those experiences meant to them. Questionnaire data were transcribed and analyzed utilizing qualitative thematic analysis that summarized themes in the written reports. Boyatzis (1998) emphasized that thematic analysis is a process of using codes to denote themes and patterns in order to understand the data in a systematic manner.[3]

Participants also completed the SCL-90-R or Symptom Checklist-90-R developed by Leonard R. Derogatis, Ph.D. (1994). This self-report measure of psychopathology was designed to reflect psychological symptom patterns of psychiatric and medical patients. It measures nine primary symptom dimensions:

1. Somatization
2. Obsessive-Compulsive
3. Interpersonal Sensitivity
4. Depression
5. Anxiety
6. Hostility
7. Phobic Anxiety
8. Paranoid Ideation
9. Psychoticism

It also measures three global indices of distress:

1. The Global Severity Index
2. The Positive Symptom Distress Index
3. The Positive Symptom Total

A detailed description of each symptom and index can be found in appendix B, along with the summarized scores of the interviewees.

STUDY LIMITATIONS

It must be noted that this sample size is small; only seven people participated. Certainly there are many more people throughout the world reporting experiences on other planets, moons, or stars. These participants were selected for their ability to adequately articulate their experiences. In addition, this study did not uncover any physical evidence concerning their reports such as photos, artwork, or implants. Therefore, more research is needed to continue gathering information and collecting data on this topic.

Another limitation of this study is that participants were not tested for conditions such as fantasy proneness, trauma-related illnesses, traumatic birth memories, sleep disorders, planted memories, or temporal lobe involvement. Such conditions have been hypothesized to account for reports similar to those that are a part of this study, as detailed in chapter 2.

The primary focus of this study was on the life changes in people resulting from their experiences. Other changes that could have been explored would have been biological, neurological, or physiological. Do people who believe that they have had extraterrestrial experiences have a different biological makeup, such as different DNA or brain activity? This research offers no answer to that type of question.

FUTURE RESEARCH

One recommendation for future research is to delve deeper with the same participants involved in this study. More quality time spent with these individuals might lead to more comprehensive reports. Another recommendation is to establish support groups, such as one involving this particular group of participants, who are willing to unite, support, and share experiences with each other. During the course of this research many of the participants expressed curiosity regarding whether others in the study had similar types of experiences.

Another recommendation for future research would be to provide a larger sample of experiencers, along with experiencers from other countries, cultures, and ethnicities. Additional suggestions include improving reliability and validity with more psychological testing of the participants. Further research in these areas needs to be conducted, should sufficient long-term funding become available.

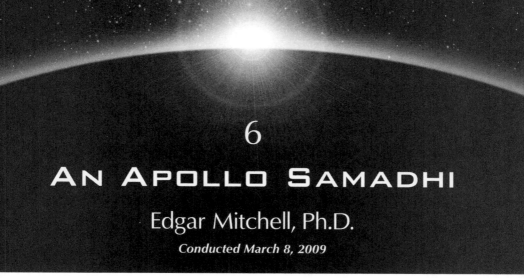

6

AN APOLLO SAMADHI

Edgar Mitchell, Ph.D.

Conducted March 8, 2009

Edgar Mitchell (1930–) became the sixth man to walk on the moon. Recipient of four honorary doctorates, he earned bachelor of science degrees in industrial management and aeronautics, followed by a doctorate in aeronautics and astronautics from the Massachusetts Institute of Technology. The first part of his career was as a military officer, test pilot, engineer, and astronaut; the second has been as a student, researcher, and teacher exploring the inner experience with both subjective and objective methods. In 1973 Mitchell founded the Institute of Noetic Sciences to conduct and sponsor research programs on the nature of human consciousness. He is the author of numerous essays and articles in professional journals.

▼

T. J. Streicher: I really appreciate this opportunity to talk with you with regard to a topic that's important, I think, for both of us. So I want to thank you for this opportunity. I am creating some sacred space between us right now, so that we can be up front and personal about some of these issues with regard to people who have experiences on other planets or other worlds. What was it like for you to visit another world?

Edgar: Well, in response, what more could an explorer want than to go where humans have never been? Look around, gather data, come back to tell the people what you saw? That's what explorers do, and that in itself is pleasurable, a highlight in an explorer's life, so that's my answer. What more can I ask than to do that?

T. J. Streicher: So it sounds like you look at that as a privilege?

Edgar: Yes, for sure.

T. J. Streicher: Can you clarify where this other world was?

Edgar: It was our moon. I think our explorations were the beginnings of Earth beings becoming extraterrestrial citizens—the beginning of our exploration of the larger universe.

T. J. Streicher: Where do you think the moon came from?

Edgar: According to astronomy, cosmology, and astrophysics, the moon was captured as our sun and solar system were organizing. It was part of the debris that made up the solar system.

T. J. Streicher: So, stellar debris maybe?

Edgar: Yes, stellar debris. The academic answer is, of course, that the big bang created all of this. I do not believe in this theory.

T. J. Streicher: You do not believe in the big bang theory?

Edgar: I think the evidence is more supportive of Fred Hoyle's concept of continuous creation.*

T. J. Streicher: I think it was featured in *Astronomy* this month, wasn't it?

Edgar: I have not read the *Astronomy* magazine this month, but I have believed for some time that continuous creation is likely the right answer. We now have the scientific methodology to show how this can be viable. In the past we have not had the mathematical formulas to

---

*Basically, this concept states that the big bang theory of creation is on the way out, because the universe is in a state of continuous creation.

support continuous creation theory. Which one is the right answer? We still don't know; we won't know for a while.

T. J. Streicher: Your experience seems phenomenal to me. What is the size of the moon?

Edgar: Well, it's roughly one-quarter the size of our planet and, as far as mass and gravitation are concerned, it is one-sixth as massive. With regard to visibility, it appears to be about one-quarter the size of our Earth when viewed from Earth as opposed to looking from the moon toward the Earth. It is a bit lop-sided, because only one side continuously faces the Earth. Over thousands of years the gravitational traction on the Earth side of the moon has caused the lava from inside the moon to come out the front side, filling all the big craters on the front side with lava. This lava was subsequently beaten up by meteor impact and particles. On the back side it looks a little different. It doesn't have the dark crater mass filling in the craters like it has on the front side. The backside looks like brown dust and craters. The front side is clearly dark. It was called *Mare* (Latin for "oceans") by the ancient observers. The front side has seas of lava, and not water seas.

T. J. Streicher: What year was this all happening?

Edgar: 1971.

T. J. Streicher: When you recall approaching the moon, what was going through your head at the time, or were you busy?

Edgar: I was busy preparing, following our plans, following procedures of readiness. We had a full schedule of events to keep up with, flying the spacecraft.

T. J. Streicher: So there wasn't a continual visual contact?

Edgar: Well, there was, but we were busy. Sure, we looked out and saw it; one could see it, but we were so busy going through our checklist with the procedures that we have to go through in order to fly the spacecraft and get ready to go down. We weren't just sitting in pastures all the time; we had work to do.

T. J. Streicher: About how much time elapsed from the time you saw the moon until you actually physically landed?

Edgar: We spent three days getting there. Once there, it was only a few hours until we went into orbit around the moon. We then transferred into the lunar module. A few moments later we went down to the lunar surface. We had some problems along the way that we had to solve and it was actually three and a half days. We left on January 31 and landed on February 5, East Coast time.

T. J. Streicher: When you were on the moon, did you see any signs of civilization or signs of life?

Edgar: No, this is a totally dead planet.

T. J. Streicher: Everything on it looked dead to you?

Edgar: Yes, except for natural structures like craters. There were lava-filled craters on the front side, and craters with powdery brown dust on the back side.

T. J. Streicher: Did that seem interesting to you?

Edgar: Yes, of course. I was pretty well trained in geology and I was prepared for what I saw, which also matched the predictions of the geologists. It shaped up to former geological assumptions of the moon's surface. Our tasks on the surface were to do scientific experiments, to take a geology trek, and to collect data. We collected roughly a hundred pounds of material for our data. We took thousands of pictures.

T. J. Streicher: Were most of those pictures made available to the public?

Edgar: All of them were available. Everything was available, although some pictures were not worth developing.

T. J. Streicher: Where are the moon rocks?

Edgar: In the receiving lab at Houston.

T. J. Streicher: Are they still there now?

Edgar: Well, those that haven't been parceled out to investigators and geologists over the years for further study. The receiving lab was the depository of all the specimens and samples that were brought back. Things were parceled down to investigators, geologists, and any other type of scientist who could justify having specimens.

T. J. Streicher: Do you think there were signs of different seasons on the moon?

Edgar: Well, certainly the moon goes through cycles of light and dark, days and night. The same side of the moon is always facing the Earth. The difference is that the moon [revolves] once every revolution. A day on the moon is twenty-eight Earth days long. There are fourteen days of light and fourteen days of partial darkness.

T. J. Streicher: Were you able to detect varying degrees of temperature?

Edgar: For sure, it gets very hot on the sunlit side and very cold on the dark side.

T. J. Streicher: Can you give us a temperature range in Fahrenheit?

Edgar: I don't have this information memorized, but it is about forty to fifty degrees below freezing on the dark side, and well over 150 degrees on the sunlit side. That was part of our constraints; we wanted to be there during the day, but we kind of wanted to get off before midday because it got too hot, too hard on our equipment and stuff.

T. J. Streicher: What did the sky look like from the moon?

Edgar: Well, it looked like on Earth; the stars are out there, but you can't see them because the pupils of your eyes are shut down. To look at the stars would be blinding. [Unlike on Earth,] there is no light or atmosphere to reflect light, so if you were to look up you could see right into the heavens. You cannot see the stars with the naked eye or with a camera lens, unless you squeeze the camera lens down. If you were to look through a tube or a telescope, you could see stars.

T. J. Streicher: Were you able to utilize the telescopic view like you mentioned? If so, what did you see?

Edgar: I saw the same stars that you see from Earth.

T. J. Streicher: You mean it was similar to what you would see here?

Edgar: Yes, and we had a telescope that was shielded. We used the stars to align our telescope with a navigational platform.

T. J. Streicher: What kind of feelings did you have while you were there on this dusty other world?

Edgar: Well, it depends on what angle you were looking at it from and depends on the angle of the sun. Looking straight down with the sun it was a brownish color, and the down side would be grayer. If you look horizontally, it would look more of a true brown color. So the particular variation in color that one sees is a result of the symbiotic relationship between the reflection and the angles of the sun.

T. J. Streicher: If you picked some of this up in your hand and held it close to your eye, what color would it be?

Edgar: Gray, a dark gray. We did find rocks with certain colors in them that had been thrown out of the interior impact craters. By and large the moon dust was gray or brown depending upon the angle of the sun and the quality of its reflection.

T. J. Streicher: Were there any caverns where you could go into the moon?

Edgar: Well, there may be some, but we didn't see any.

T. J. Streicher: When you were out looking at the curvature of the horizon, what were your thoughts?

Edgar: The part that it is smaller is very deceiving. You cannot see the near horizon, as it is much closer than it is on Earth. We were in the highlands area. It was pretty darn flat; we found some relief, but roughly it was a pretty flat surface. We had no experience in measuring or gauging distance. It seemed impossible. It's like being here on Earth and being out in the desert and seeing a mountain way off in the distance. It may actually be many, many miles farther away than it looks at that point. When on the moon, because of the curvature, it looks even farther away. The curvature is deceiving, because something is poking up from its base. It may be actually extended even further over the base than it appears. There is confusion on the exact point of entry.

T. J. Streicher: What is your belief on the actual consistency of the moon—do you believe it to be a hollow world?

Edgar: I don't think anybody knows the answer to that. Certainly you can tell it is volcanic, or was volcanic, but how much is left inside we don't know. We still have a molten core inside the Earth, but it doesn't appear that there is a molten core left on the moon, so there may be hollow in there somewhere. I haven't studied the recent data of what the current thinking among geologists is; they are still studying it.

T. J. Streicher: Did you experience any noises or lights when you were there?

Edgar: Oh, no.

T. J. Streicher: Any abnormal lighting?

Edgar: No.

T. J. Streicher: Did you see any buildings, vehicles, or underground tunnels?

Edgar: No, the only thing that comes close is the pictures of what looked liked collapsed lava tubes. In other words, like a little canyon running across the surface. It was probably a lava tube that collapsed and left an impression.

T. J. Streicher: How deep of an impression?

Edgar: It was hard to tell; it could be a few hundred yards across and maybe a dozen yards deep. There are some lava tubes that clearly run between craters. There are pictures of craters that show the lava tube impressions going between them. My guess is that these are lava tubes that had once carried lava and dumped lava out into these craters.

T. J. Streicher: I am just taken by this phenomenal experience and just imagining what it could have been like.

Edgar: It is a powerful experience; to be one of the first generations of space explorers and to see the Earth from that perspective was very powerful. This experience affected all of us very strongly.

T. J. Streicher: Was it so inspiring that it was hard to put into words? Did you ever doubt your own perception at any time?

Edgar: No, you just say what you think, what you're feeling, but then back to work. We only had a few moments here and there to grab insights or admire the scenery; then it was back to work because our checklist was our primary concern. We expected something to fail. We expected the equipment to fail, and we didn't want to waste time. By and large, we had created a time line that was about 120 percent of human capacity, if all went well. Well, in our particular case, we didn't have any failed equipment. We had to work at 120 percent of human capacity, following our timeline and working at full-out capacity.

T. J. Streicher: Did you ever feel like your safety was jeopardized?

Edgar: No, we were in control.

T. J. Streicher: Was there stress involved in this?

Edgar: Well, yes, there is stress, but we practiced and practiced and practiced the checklist and the maneuvers with the equipment, until we were comfortable. Nearly all of us were test pilots, except Jack Schmidt. Most of us had been pilots in wartime. We had to learn how to control our feelings and our emotions, so we would not get rattled with the things we were required to perform. We had to stay on top of everything; it's just the type of guys we are.

T. J. Streicher: Yes, you had considerable training, but was there anything different, unexpected?

Edgar: Well, sure, there are things that are unexpected, but I do not think there was anything that was so different that we were really surprised by it. Everything was planned and simulated; we were really taken with how good the simulation worked in regards to preparing us for our flight. It doesn't mean that we didn't have surprises. We had a few things go wrong on the way out that we had to work around, and the landing radar didn't work when we started down. We did have problems to overcome, but it was amazing how well as a team we were able to overcome these problems, causing no detrimental impact to the mission.

T. J. Streicher: Can you recall the actual first step on the moon?

Edgar: The landing gear had a compression strut in it, a shock absorber, yet we landed so gently that we didn't even compress the landing strut. The last step on the ladder was about three feet from the surface. When you hit that last step facing front, you had to push off and drop forward down to the landing pad, which was a little bit of a surprise. We had the television camera set up to capture that moment. Regardless of surprises, we did whatever we had to do.

T. J. Streicher: Did you leave a footprint?

Edgar: When we came down the ladder, we landed on the footpad on the front of the spacecraft. We had to step off the footpad to get onto the ground.

T. J. Streicher: Did you leave actual footprints?

Edgar: Sure, because the soil is soft; we stepped into it about two inches, depending on if we were on the edge of a little crater or something. The moon is pockmarked with craters all over it, tiny little craters ranging to great big craters. Around the edges of these craters the sand or soil is soft or hard depending on the size, depth, and stability of the crater.

T. J. Streicher: How do you think this experience affected you?

Edgar: If you have read my *Way of the Explorer* book, I describe how I was affected there and on the DVD, which is included. It wasn't the experience of being on the moon so much as it was the experience of seeing Earth and the heavens from deep space. Seeing these from a different perspective and seeing the "big picture effect."

T. J. Streicher: But what about the actual experience of traveling in a spacecraft and arriving on another world—did this impress you?

Edgar: Well, "impress," of course, but we trained. You've got to understand—we practiced and practiced and practiced to do just that.

T. J. Streicher: Yes, but this is the actual event.

Edgar: But you have got to understand, you asked if we were frightened—we had to stay alert. We were alert to everything that was happening. Certainly in my case and in the case of most of the guys I know, we are very focused on carrying, going, doing what you are supposed to do. It is a job; we were there to do a job. We were working against time, we only had so much time to do this job, and we did not have time to gawk and look around, we had to do what we had to do. Okay, you steal a few seconds now and then every so often—Wow, look at that!—but then right back to work again.

T. J. Streicher: It sounds like you must be very work-oriented, always focused all of the time.

Edgar: Yes, no question, you're absolutely right. When we climbed up Cone Crater, we could look out and see the old lunar module sitting there two kilometers away. That was like being on a plateau and seeing that old lunar module out there—"Wow, that's interesting! Look how far away it is."

T. J. Streicher: Now there are signs of civilization; there is a spacecraft out there.

Edgar: But when you climb up a mountain, as it were, it was a tough climb, so we huffed and puffed till we got to the top, and then the medics monitoring our heart rates said, "Okay, slow down, you're working a little too hard, take a little break." We did, so we took a look around, and then went back to work.

T. J. Streicher: What were your thoughts at this time?

Edgar: I am so job-oriented, work-oriented, get-the-job-done sort of thing. Most of us were that way; we were not the sort of guys who were poets or who would be sitting there gawking and marveling at things. We could see it—"Got that, but go on now."

T. J. Streicher: What kinds of changes have occurred with you?

Edgar: The changes are the result of the big picture effect. You see things differently, and of course there is the epiphany in coming home. The epiphany is, "Wow, I am seeing things in a different way, and then trying to put that together into a story as to what it is." I still don't have an answer from a cosmological sense as to what causes humans to have a peak experience. In ancient Sanskrit it is called a *samadhi* experience, and in the Buddhist tradition it is called a *satori*. What causes a peak experience, I cannot say. Even after having studied a lot of physics, biology, and psychology on this subject, I still can't answer what is the physical process that nature allows to take place; I only know it shifts your perspective.

T. J. Streicher: Yes, that's what I am interested in, that shift in perspective; how has your perspective changed?

Edgar: I can tell you that I feel differently. I appreciate the complexities of the universe. I appreciate now—from our modern Hubble telescope data—that the universe is much larger, much grander, and much more complex than we ever thought it was in the past. We are still ignorant. We think we are a pretty smart species, but I usually say we are just barely out of the trees. We have learned a lot, but we haven't learned nearly as much as we like to think we have, and there is still a long way to go. It's amazing and inspiring. Even though I went off to war because of the draft that we had in place when I graduated from college, and I did my duty as a pilot, I learned to appreciate that war is a fallacy. Killing people is not what we are supposed to be doing. We have to evolve past all of that.

T. J. Streicher: Were you involved in that war?

Edgar: Well, I was shot at!

T. J. Streicher: Is this the Korean War?

Edgar: Yes. I do not believe in war. I believe we have to evolve past that, but we have not. Our destiny, if we are to be citizens of the universe, is to be peaceful citizens of the universe. The real question pertains to both the "trans" experience and the epiphany that I had in space. The question is, what is it in nature that causes that shift, that type of shift that spills over into an entire value system? Why is war no longer acceptable to me? And it is not acceptable that we humans are warlike and are threatening our own species and our very own existence on this planet by multiplying the way we are. We are not on a sustainable path. It is disturbing that the population continues unabated and refuses to sincerely adapt a consciousness that embraces renewable resources as a solution. Sustainability remains as a major thrust and focus of my thinking at this point. What is it in nature that allows us to have transcendental and transformational experiences like I have had? I don't know the answer to that yet.

T. J. Streicher: Are you searching for that?

Edgar: That is a part of what my Noetic Foundation is about, trying to understand consciousness and transcendental type experiences. They are recorded throughout history, and the great mystics of all times have talked about them and we humans know about them, yet we continue to spend our time killing each other and arguing over whose God is the best God.

T. J. Streicher: But you're not doing that—your consciousness has been raised?

Edgar: To me raising consciousness means shifting the ethical structure of our thought, to be more concerned for the greater good, for the whole. And to accept our individual role in doing that.

T. J. Streicher: That's a start.

Edgar: Yes, it's a start.

T. J. Streicher: Would you talk a little about your newfound cosmology? Do you think, for instance, that there is life on other planets?

Edgar: Oh, I have no doubt about it. The fact is that we have been visited, and the whole UFO phenomenon—we have been visited. There are a lot of people who have more experience with that than I do. I have no firsthand experience with visiting aliens, except for the Roswell experience where I grew up. I grew up near Roswell, New Mexico. I was in high school in 1947, when the Roswell incident took place.

T. J. Streicher: Did you get some firsthand information about that?

Edgar: Oh, yes, during that period it was hushed up right after it was announced. One day it was announced; the next day it was hushed in the newspapers.

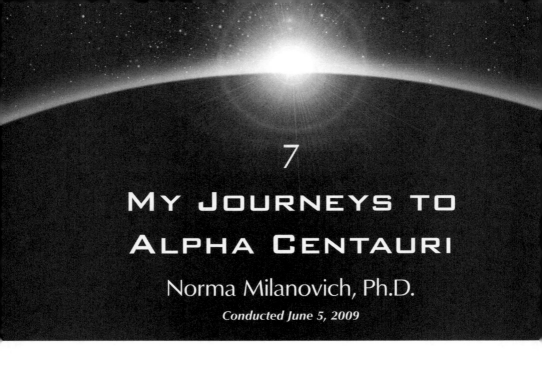

7

My Journeys to Alpha Centauri

Norma Milanovich, Ph.D.

Conducted June 5, 2009

Dr. Milanovich was a professor of education at the University of New Mexico in the 1980s, when she was "contacted and awakened" by Celestial Beings. Although her twenty-year career was in academia, she also served as a consultant to many business, industry, and government organizations. As a result of her contacts with Celestials who claim to be from many areas of the universe, she wrote *We, the Arcturians; The Light Shall Set You Free; Sacred Journey to Atlantis;* and *Celestial Voices.* Today Dr. Milanovich is a popular speaker, workshop facilitator, journey coordinator, psychic, intuitive, and writer, perhaps best known as a voice for the Ascended Masters, who work endlessly at this time to bring the Earth into the fifth dimension.

▼

T. J. Streicher: I want to thank you for this opportunity to talk with you. I think that this information could be considered important for a lot of people, especially for those who have had similar types of experiences. Basically, the interview will be divided into three sections. The first will involve describing your experience on another planet. The second will involve your reactions to that experience. The last will involve your reflections and possible new philosophy obtained from your experience.

Would you describe to me how large this other planet is, where this other planet is, and what is the name of this other planet?

Norma: The name of this other planet is Alpha Centauri. It is in the Southern Cross, which can be seen only from the Southern Hemisphere. It is a rather large planet, and it is hard to find something to compare it to, but I believe it is larger than Earth.

T. J. Streicher: Is there a civilization there?

Norma: Yes.

T. J. Streicher: Would you describe it to me, please?

Norma: The civilization seems to be composed of Beings who are more etheric than we are here on Earth. Many of them are very tall and thin. When they leave their planet, they have more of an ET look—tall, thin necks and faces, and so on. They look more like the traditional extraterrestrial that is portrayed in movies. But when I am there, there is a tendency (or it may be my own bias) to view them as tall and looking somewhat more human.

T. J. Streicher: Would they look humanoid, then?

Norma: On their planet they do, but when they are in other places around the universe, such as here, they seem to carry more of an alien kind of presence, like you would see in a movie.

T. J. Streicher: Do you mean that they actually change their physical appearance?

Norma: Yes. I have never questioned that. Maybe there is more than one type of Being on their planet and that is why I am seeing two forms. A possibility is that when they appear here they are in their Light Bodies, and their Light Bodies are quite different from the presence that I see on Alpha Centauri.

T. J. Streicher: Are there seasons on this planet?

Norma: No, I am not familiar with any.

T. J. Streicher: How many times have you visited there?

Norma: Oh, probably about fifty.

T. J. Streicher: Do you recall what the climate was like or the temperature range? How did it feel?

Norma: It was very comfortable, but I don't think that "temperature range" would be an accurate way to describe what we would believe the temperature to be. It is more nurturing to you as a person being there, rather than feeling cold or hot or something like that. My recollection is that it is more nurturing to the person or alien Being who is there.

T. J. Streicher: When you say "more nurturing," would you be more specific on what type? Was it emotional, spiritual, or what?

Norma: I'd say it was mental, in the sense that mental nurturing would embrace whatever mood you would be in at that time. Alpha Centauri is a planet (or star—whichever is more appropriate) that is concerned more with theory or theoretical issues. The Beings are at a very high level. They are very etheric (from my experience), and they deal more on the level of creation than with putting things together as we do in the third dimension, such as creating with bricks and mortar and things like that. They are more into their minds—*everything supports their minds.* The temperature on Alpha Centauri is like your experience of the environment around you—you just experience it when you are there. You feel it. You see it. It's as if everything, including the temperature, is supporting you and wanting you to succeed. Everything supports your mental abilities.

T. J. Streicher: Did you find that supportive of your well-being?

Norma: Yes.

T. J. Streicher: What does the sky look like?

Norma: It's a bluish-gray color that is very ethereal. I described it to some friends once as the color of the Dallas Cowboy football uniforms awhile back, when the uniforms weren't gray and they weren't blue. It was kind of a combination of the two. Whenever I am on Alpha Centauri, that is what I pick up. That color is everywhere.

T. J. Streicher: Did you recall seeing any vegetation or animal life?

Norma: No.

T. J. Streicher: Would you say that there are natural resources available on this other planet?

Norma: The greatest resources, I would say, are the mental abilities of the people. They reason at such a high theoretical level that they have already figured out universal networking. That's what they need on their planet to trade or to sustain themselves. They are so intelligent. They do not have to deal with a hand-to-mouth existence. Everything is already created and structured because their mental and theoretical abilities are so highly developed. They get things done quickly at a very high level. Their mental abilities are so pronounced that they can solve problems almost before they develop.

T. J. Streicher: Did you recall seeing any buildings?

Norma: Yes, the buildings are very crystalline in nature—almost like quartz crystal. They are translucent with tall spires on them. Portions of the buildings are tall and thin and somewhat like the way the New Age artists represent them to be, such as crystalline temples in the sky. They have a lot of these structures in their architecture.

T. J. Streicher: Did you see any vehicles?

Norma: I didn't see any cars. They have vehicles that hover. They move on a seamless path and do not stop and go the way they do here. They just glide and move gracefully, anywhere they wish to go.

T. J. Streicher: Did you see any underground tunnels?

Norma: No.

T. J. Streicher: Do you recall the color of the planet, or the ground?

Norma: Here again, mostly what I saw is this bluish-gray color with white, silver, and a little bit of gold sometimes. Their colors are more like metallic colors. Even the white and the blue parts of them are like our new cars today, where they are called metallic blue or metallic white because there is a sheen or a metallic glisten to them. From my experience, everything there reflects that kind of coloring.

T. J. Streicher: Did you see any type of landscape?

Norma: No. I saw that the buildings and everything have a purpose. I saw Beings with extraordinary grace, and there was no anger in them at all. They were almost Creator Beings that have a purpose for creation. They appear to be so highly evolved that I don't think they understand what destruction is. I didn't see trees or anything like that. I just saw these crystalline buildings and that everything supports their minds and what it is they are to create.

T. J. Streicher: You mentioned that they were tall and thin—would you give some measurement to that?

Norma: Yes, they were about seven feet tall, but when I saw them in other places (like here on Earth), they were much taller.

T. J. Streicher: Are they wearing any clothes?

Norma: Yes, there is a garment, like a Roman garment with a cape or something like that. They have arms, they have legs, but they are so thin. When I am on Alpha Centauri they look more humanoid, like humans, and they wear clothes that are similar to our clothes and uniforms. They wear space uniforms, more like you see in movies such as *Star Trek*. Their bodies were very similar, except that they were all very attractive. It was like they evolved out of having ninety-five varieties of ugly to beautiful. Somehow their minds are so developed that they have been able to get rid of ugliness, so everyone is rather beautiful. Because they are so thin, their garments fit almost like they are models, but they are not interested in that. They are only interested in the development of the mind, and everybody there has that innate high mental ability.

T. J. Streicher: Are they interested in longevity?

Norma: They are the *epitome* of longevity.

T. J. Streicher: How many Earth years?

Norma: Probably anywhere from seven hundred to one thousand.

T. J. Streicher: Do you recall looking in their eyes?

Norma: Yes, I do. They have these steel-blue, piercing, radiant eyes, filled with Light. When they look at one another, with their mental abilities so highly developed, they gaze with a tremendous amount of love and compassion in their eyes. They command some of the wisest eyes you could ever imagine. You just know they can read everything about you. They have wisdom in their minds that far surpasses whatever we can command on Earth—at least that is true with the group I know. I know there are many who are much more intelligent than I am (or my colleagues). These beings appear to have an IQ of (probably) 250, in comparison to our measurement of IQ on Earth as averaging 100.

T. J. Streicher: Did you communicate with them, and, if so, how?

Norma: You can communicate with them because they are multi-lingual. They have an ability (in their minds) to translate all languages, whether a person is speaking words directly out of his or her mouth, or if someone is thinking in Spanish or German. That language development portion of their minds must be based in the universal language of symbolism. Our languages must penetrate their minds with symbols and the symbolism translates everything in their brains (if they have brains). Consequently, they are then able to speak to you in your own language. It's like they don't even have to go to school to take a course to learn French, German, Spanish, and so on, because they already have achieved a level of communication that bypasses what comes out of different peoples' mouths. They are already on a higher level with the universal language of light; therefore, their brains automatically translate words for them, so they can deliver back to you what you need to understand.

T. J. Streicher: Have you acknowledged any telepathy or mind-to-mind communication with them?

Norma: Oh, yes. I seem to be visited by them a lot, and my communications are not just facilitated by me going there. I feel I'm in constant communication with them.

T. J. Streicher: What type of communication is this?

Norma: Telepathic and experiential.

T. J. Streicher: But they are able to speak with you in the literal sense also?

Norma: Yes, absolutely.

T. J. Streicher: Do you ever feel like they are reading your mind?

Norma: That's the whole point. Whether they are reading one's mind or not, they appear to have a mechanism in their brain structure that gives them the ability not only to translate what you are thinking and saying but also to see right through you. They know so much more than we can imagine.

T. J. Streicher: As we close this first section, is there anything else you want to say about the descriptions of this other planet?

Norma: No, I think I have covered many of the main points.

T. J. Streicher: What was your experience on another planet like?

Norma: Everything was positive.

T. J. Streicher: And nothing was negative?

Norma: Never, not once.

T. J. Streicher: How did this experience affect you?

Norma: In my everyday life today? Having experienced these situations, I came to understand and realize that very deeply in my soul there are higher places to live, and in some respects it makes me yearn to be in a community where everyone respects one another, where destruction isn't on anyone's agenda, and where people want to debate issues and theories to learn and create a better world or society. It almost gives me something to which to aspire. Maybe someday I will be lucky enough to be with a group of people who will model their own behaviors after these behavior traits.

T. J. Streicher: I have a couple of your books that you recommended, and I was trying to understand how your initial contact started. It sounded like it was in your middle years. Do you recall earlier contact in childhood?

Norma: No, nothing.

T. J. Streicher: Even now in retrospect?

Norma: No, I remember nothing. I am sure it happened, but I don't recall anything.

T. J. Streicher: What changes took place in you?

Norma: When communicating with these Beings—whether by remote viewing, telepathic, or other forms of contact—I have had only positive experiences. I have received many messages and lots of information from them on topics that I was not skilled in understanding. However, when I applied their guidance and some of the concepts they introduced to me, I began to find that they worked, and my life got better and better.

T. J. Streicher: Would you give me an example?

Norma: Well, twenty years ago visualization was hardly understood. When my book came out, there were many messages there from Celestial Beings teaching us how to use our minds at higher levels for creation. I actually learned to respect this skill through their guidance and messages. I never purchased any other books at the time, but I did find that, by following their advice, I could influence my destiny and future even more. I slowly began to use the innate powers of the mind to literally bring things to me and to create things around me. Instead of feeling that I was alone in the world, that everyone was against me, or that I would have to always work hard for everything in life, I began to manifest my dreams with my mind. It was only years later that other books were written about this. The Arcturians were some of the first extraterrestrials who started providing me with this information. Later, I began to connect with other Celestial Beings. It never mattered what world, planet, or star they were from, because so many of them were fifth dimensional Beings (or higher). Since they had traveled the same path of evolution, they all had similar information. It was always knowledge and information that was not yet on Earth.

T. J. Streicher: You mentioned these innate powers of yours. Are you describing paranormal skills, or could you be more specific?

Norma: Not too many people can channel and receive messages from higher intelligences who claim they are from another part of the universe. My skill is a teachable skill. My abilities to channel must be originating in an area of my mind or brain that humans, in general, have not fully developed yet. It must be that way, or my ability to communicate telepathically would be more common. The first messages that I received taught me how to use my mind in a variety of ways that accomplished changes in me—physically, emotionally, spiritually, and mentally. What these Beings taught me were concepts that have not yet been taught in schools, nor had I learned them from my parents or from religious institutions. These Beings provided extraordinary information to me. I witnessed my life changing for the better, and there was a freeing effect occurring within my mental body. My mind began to know things that were true, and I knew these things without having to read books or learn the information in traditional ways. I hope that makes sense.

T. J. Streicher: Yes. Do you recall ever witnessing the Beings consuming food or drink of any kind?

Norma: Never. I have never witnessed that.

T. J. Streicher: Is it possible that they live on another form of energy? How do you perceive this?

Norma: Because I have never seen or observed them consuming food, the only thing I can explain is what they mentally transmitted to me.

T. J. Streicher: While you were with them, did *you* consume anything?

Norma: Not to my knowledge. I think they are beyond eating.

T. J. Streicher: But was there some sort of energy exchange?

Norma: Oh, yes.

T. J. Streicher: Can you talk a little bit more about the cosmic change that took place in you?

Norma: I began to understand my unity with all life and all energy, including the universe and the cosmos. One of the things that started to develop rapidly within me was my experiencing no fear. Before my communications with them, I was cautious, concerned, and worried about things. Little by little, by connecting with them over and over again, I began to feel a self-confidence growing within me, and I no longer saw the world as something to fear. I began to see the interconnectedness of everything, and I began to realize the power I had to shape my own destiny.

T. J. Streicher: Do you recall, while you were on this other planet, what you were thinking and feeling?

Norma: I was pretty much focused on the work, on the mission of their planet, and what they were doing. I experienced it. I could tell that they thoroughly enjoyed creation and worked to develop the mind. Everyone was always working, every day. I never did see them sleep. They came together in anticipation of having a great time, because they were all on the same page. They know they will always move forward, and they want to see what the outcome will be when they all put their minds together. That's what I experienced. I was always aligned with work when I was there.

T. J. Streicher: When you say "work," are you talking about creation?

Norma: I am referring more to their mission. They are advanced in understanding theory. In our universities, some professors have difficulty teaching students how to theorize. Most students do not even have the mental abilities to operate at that level. As a professor for twenty years, I saw students struggle writing their dissertations, because one of their weakest areas was in their ability to theorize or conceptualize. They struggled in writing down variables and defining the relationships between them. They could barely define their problems or the purposes of their studies, much less write hypotheses. These Beings, on the other hand, *live theory*. They see the interconnectedness of all things. They come together to support one another at that level of understanding and see everything else below that level as being like learning the alphabet. It's so easy for them. So that is what I picked up every time I was there. They were focused on knowledge, but it was more than that. It is the wisdom that comes from the knowledge, and how they can use it, that drives them.

T. J. Streicher: What would you say was the most meaningful part of the experience on another planet?

Norma: I never saw anything (that I recall) that demonstrated things that contributed to the advancement of their society. So, for me personally, the most meaningful thing I came away with was a higher way of living. Also, I now understand the value of it. I cherished the knowledge, as I brought the ideas back into my everyday life. I now consciously try to have a better life around me (with more grace). I value wisdom, Light, and things like that, that feed my soul.

T. J. Streicher: You mentioned they were peaceful Beings, so maybe you brought some of that peace back with you also?

Norma: Exactly. Not fearing anything anymore made me automatically seek a higher level of existence in everything that I was doing.

T. J. Streicher: Were you able to obtain that here on the Earth plane?

Norma: Perhaps on some level, but I never operated like that before, when I was acting normal. I don't even presume that I could operate at the same level that I witnessed out there.

T. J. Streicher: When did this experience occur, and about how many times?

Norma: About fifty times. As I said, every time I go there I witness the same thing.

T. J. Streicher: Why do you think this is?

Norma: Because I think my soul is very familiar with these higher dimensions. I believe in reincarnation—on some level, I believe that I have shared experiences with that civilization. I think that is one of the reasons why it is easy for me to go back there.

T. J. Streicher: Is it still happening for you now?

Norma: Yes, any moment, any time I want it to.

T. J. Streicher: Has this experience given you a different connection with humanity?

Norma: I think it has made me lighter, made me appreciate other life forms and the interconnectedness of all people and Beings. Therefore, I would say that I believe it has made me a more loving person. It's made me a person who is now able to love and appreciate all because of their grace and everything that they command. If I took a piece of it here, I would have to be kinder, more compassionate, more loving to other people, because that's the way they are.

T. J. Streicher: Has your concern for the material things in life changed?

Norma: Yes, I actually appreciate the material things of life even more, not less. I appreciate beautiful things, things that have historical meaning, or greater artistic expression—things that are more eloquent. Yes, it is like evolving up to a higher level, but I don't have a desire to buy things or be in a societal position. I don't even need that. I could stay home and never leave the house, but I could no longer live in an environment that is broken, dirty, and in need of repair, with chaos all around. Everything must be in order, just like theirs is. The more eloquent my environment is, the more it feeds my soul. That is the way I would describe it.

T. J. Streicher: How would you describe the Beings? They do not seem very materialistic.

Norma: No, but they are ordered in their minds, and everything there is so perfect. There is no crime, no clutter, no dirt. Their minds are clear and organized. That is the part that I would say has rubbed off on me—I really have a great respect and appreciation for that, and it is a kind of yearning to have something similar, because it raises you up from the problems of the mundane, hand-to-mouth existence that resides on Earth. In my life, there is hardly a country that I have not visited, and most of the people in those countries (because most of them are third-world countries) are living a hand-to-mouth existence. Broken shacks and dirt are everywhere—just an unbelievable kind of existence. My experience with these Beings has really shifted me not to want to experience that kind of existence. In other words, I do not think I could ever become Mother Theresa now and live for the rest of my life in the villages of India, sleeping on the ground. Some people can, but I can't, because there is something programmed in me now that says there is a much better way to save the world, and that is through my mind. From my skills, knowledge, and wisdom, and through order, grace, Light, and beauty, and things like that, will I contribute to a better world. So I am really hooked now in trying to use that arena to help more people evolve.

T. J. Streicher: What is your intention when visiting all these other countries—are you lecturing, or something like that?

Norma: Yes, all of the above. I can now remote-view them and observe. That's another skill I have automatically picked up. Since the Beings are telepathic and clairvoyant, I now have all those skills too. So, obviously, I am going to suck in the experience like a sponge. I like what they have more than what I see down here. If all people on Earth were focused, if they lovingly cared about creation and one another, and if they were organized, I think our Earth would be a much better place. I think it would help eliminate diseases, because it is my experience that they don't even have diseases. It's like everything is so clean, neat, and organized that they don't have viruses and bacteria that eat their flesh and do all those things. They reside on a level so much higher than that. They have already conquered that. They understand it and accept it, so they don't even have to go there.

T. J. Streicher: Would you say that you give people hope?

Norma: I hope so. Yes.

T. J. Streicher: Has your desire to help others changed since your initial experience?

Norma: No, I was always geared toward serving others, from childhood on. What these experiences did was help me find myself and grow more quickly. I now serve others better, by learning from them and adopting higher modes of behavior.

T. J. Streicher: Is that what you are doing now?

Norma: I would hope that I am. I strive to do that.

T. J. Streicher: Have your concerns for planet Earth changed?

Norma: I don't know if they have changed because of my interaction with them so much as my concerns have changed. My concerns are more focused now on how people perform on this planet—I look at overpopulation, at how people don't care that animals are going extinct (and they are still killing them), drugs, child pornography, violence—the list goes on and on, as one human preys upon another human. This is getting so out of control that the world itself is spinning out of control. My concerns are probably more from my experiences in the third dimension and from caring so much for this planet, rather than from my extraterrestrial experiences as such. I think it is just a reality thing. You can't watch TV, read, look at the internet and computers, and not care, because problems are everywhere. If you don't care, then I would say that you are subhuman, or you haven't developed.

T. J. Streicher: You mentioned earlier your concerns about chemical trails [streaks of chemicals that are left in the sky from spray systems on airplanes]. Do you think you would have had all that knowledge before these experiences?

Norma: It's hard to say.

T. J. Streicher: Have your concerns for the welfare of the Earth expanded to the inhabitants of Earth?

Norma: I have always been a person with an open mind. I came into this world with an open mind, and this is one of the reasons why I believe that I have had these experiences. I can communicate with Beings who claim that they are from other parts of this galaxy or this universe. This has helped me be open and understand. Over and above all that, I do think that my experiences with these extraterrestrials have actually enhanced my concern through the role modeling, words, ideas, and concepts that they constantly transmitted to me. Everything enhanced what was already in me.

T. J. Streicher: How do you feel about being back on Earth now?

Norma: The same way I did for the last twenty years: it's a beautiful planet. It's incredible. There are many loving people, but I am much more detached now, and from what I have seen in these other worlds, I think the agendas and curricula of these other worlds fit my personality more than here on Earth. I can appreciate the beauty and see the beauty in people and I know their plight, but I am detached from it all. I am also determined to help in any way that I can. I have a sense that the determination that flows through me—a strong work ethic—comes from my connection to these Beings.

T. J. Streicher: Has this been a spiritual/religious experience for you?

Norma: Very spiritual and religious. Everyone, every Being that I ever contacted, has always talked about the God Force, the Great Central Sun, and the Light within that connects us to a Higher Power. They are adamant. They don't bend from these concepts. It has really instilled in me a great respect for this Oneness, this interconnectedness, through this Higher Power. Then, by traveling the world over the past twenty-five years and meeting people of all religions on my journeys, I really now appreciate people and these higher concepts in all religions. So it has made me more eclectic. I now embrace all the people and the highest principles from all the religions. I don't differentiate very much anymore. I don't judge, because of my experience with these Beings.

T. J. Streicher: Do you think that maybe all the religions are talking about basically the same thing, the God Force?

Norma: I think, in part, some are, but then I think that there are sections in these religions that are not on the same page, one with another. The basic tenets in most religions are really beautiful. Buddhism, though, is more of a way of life and of the mind. It teaches how to shape your life and use the power of your mind to become a better person in your connectedness to a God Force. But I think all religions have a piece of this mosaic. I think that somehow they all have to be connected. The best of all of them, or the smartest and wisest concepts from each religion, has to be shared in higher teachings. All humanity will now take a quantum leap—to start walking that talk—following those principles that most religions embrace.

T. J. Streicher: Do the Beings from Alpha Centauri talk about any type of religion or spirituality?

Norma: No, but the Arcturians and the Ascended Masters do. They refer to a Being who is coming back to this planet, whom they call the Most Radiant One. They say that He is also the soul of Jesus, the Christ, who came to Earth two thousand years ago (and that He had other incarnations as well). But they said they would never call him Jesus. They said that, when He returns, every religion and culture on the planet will recognize Him as their own. For example, in Mexico, he would be called Quetzalcoatl. In South America, he would be called Vera Quacha, and maybe the Second Coming by the Jews. He will be called Jesus by the Christians. It doesn't make any difference what the name is, because when we recognize him it will be like stepping above the pettiness of all the differences down here, and suddenly the lines will connect to something much, much greater. [All religions] will claim Him. They keep calling Him the Most Radiant One, but they won't go into specifics. They say if they started saying Quetzalcoatl or Jesus, for example, other groups would turn away because of their prejudices regarding the name. They say He is worthy of more than that, so they just keep calling Him the Most Radiant One.

T. J. Streicher: Have any of your personal goals in life changed?

Norma: These experiences have put me on the path of sharing my truth and the truths learned from my communications with these Beings. The information from the messages that I received (when followed) brought a better life to me and to other people, because I lived and practiced the wisdom and I saw what it did for me. So, yes, I became (1) a seeker of truth, and (2) someone who only wanted to live my life in truth. As a result, I published books. I now take people on journeys, guided by these Beings. I have taught people telepathic skills, how to communicate, and so on.

T. J. Streicher: Didn't you also make a dramatic career change?

Norma: In some ways, yes.

T. J. Streicher: Weren't you mostly into academia at the time?

Norma: Well, yes, I was. I was a professor of education. I taught teachers how to teach. It didn't matter what the subject matter was. I would teach them the process of developing lesson plans, and then they would put the content in, so it made no difference what subject it was—history, math, science, whatever. I did not want to stay at the university after twenty years, because I wanted to be an entrepreneur. I wanted to own my own company. I wanted to go into human resource development and training and education. I wanted to expand myself. When I left the university, I left with a great repertoire of skills. I knew how to teach, and I could train in many areas. I became a consultant in corporate America; I taught team building, job task analysis, strategic planning, and so on to Fortune 500 companies, the Navajo Nation, government workers, and so on. I taught many courses on human empowerment.

When I left the university, I began to develop some of the concepts these Beings were teaching me, realizing that they see the whole world as energy (where we see it here as physical matter). You see a chair, a table, a car, but they don't look at the world the same way. They think of it as energy; everything is a vibration. When you understand that everything is a vibration (even higher intelligence), you begin to see a curriculum lying dormant that could certainly help people change their approach to life, a dynamic curriculum of energy, rather than a stagnant curriculum around objects and forms.

I took the concepts that these Beings taught me (for fifteen years), and I began to teach these innovative and higher concepts, so people could remove struggle, pain, suffering, depression, or whatever from their lives. I taught them how to embrace beauty and love, and to let go of fear. I gave them the curriculum in such a way that they could understand how to raise their vibrational frequencies and thus continue to raise themselves in their worlds, their jobs, and their society. I taught them how to manifest things with their minds. What I believed was that this was futuristic, and, in my opinion, definitely what humanity needed. So I didn't teach at the university anymore, and this is what I've been doing now for twenty years. I have still been teaching; I just changed the subject matter of what I taught.

T. J. Streicher: Would you consider yourself somewhat of a counselor, then?

Norma: I consider myself to be a teacher and a guide. A counselor is somebody who helps people out of their problems, and a counselor is a healer. I'm a different kind of healer—I'm a healer with words. The wisdom is what one gets from words; once they assimilate the messages and understand them, I have the power to change people's lives. Knowledge is power, and knowledge has power. When you experience it, you can change the conditions around in a better way.

T. J. Streicher: Have you actually made a business out of this, then?

Norma: Well, I did, because the spiritual business or the content of spirituality includes channeling and connecting with these Beings and with UFOs. It is a whole new paradigm. My business now sits on a new frontier that humanity is slowly entering. I realize that concepts like team building, strategic planning, sexual harassment in the workplace, and communication in the workplace are very different from teaching people (1) telepathic communication, (2) how to vibrationally change their lives, or (3) how to become more Light at the cellular level, through the chakra systems, and so on. I realized years ago that I couldn't advertise the same company with these two opposing views, so I started two companies. I am now doing what I love! Like the old saying goes: Do what you love, and the money will follow. I began to follow my heart, because this is my truth. This whole experience sent me on a journey to discover truth, and this path made me the happiest.

T. J. Streicher: Would this be considered your life's work?

Norma: Oh, yes, but this too will change. Higher things will blow gently across my path and bring in other changes, I am sure.

T. J. Streicher: Has your fear of death changed?

Norma: I don't fear death at all.

T. J. Streicher: Have you always been that way?

Norma: I have always been that way.

T. J. Streicher: So there was no fear of going into these episodes with the Beings?

Norma: No, absolutely not.

T. J. Streicher: Do you think of going back to this other planet, and if so, for how long?

Norma: Having been there so many times, I think it is embedded within my cells and mind to do so. So my answer would have to be yes. It grows on you, because it is so much better than what is around here.

T. J. Streicher: For how long?

Norma: I could very easily go out of embodiment, if I was accepted to have an existence there. I would stay for a while. I think the universe is diverse with places and experiences that are wonderful and great. It would be whatever my soul wanted to create—whatever would support new growth for me.

T. J. Streicher: So you do somewhat consider going back and for an indefinite amount of time?

Norma: Sure. I don't really need to know for how long.

T. J. Streicher: What is your response to people who think your experience is fantasy, illusion, or just crazy?

Norma: I don't care, because I know my experiences are real. I have had these experiences for twenty years. I am beyond the debate of whether it is real or not, and personally, I don't want to have conversations with people anymore who are still trying to decide whether or not UFOs are even real. We are so far beyond that. That wastes my time. So I just let go of things that drain me. If somebody happens to be in my presence (who is at that level), I just find a convenient way to walk away, because I no longer enjoy talking with people who, I perceive, are at such a low level of awareness or consciousness. That doesn't excite me anymore. I will no longer play these games, and I don't even go there anymore. I just walk away. It drains me too much to be at that level.

T. J. Streicher: You have mentioned UFOs several times now. Do the Beings use UFOs?

Norma: Yes, they do.

T. J. Streicher: Do they use spacecraft?

Norma: Yes. They can also manifest themselves to be in other places. I think they can also shapeshift, as they are already evolved to that level. In my opinion, they can do just about anything they want. Anything would shock us here on Earth. I think many people have captured (in scripts, movies, and visuals) some of the things that are potential possibilities for what these other Beings can do. It isn't just me with the visions. Others can access this, and I think we have some very skilled people on Earth today who are putting their visions into movies, books, and stuff. I honestly think there is a little bit of truth in everything that is produced today.

T. J. Streicher: How long did it take for your experiences to sink in?

Norma: It took about a year or two, but I somehow knew, instantaneously, that it was real. On another level, to merge this with people around me took about a year.

T. J. Streicher: Do you consider yourself to be a person of two worlds?

Norma: More than two worlds—because I can communicate with Beings from the Pleiades, Arcturus, Alpha Centauri, or the Ascended Masters from other dimensions of time/space. My citizenship goes far beyond being in a single spaceship coming to Earth. This reality I'm describing is so multidimensional and multifaceted. When one is skilled in remote viewing, soul retrieval, astral projection, and telepathy, all of these things become endless opportunities to explore. I am always open-minded and say, show me a new idea. It isn't just being a person of two worlds. It's much more than that, because it is all in the mind. Everything is in the mind, and mind is more than the reality of two worlds.

T. J. Streicher: Would you consider yourself to be a galactic citizen?

Norma: Well, I think it's even more than that. It's more of a cosmic or universal figure or something like that. I think humanity really needs to get up to those higher levels.

T. J. Streicher: How will you integrate this experience into consciousness?

Norma: I already have done this by being grateful every day, by allowing and learning, by being a student, and by being open to receiving more ideas. I choose. I evaluate whether the new experiences are for me or not. If I like them, then I say, thank you. If I don't, there is no judgment. Everything that I have learned in twenty years from my experiences and communications with them has made my world better.

T. J. Streicher: Did you have any problems with integration or ontological shock?

Norma: Absolutely not. No.

T. J. Streicher: Did that come instantaneously for you?

Norma: No, that took about a year, and after that it was okay, and everything was fine.

T. J. Streicher: That was the last question of the interview, but I would like to ask if there is anything else you want to add before closing.

Norma: I think people everywhere in the world have to get on the same page and start acknowledging the existence of life and consciousness beyond this planet. We need to stop debating the basic questions if it is real or not, or does it exist or not. That wastes time. I think we need to force the governments to reveal more of the documentation they hide from the people, regarding the truths of the extraterrestrials here on Earth. That would encourage humanity to grow up. We are deserving of this knowledge. We are not going to panic as they keep telling us we will. I think humanity literally needs to evolve, and now is the time. We need to open our minds; we need to take our power; and we need to open up to higher knowledge and information, and then accept the responsibility that comes with it. Every time a person changes, what comes with it is responsibility, which is why most people don't like to change. They are basically lazy, I think. They don't want responsibility. So, my last words are, let's get off our duffs and get on with this. Let's now move into these higher worlds with these other Beings and start enjoying another way of life.

T. J. Streicher: We are hoping that this study may help raise consciousness toward the goals you just mentioned.

Norma: I hope so, and good luck to you, too, because we need more of this and we need professors who will support this kind of work—not frivolous work, but meaningful work that can make the difference for our future.

8

THE CRYSTALLINE TOWERS

Marilynn Hughes

Conducted February 23, 2009

Marilynn Hughes, whose career was in broadcasting as a news anchor, reporter, and producer, has experienced, researched, written, and taught about out-of-body travel and mysticism since 1987. She will be featured in the documentary film due for release in the summer of 2012. Marilynn founded the Out-of-Body Travel Foundation in 2003 and has written over fifty books and thirty magazine articles on out-of-body travel and comparative religious mysticism. These books, along with accompanying music and art, are available for free download or can be purchased in print.

When Marilynn was nine years old, she had her first profound vision, wherein she saw the heavens open and a beautiful marble staircase surrounded by angels leading to the throne of God. When she was twenty-two years old, she had her first out-of-body experience completely unexpectedly; thus began a process of journaling that would unleash thousands of out-of-body travel and mystical experiences over the next decades.

▼

T. J. Streicher: Hi, Marilynn!

Marilynn: Hi. Thanks for meeting me here today; this is really great, and I want you to know that I appreciate and respect this time we are spending together. I will try to hold it as sacred space between us.

T. J. Streicher: I feel the same. I really think that this is important information, and that is why I wanted to meet with you today and talk a little bit about your experience, or experiences, that might help in this study of people who have experience on other planets. What I would like to start off with is to ask you, if you can recall, when you think of another planet and how you may have approached it, along with the techniques you used such as out-of-body travel. Are there any other ways to do it? Maybe you can give me an idea of how you would travel to another planet and how you have, in the past, traveled to another planet.

Marilynn: The way it happens to me is *absolutely not* something that I induce myself. It is through out-of-body experiences. I will usually be in a very, very, deep state of consciousness or sleep, and suddenly then I will become aware or conscious of the presences around me. They will pull me into this energy, which I immediately recognize, because I've experienced it so many times now. But in the beginning, it was more of a sense of awe. However, I still have new experiences with races I haven't yet been introduced to that will instill within me a sense of awe again. Sometimes I can even tell which ones they are. For example, the Pleiadian experiences I have had are probably more numerous than the ones I have had with some of the other ones, so I can recognize the feeling of it and I will be pulled out of my body. There are usually beings there. A lot of times they are hooded; they wear almost what I would call monk robes. A lot of times I am not allowed to see their faces or what they actually look like underneath their robes. There have been many times where they appear in a light body.

Sometimes I have seen other less ethereal extraterrestrials and can feel that they are different—the greys that people speak about. But my experiences with them are very different from the ones I have had with those whom I would consider to be more advanced life-forms, where the civilizations they come from are more spiritual and they have a purpose in coming here that is spiritual. It is eternal, a work of God. One way I explained it to someone recently, after having an experience with the Pleiadian ships, is that oftentimes, as soon as you are pulled out of your body, you will see them hovering. There is a mother ship along with several craft that surround it. And you always become aware of the ships before you encounter anything else, because they emanate the power and it draws you to them. It's hard to describe. I hope I'm doing well.

T. J. Streicher: The only question I had is, do you ever contact these beings before you are in a semiconscious state or subconscious state?

Marilynn: No.

T. J. Streicher: Do you put yourself in a trance state or some other kind of state?

Marilynn: I do not put myself into a state, but I will be drawn naturally into a very deep state of sleep. What happens with out-of-body travel is that you are completely unconscious and at a very deep level of consciousness. And suddenly your spirit becomes totally conscious, so you have these very, very intense experiences; you go through vibrational states when you are exiting the body and stuff like that. You are as conscious as you and I sitting here talking, but your body is completely unconscious. Your spirit is not. So I have never seen them myself while in a physical waking state. I have had a couple of experiences where I have seen some things—when I was in Sedona, for instance, when I was in my physical body—that appeared to be some kind of spacecraft in the night sky, but that was it. Usually for me it happens in the out-of-body travel state, so I am very unconscious of my body, but not my spirit.

T. J. Streicher: Can you anticipate this event?

Marilynn: No, it happens spontaneously. It can happen when you least expect it.

T. J. Streicher: But always during a state of sleep?

Marilynn: Yes. I have three kids, and one of them would often have the same experiences I was having at night with the Pleiadians. They would be around the house, and we would see them the same night, and there would be no reason to expect it to occur. We would both have the experience the same night.

T. J. Streicher: So you shared these with your child the next morning?

Marilynn: Or vice versa.

T. J. Streicher: Somebody would say something in the morning like, I had a dream, or I dreamed something? What would be the difference between this experience and a dream experience?

Marilynn: Well, that is a good question. What I think happens with out-of-body travel is that you are more conscious, and you are aware that you leave your body. You're aware of the vibration, you're aware that you are walking through matter, walking through the ceiling. You're aware of the spaceship over there, and they take you in a totally conscious way in a dreamlike experience. But it's really like being totally awake. Does that make sense?

T. J. Streicher: Yes. There is such a thing as lucid dreaming where you do know you are dreaming. This is a different state, correct?

Marilynn: It is different. You are totally aware. Probably not in the beginning, but now it has been twenty to thirty years since this started, or maybe twenty-two or something like that. Now I am very much aware of when I am not in my body anymore, whereas when I am dreaming I am aware that I am dreaming. So it is different. There is a lot of similarity. My conclusions over the years have been that a lot of these things are probably happening on different levels of consciousness. So someone who experienced a lucid dream or even left the lucid dream can very well be remembering portions of what might be out-of-body experiences. They're not just totally conscious, and so there are different levels of consciousness for these experiences. Does that make any sense? One of the things I talk about in my books is about subconscious astral spirits, those who are dreaming but absolutely subconscious. They will not remember the experience as a dream or anything. Because you meet people in these out-of-body travel states that you know are subconscious, which means they are out of their body but not aware of it. And you see this with the extraterrestrial life forms a lot, and you can tell immediately that many of these people will not remember what is happening to them. But I remember it completely, as if awake.

T. J. Streicher: Can you recall all of it?

Marilynn: You can recall however much they allow you to, because there have been many experiences where they will show you things that are just so awe-inspiring, awesome, and you feel like, I have to remember all this. There is often a sense of holy awe. And then they will take a portion out of your mind that they do not want you to remember, for whatever reason. So they let you remember whatever they want and no more.

T. J. Streicher: Do you have the feeling that they are in control of the situation?

Marilynn: No, it's not a feeling. You *know* they are in control, as with the Pleiadians. With the civilizations that I consider to be higher and here for a greater purpose, you feel completely comfortable with them being in control. Except for the fact that you're disappointed that they take away certain memories, because you remember you saw something spectacular, but it's just taken away.

T. J. Streicher: Is it erased?

Marilynn: Yes, it is, so you're really disappointed, and you want to try and bring it back. But you can't. There are certain things that they do not allow you to remember, and then there are things that are so beyond our comprehension. There was something, ironically, about one of my children, which I was shown. I can't remember where it was that I was shown, and this might sound a little bit out there, but we were sharing sacred space.

T. J. Streicher: Nothing is too far out there for me.

Marilynn: I was shown that some of us have other origins before we incarnate here. We have some of these elements, and sometimes it has to do with which civilization hangs around us, because it is something we are supposed to do. I was shown this civilization that one of my children had come from, and I was taken really far out; we went to a place that was so far beyond anything that I understood astronomically, I had no idea where it was. I just know it was so far out, and beyond that I did not know where it was, and I don't have a name for it. But I experienced the level of spiritual evolution of the civilization for maybe twenty to thirty minutes, and they were downloading into me. It was an incredible experience and I was just awestruck by it when I came back. While at the same time I will never forget the experience, I can never really put it into words completely in terms of how I felt—like, "Wow, they wanted me to realize that they had come from a very advanced place." One of the things I have been shown about my own kids is to always remember that they are just little people in bodies, and you have to respect that they may have purposes beyond what you might even be able to comprehend as their parent. I think they were trying to give me more respect for their souls and were making sure I was leading them correctly, while also being respectful. They might develop and know things that I didn't understand as they got older. Does that make sense?

T. J. Streicher: Sure. Are these beings familiar to you now? Are these the same beings that come to visit you?

Marilynn: No, I've only seen this civilization that one time. I see the Pleiadians most often. With the Pleiadians, you do get a certain sense— it's more like a group; there is a huge mother ship that I have seen repeatedly, and there are always separate crafts. And it's almost like a consciousness with them, because they never speak; everything is communicated telepathically. You always get the sense that when you see many of them they are all telling you things. They are communicating with their thoughts, and so there is a sense of familiarity with them every time they come. A holy silence, as well. But as to whether they are exactly the same ones, I'm not sure, because it is more like a consciousness of one.

The last experience had come totally out of the blue, just a couple of months ago. It is hard to put into words, but I will try. I was sitting inside our Catholic church and the roof was off. It was an out-of-body experience, and I looked up and all of a sudden . . . When they come you have that sense of what I've seen others experience during Marian apparitions, when the Blessed Virgin appears. The attention is immediately on her, which, ironically, is another thing I can point out in a minute about the Blessed Virgin Mary, because I had an experience with her and her extraterrestrial origins. In this experience the roof was off the church, and they were getting ready to celebrate the Holy Mass. And in Catholicism a Holy Mass is the most holy event that we celebrate. And the mother ship was above the church, and I was mesmerized looking at it; there were crafts around it, and I immediately understood what they were bringing (even though it felt very odd to me to realize this at the time as a Catholic) was so far beyond what we already had understood spiritually. It was more important that I was fixed upon them than on what was about to be celebrated. Why? Because they were creating a galactic link between our religious rituals, which are important, but they were taking it to an even higher level in the galactic heavens. It was profoundly intense, in the sense that communicating to me was such a huge evolutionary leap for those who could accept it. I'm not sure how it will end up manifesting in the real time and real world, but it's there and it's important. It's a galactic linkup, so to speak, a raising of our level of humanity to a level that can receive those things, which are coming from these higher spheres wherein many of these extraterrestrial life-forms reside. They are trying to help us to achieve a higher level of spiritual understanding.

The thing that I get when I see them is that they're ever present and they are around. When the Iraq War started, I had an experience where they were hovering and watching to see what we were going to do. We could either take a huge evolutionary leap forward or blow ourselves back to the Stone Age, and they were anxiously waiting to see what we were going to do at that point. It was interesting.

Going back to the Blessed Virgin, I had a really cool experience with her and it was with the Pleiadians. They had come, and I was running after them in spirit; they always have this sound when they come. It's very loud, vibrational, like the sounds of a perfectly humming but profoundly powerful jet engine that somehow reaches you on a soul level. A beautiful lady had exited the bottom of one of the Pleiadian craft, and I knew her name to be "The Lady in Light." I began running through the crowds to get near this beautiful lady who had descended from the Pleiadian ship, and when I came up behind her, she turned to look at me and smiled. Instantly, I knew. And I said to her, "You're the Blessed Virgin Mary." But yet, she had just gotten off of a Pleiadian ship!

T. J. Streicher: You say "they"—now are you talking about the Pleiadians? I was wondering, because you have some ability to distinguish the Pleiadians from other visitors. How do you know that they are Pleiadians?

Marilynn: Well, I have been taken to the Pleiades a couple of times, for one, and they would point out who they are. There was one in particular who came first. His name was Antonique, and he taught me a lot. But he was only the beginning of many who would come after him. Their spacecraft come with a particular vibration that is unique only to them.

T. J. Streicher: When you are ready, I would like you to go into greater detail on one of these experiences when you felt you did travel to another world or planet.

Marilynn: I will go ahead with the one when I went to the Pleiades for the first time, if that is Okay.

T. J. Streicher: Yes.

Marilynn: Only because I'm more familiar with them, but I have seen others. The Pleiadians had come and there was a craft. It was silver and had a blue light underneath. And they told me that they were going to take me to see what the Pleiades looked like.

T. J. Streicher: Did you have previous contact before this? For about how long?

Marilynn: Yes, about six months. But they had come to me on Earth; I had not been taken to where they had come from yet. So they put me into this vessel, and it wasn't long before we reached the Pleiades, and we landed on what I believed to be a planet. I'm trying to remember the details about the soil. I remember the Pleiadian sky was a deep purplish-blue. It was very intense, because instead of having one sun, it was darker. You could see the Pleiadian stars all around—I think there were six or seven. You could see them all from the ground. There were a lot of crystal-like formations.

T. J. Streicher: Crystal-like formations on the ground?

Marilynn: Yes, and all around. It was more like a mountainous but desert-like landscape; there were no trees and little water. It was very beautiful, and the feeling was like a humming high vibration of love. But it was kind of—in terms of landscape, it felt like there was a lot of rock, mountains, and crystals that would protrude from the ground and inside the caverns and things. Many of the mountains were embedded with a purplish rock similar to amethyst, but that amethyst formation would encase entire mountain formations. The beings there appeared to me as beings of light; they were pretty much light bodies. You didn't see arms and legs, but we flitted about the planet with ease. It was like you were in that light body, and you could travel at the speed of light or higher; I don't know.

T. J. Streicher: You were out of the craft at this time now. When that happened and you looked at this remarkable place, how large did this planet seem? Was it immense? Could you see a horizon?

Marilynn: It didn't seem immense. You know, it wasn't like here where you can look out forever; it didn't seem like it was huge. I remember seeing these huge butterflies. The horizon was probably as if I were on a moon.

T. J. Streicher: What was the color of this planet—could you tell by the ground?

Marilynn: The ground had a grayish nature, and there were crystalline things that were like quartz crystal. I remember there being a lot of purple and blue—the amethyst on the mountains and in the caverns. But the sky was very purple-blue. The landscape was not like the moon in the sense of the barrenness of the moon, but in terms of the light, the sunlight, it was different from what we have here where you just see the obvious day, obvious night. It was more like twilight. Does that make sense at all?

T. J. Streicher: Kind of in between?

Marilynn: Yes, it was more like what to expect on the moon, but then again some obvious differences. But in terms of astronomically, it is what I would expect if I were going to be on the moon. It's like what we see from the twilight. I know that the moon gets totally dark on one side too, but when you see the moon landing, there is, like, a twilight sense. Does that make sense?

T. J. Streicher: Yes. Was there a name for this planet?

Marilynn: They did not tell me.

T. J. Streicher: You said they were going to take you to their planet, correct?

Marilynn: This was one of them. We know there were more. What they were telling me was they wanted me to experience what it felt like to be truly and totally free, because they are in a different space than we are. And it was really awesome, because the moment was so simple. Everything was so simple. You could fly across the landscape and go inside the mountain. And there was a lot of crystal and structure in the mountain, I remember that. There was a lot of healing energy. Unconditional and intense love . . .

T. J. Streicher: So did you go under the planet then, inside the planet?

Marilynn: Well, it was more like I was on the surface when we landed, and then they took me inside some kind of a mountain. I don't remember right off hand if it was like a cave that went inside, but there were more crystals in there. It was inside this mountain. I don't recall seeing any plants. It was very crystalline. It was primarily these huge quartz structures and things that could be compared to amethyst. But there were also purplish quartz structures, so that is not exactly amethyst, but it was like that color. I remember being mesmerized by the sky because it was a beautiful deep bluish purple, and you could see several of these Pleiadian stars in the sky.

T. J. Streicher: How could you see them—were they shining?

Marilynn: Yes, they were shining, and you could see this interesting look of the stars. I have painted these. It's more like twilight in a night sky than a daytime sky. There were these huge stars.

T. J. Streicher: Like a sun?

Marilynn: They were huge like a sun, but they were for whatever reason not like the daylight that we have. It wasn't like that. For whatever reason, it wasn't emanating that kind of light to the place where we were—why, I don't know.

T. J. Streicher: Can you remember the temperature?

Marilynn: Yes, that is a good question, because I remember writing that the temperature was perfect. You never felt cold and you never felt too hot. You always felt like you were the perfect temperature, but you were in a different kind of body. It was kind of like a light body at the time, so I remember that as being really an unusual thing, since in my physical body I had a tendency to get very cold. It was really beautiful; there was this sense of profound unconditional love. There was a real sense of intelligence that was more than intelligence. It was like an evolution of these beings that are different from us, greater than us.

T. J. Streicher: Did you get to go any other places? You mentioned the caverns.

Marilynn: That particular visit I was not allowed to go any other places.

T. J. Streicher: Did you get to go to the same place another time?

Marilynn: I don't think so. I have never even checked to see if there are other planets there.

T. J. Streicher: What really matters is your experience on another planet.

Marilynn: I was also taken to see Alpha Centauri, wherein I was taken on another spaceship. These two beings were dressed all in white and they appeared to be human, but they weren't. They told me that they had changed their appearance for my benefit, and they wanted me to see the Alpha Centauri planet, so I was taken to see it. It was more Earthly, except that it had this huge sun. The thing I remember, I was not allowed off the spacecraft on this experience. But I could see there was lush greenery and it was much more Earthlike, except there was this huge sun, about half the size of the horizon on this planet. You can't help but ask these questions, like how could they be so close to the sun? But I didn't know what kind of life form they are; I could not explain that. But the sun was the size of half the sky. In a separate experience relating to the planet Venus, I saw some similarity, but Venus is not inhabited with physical beings.

T. J. Streicher: How did you know it was the planet Venus?

Marilynn: Because they always tell me.

T. J. Streicher: Always?

Marilynn: Well, I have had some experiences with the greys; they never told me where they were from. I still don't know where they are from. In regards to the Venus experiences, they came to me in a crystal-faceted spaceship, and it was bluish green, with maybe some purple in it.

T. J. Streicher: Would you like to draw it?

Marilynn: Sure. It was like a crystal-faceted spacecraft. Almost like a bottle shape, wider on the bottom, narrower on the top. It was *very* beautiful, and when you would go to the planet there were buildings that were not so different from what you see on Earth.

T. J. Streicher: Did you see buildings on Venus?

Marilynn: Yes, and on Alpha Centauri there were buildings. There were some similarities between the buildings we have here and some that they had there. The similarities are like the new modern architecture that we're seeing, like the shiny buildings. They were not skyscrapers, but they had that metallic mirror reflective surface. And I remember that the atmosphere was more gaseous, as if there was a haze, but there was a bright light. It was different from the Pleiades, where it was darker and you can see all these stars.

T. J. Streicher: Did you see signs of civilization?

Marilynn: On the Pleiades, no, not there—only with their spacecraft. You would think based on my other experiences that there would have to be signs of civilization, but I was not shown them.

T. J. Streicher: What about under the surface of the planet?

Marilynn: Maybe. I remember seeing inside the cavern they took me into all these crystalline structures that seemed important, like perhaps it powered or controlled something. The Pleiadians do have very sophisticated spacecraft, after all.

T. J. Streicher: Can we go into more detail concerning what the planets looked like?

Marilynn: On the Pleiades, I don't think I saw a single building; I saw a big rocky mountain, but it didn't have trees or plants. It had protrusions of crystal structures, a big scale version of amethyst. The primary colors were crystal clear and purple—a beautiful purple.

T. J. Streicher: Did it resemble the sky?

Marilynn: Yes, it was similar to the sky, but the sky had a darker hue, because it was very twilightish and more purple.

T. J. Streicher: Could the crystals be reflecting the light from the sky?

Marilynn: I think that is possible, but I'm not sure.

T. J. Streicher: Did you touch these crystals?

Marilynn: Yes, and when you touched them there was an energy emitted, so part of the fun was going from crystal to crystal. It was powerful. When I went into the mountain, there was something under the mountain that had to do with how their souls were powered, perhaps how their ships were powered. It was like the crystalline structures were a power plant.

T. J. Streicher: Were you inside the mountain?

Marilynn: Yes. I received information from being in there from a male who was in there. These crystal structures provided some kind of power, and I don't know what it is. The spacecraft are very loud, there's a low rumbling. The whole planet vibrates. The Pleiadians have this heightened spiritual evolution. I'd mentioned before seeing the Blessed Virgin Mary coming out of a Pleiadian ship. She was dressed in purple and white and I touched her hand. I understood then that she had Pleiadian origins. I had also been told that Christ has Pleiadian origins. That was a very powerful experience I had with her, and a profound understanding that there are a lot of holy people who may have origins like these. I write a lot about all the different world religions. My own personal belief about the holy people who have come, like the prophets, avatars, messiahs, the great saints and mystics and stuff, is that a lot of them may have come from far away (however this works, because I don't know how it does), where they have these aspects of other star systems.

T. J. Streicher: Do you consider all of them to be extraterrestrial then?

Marilynn: No. I have had innumerable experiences with spirits and beings. One of the things I write about is lost souls. The majority of the types of beings that I deal with are either human beings who have died, or angels, demons, people in between heaven, hell, and purgatory. And there are many different realms of those, and there is a planetary connection to those realms as well. Each of these planetary systems serves a different function. For instance, the Earth is a world that I would consider a mortal realm, where the battles between good and evil exist. But there are other planetary systems where they are beyond the battles of good and evil. There are also other planetary systems where there are other mortals like us, as well.

In my writings, I explain how the systems of evolution can be understood through a system I have been shown—a star map—the Universal Sphere of Realms. But this star map shows planetary locations and our own location according to the level of evolution, not a physical location. But somehow it works out that these physical locations all merge and make sense when you see them overlapping the Universal Sphere of Realms. In a nutshell, the most interior realms one and two are lower realms—realms where dominant darkness and evil reside. Realms three and four are borderlands, the mortal realms—realms where the battle of good and evil both within us and outside of us takes place. Realms five and above are worlds of ever-increasing light. One of the most powerful experiences I have had, because I have had several of that type, is that of all these civilizations coming together. I mentioned to you before about the Galactic Council?

T. J. Streicher: Have you met with the Galactic Council?

Marilynn: Yes. I don't know where it was; it was not on Earth.

T. J. Streicher: What did the Galactic Council consist of?

Marilynn: There were five people from the Earth that particular night that I was taken, and there were representatives from, it seemed like, every star system in the universe. There were many beings, and they all looked different. But the purpose of the council had to do with bringing members of mortal races, in our case humanity, into touch with the higher Galactic Council. They are actively seeking to create within the consciousness of mankind a galactic linkup in our spiritual and psychic bodies, which will help us transcend where we are on the evolutionary scale of things.

T. J. Streicher: Do you recall about how many beings were at the Galactic Council?

Marilynn: Between one and two thousand. There are so many different ones that you have a hard time recalling their differences when you come back. I was very overwhelmed when I first woke up. I had another experience years ago, when I was taken to another Galactic Council, but it was something similar, where there were several species, races, several different kinds in one location. And that was very interesting because there are so many different-looking creatures or forms of life, perhaps I should say.

T. J. Streicher: What was your experience on another planet like?

Marilynn: Ecstatic. It is very similar to the experiences that the mystics might describe as ecstasy or samadhi in Hinduism. You go into an altered state like you are in ecstasy. It's the unconditional love that you feel, and the power, and it's almost a sense like I am home. There is a sense of being home for just a moment, of being in a more perfect world. It's a real break from a mortal realm, at least these ones. I had experiences with the greys, and those were not always positive. But the ones I'm referring to now are the ones in whose presence you feel that you are surrounded by God, in a sense. It's not that these beings are God; it's just that you are in such a higher place—these extraterrestrials are much closer to God. The unconditional love is palpable, but it is so hard to explain to a mortal realm what unconditional love really means. Those who are able to reach into these realms do so because of the correction they've already received when they, too, may have traveled beyond mortal realms. Unconditional love is felt as something that can only be experienced within the natural confines of understanding. Understanding comes about through correction.

Those of us in the mortal realm often misinterpret unconditional love as staying where you are, when in fact it is the opposite. Unconditional love is achieved by races who have reached such a state of love and a heightened understanding of God that they naturally stay within certain boundaries. We are in a mortal realm, because we must learn those boundaries that unleash that kind of love, which means, in essence, we will have to receive instruction, guidance, and learning on virtue and attaining to this higher understanding, which naturally amends and controls itself within the confines of God's will without disturbance. It's a beauty and power; it's energy that they fill you with. They always have a mission for you, going in steps. There is something that they want you to do. You are always excited to see them again. You can't wait to see what they have to tell you this time. And every time you see them, you bring something energetic back with you, something more than the last time.

T. J. Streicher: Sounds like a family that cares about each other?

Marilynn: Yes, very much. It is very similar to going home. That sounds odd, but it feels like I'm home for a few minutes. Does that make sense? Oh, and how I miss it when I have to come back!

T. J. Streicher: Yes. So how did this experience affect you, now when you look back?

Marilynn: It just affected everything. It changed the entire path my life was taking. It was laid out for me, and I felt compelled to follow. When I was in my early twenties I was in the news business. I was a radio news anchor and reporter. I was heading in a pretty good direction there, and I completely changed my direction. If I had continued to do what I was doing, I would probably be doing that kind of stuff now. But it felt like I was being called in a completely different direction. Sometimes I say that God assigned me to be a reporter in other realms. My spirit began to travel through what I call "star tunnels" but which are very similar to what science terms black holes. But when you mystically travel through these "gateways" you enter into the sphere that I term the "galactic heavens." It is another dimensional reality of the universe, and within it is heaven. It encompasses everything we have that is knowledge-based here on Earth with everything that the galactic heavens contain in terms of knowledge. Those who reside in heaven are not just spirits from the Earth but from other planets. But when you're there, that feels very natural. Everything that I have done in my entire life has completely changed.

T. J. Streicher: Can you recall what you were thinking and feeling on this other planet?

Marilynn: Very ecstatic. You are in awe the whole time—remember, you are seeing the Kingdom of God.

T. J. Streicher: Was the whole time ecstatic?

Marilynn: With the few exceptions of when I was being shown the many different civilizations. Some of them are higher than us; some of them are similar to us. I don't know if I've ever been shown any [extraterrestrials] that were lower than us. I don't think I have. But I've seen much of the lower realm as it relates to human souls. There are some extraterrestrial races that are raging with the warring between good and evil, and those are just as dangerous as we are. There can be mixtures of good and evil in each one of them; they can have bad intentions, or they can have good intentions and do stupid things.

The experience that I had with the greys was not good. The reason was that they took you completely out of your own control, and there was no free will involved. I was warned by, I think, the Pleiadians to be careful with the greys and other mortal extraterrestrial races, because there are races that are no higher than us and they can do things that are not necessarily good or helpful. They might think they are just like human beings who can do bad things with good intentions . . . whatever. You know how humanity often tries to do the right thing with good intentions but later realizes it was the wrong choice? They're mortal, like us. But there didn't appear to be that many races like these out there. There are many mortal realms other than Earth; many of these are purgatorial realms filled with many human spirits. But there were not many extraterrestrial races like this. By far, the experiences I've had with the extraterrestrials have shown a huge preponderance of higher races than ours who are beyond our comprehension.

T. J. Streicher: More mutually respectful?

Marilynn: Yes, very much so, especially when you consider that in these experiences I'm always being made aware of my inferiority. I am kind of aware that I am this dumb human, and they're taking whatever time they need to impart something to me. And I'd better pay attention, because I am the one that really needs it. They're not doing it for *their* benefit. They are doing it for *mine,* and for whatever the greater purpose is that they're instructing me to do things. Does that make sense?

T. J. Streicher: How long ago was it that you visited another planet, and when was the last time?

Marilynn: My first time was 1987 to 1990, sometime between there. My Venusian trip was the first one. The Pleiadian trip was probably about ten to fifteen years ago. The two other civilizations that I saw were probably in the last five years. In terms of general trips I have taken into the galactic heavens, through the star tunnel in the out-of-body state, that's going on all the time. I go into this alternate universal reality, and I am not visiting one particular planet, but I can see many of them. I am being taken through the galactic heavens and shown other things: they take me to space stations, and they show me universal truths in relation to Christ's great importance in all universal reality, not just for those who have lived on Earth.

That's one thing that people might be surprised by: in the galactic heavens wherein spirits of many life forms reside alongside each other, Christ is equally respected and revered in an even greater way than on Earth. I was probably taken to the galactic heavens for the first time in the last ten years, although that remains ongoing. In terms of the last Pleiadian encounter, it was a couple of months ago. In terms of going out into the actual heavens, I experience that frequently. And many of my experiences are not necessarily always dealing with the extraterrestrial element. My experiences run the gamut in terms of spiritual teaching. I have a lot of experiences that are not in this exact subject area.

T. J. Streicher: Would you like to go back to any of these planets?

Marilynn: Yes, of course.

T. J. Streicher: Why do you think you are not going back?

Marilynn: Because of these other things that have more urgency at the time. One of the more important things is that when a soul is in need on any level, this takes precedence over me getting such opportunities. Much of my time is spent working with lost souls, aiding souls in purgatorial and hell realms, working with souls on Earth on subconscious levels, even helping the extraterrestrials in their efforts to open the minds and hearts of other souls subconsciously to the work they are trying to do in linking us to a "galactic" connection or mindset. These trips to other planets or beautiful spheres are often a reward after months and months of hard work. Sometimes I'm not taken to another planet, but rather to a really holy place where I learn something profound and true instead. Does that make sense?

T. J. Streicher: Yes.

Marilynn: I think the one thing that has come through all my experiences is that everything is connected. These travels to other planets, all the things I am doing regarding other religions, the paths of the prophets, saints, mystics, sages, and ascetics; they are all connected. It's not just one or the other. They all come together, so it's hard to compartmentalize because of that.

T. J. Streicher: When you look back, do you think this has given you a better connection with humanity?

Marilynn: Very much so. It has completely changed my whole worldview. Everything I have ever believed has been completely changed by all of it.

T. J. Streicher: Has this changed your occupation?

Marilynn: Yes, I have devoted myself to my writing. I have more than sixty books in print on comparative religious mysticism and out-of-body experiences. I've written a twelve-volume series on all the different world religions and their sacred texts. I have done a lot of work with the world religions and bringing them together. My organization, the Out-of-Body Travel Foundation—its website is http://outofbodytravel .org—remains very well used around the world for out-of-body travel. And I have literally dedicated my life's blood to making everything that I do available for free download worldwide. I do this because the prophets asked me to, and I began doing it at a time when the technology was just starting to become available. Many times the extraterrestrials showed me how to make something work on the website that others could not figure out. My books are in print and can be purchased, but they are also all available for free download (http:// outofbodytravel.org). I've also painted some of my experiences and written some of the music I've heard in out-of-body travel states.

Those are available at the website as well, in print, on CDs, and for free download.

The mission of the Out-of-Body Travel Foundation is to reduce spiritual hunger worldwide by providing many resources, not just my own, for free, to anyone who has a seeking. What I try to work toward is unity and understanding between the world's religions. Rather than focusing only on our human need to be *understood,* we must also focus on *understanding* one another and trying to create a dialogue between people. The Out-of-Body Travel Foundation is worldwide; we hear from people of all faiths.

T. J. Streicher: How have these experiences changed your connection with humanity? Do you feel that you are an extraterrestrial?

Marilynn: No, I don't believe I am an extraterrestrial. I believe that my worldview has changed in the sense that I have become less judgmental. I have become more of a seeker. I want to know the truth more, whereas before these experiences came into my life I often was more arrogant and thought I already knew it. Even now, twenty some years after these experiences began, I don't know the whole truth. The one thing I have learned is that God is just so vast that it may very well not be possible for us in human form to understand and know Him completely. But we can know Him more fully. This has completely altered the spiritual path I've taken in my life; my experiences even led me to Catholicism.

They've changed the way I view everything, and I am all the more aware of my inadequacy even as a vessel to explain all that I've seen. Because I cannot even really say that I fully understand all that I've seen. I can only try, knowing that God in His fullness cannot be contained. What I have seen with the extraterrestrial races shows me what is possible for my own spirit and that of others, if we move toward the change that they bring, the alterations that they present, and the galactic alignment that they give so freely. Watching what they do out of complete selflessness, I have also changed my focus to be much more directed to the needs of humanity than to my own personal "needs," which are usually desires rather than needs.

T. J. Streicher: Has your concern for material things changed?

Marilynn: Oh, yeah, I pretty much sold everything I owned. I was told to move out here, and they said sell everything you own, and I said OK. I sold everything we owned, and we did the little wagon train and moved out West to these mountains. I was told about Ute Mountain in my visions before I ever knew that there was a Ute Nation or a mountain.

T. J. Streicher: You were told? Do you mean by your extraterrestrial friends?

Marilynn: There were many Native American spirits that were working with me at the time. Chief Joseph of the Nez Percé spent a significant amount of time teaching me in the spiritual realms. I wrote about it in *The Mysteries of the Redemption: A Treatise on Out-of-Body Travel and Mysticism,* Part II, "The Alteration Pathway." Many of them were just referred to as "the old ones." There was one named Grandmother Skywalker, Hunkpapa Woman . . . and they had ties to extraterrestrial regions. They told me to move out to Ute Mountain. Ironically, years before when I first started having out-of-body experiences, they were saying the word "Ute" to me. And I didn't know what they meant, because I lived in Ohio. We had the Shawnee and Cherokee, but I had never heard of the Ute. I did not know, and so they led me here. It took a while. I had to research. They told me things and I had to figure out what it was, and then we would have to put things in place and see where we were being led to go. One of the things that Chief Joseph would say to me was that we need to restore what has been lost. My husband Andy had some Calvary lifetimes, and he had to atone for that; now he works with the Native Americans, the Utes, atoning for some of the things he probably did in those lifetimes. Does that make sense? We had to restore our little portion of what had been lost at our hands in the past.

T. J. Streicher: Has your concern for the welfare of the planet Earth changed?

Marilynn: Yes, very much so. Especially when I had experiences where they were hovering before the Iraq War, and I could tell the importance of the moment. It was, like, what can I do about this? It has completely changed my view of the welfare of the planet, because I do believe that we are at a point where we can go forward or backward in evolution. I think of technology, global warming, and the things that we are doing, and there are so many more things that could throw us back to the Stone Age. And we can either do that or go the other direction toward where the Galactic Council and its members are trying to very quietly lead us in our subconscious minds through these galactic linkups to higher places and higher thinking. But it can be one or the other—total destruction or an age of peace—it could be that extreme. So it has changed my concern in a profound way.

T. J. Streicher: Has your desire to help others changed since this experience?

Marilynn: Yes. I now work more in a service capacity. For many years, I worked for the Catholic Church, so we did a lot with the homeless, the sick, and all sorts of things. But my energies are now on my family and the work of the Out-of-Body Travel Foundation, aimed at reducing spiritual hunger, but also working to restore that which has been lost—within our spirits.

T. J. Streicher: How do you feel about being back on Earth?

Marilynn: I have gotten accustomed to it, but I always look forward to the day when I am done here, when I can go back more permanently. I enjoy the experiences I am still very blessed to have when they occur, and I feel I am continually learning. There is a fine balance between helping and hurting, and I feel that, in the work I do. I find that fine balance difficult to achieve sometimes. I let myself down. But I do get back up and try to learn from those mistakes and try again when these things naturally happen.

T. J. Streicher: Have you considered this a spiritual or religious experience?

Marilynn: Absolutely, I do think it is. But perhaps not in the sense that some religious people may perceive it. It's different; it's more. It's beyond and greater than anything we truly understand here. I believe this connection between our world and the others absolutely encompasses the next leap for religion and spirituality. It's something that we just cannot fully understand, even if you've seen it. If you've seen it, you will understand what I mean in that we cannot fully fathom it. A person who is very religious may not know what I am talking about, because I mean it differently than they might mean it. However, I consider myself a religious person. Does that make sense? Sometimes religion is more structured than God, and the spirit of God cannot be contained within such structures. This doesn't in any way minimize the truth, value, and importance of religion. My mystical experiences led me to study all religion and to become Catholic. I know the truth in religion.

The extraterrestrial experience is a religious experience—unfortunately probably very hard for a person who may not have experienced it to place in this context. God is behind it all. When you're there, you know God is present. You know He is behind all of it, including the extraterrestrial experiences, but you also understand that they're all related. You get it that some of our great holy people were possibly of extraterrestrial origin, but it is all under the umbrella of God. On the other hand, some people of different faiths might find this ridiculous, and I understand that view. But I can tell you from my experience without question they are all connected.

I look at the time we are facing now and compare it to the time of Christopher Columbus. They found a new world at that time, and we are on the verge of realizing that we are going to find yet another new world beyond our own planet. The only question is that we don't know which ones are inhabited, how they are inhabited, how they exist. We know we have different laws of life in our realm than they do in theirs, because many of these beings such as the Pleiadians are not third-dimensional creatures. They are spiritual creatures, fifth dimensional and beyond. The greys, from what I understand, are third-dimensional creatures that have a physical body. But a lot of these extraterrestrial civilizations have completely different laws of existence than we have. It's *very* similar to what Christopher Columbus found in the New World. We are just on the verge of finding these new worlds now, but there are so many and they are so varied; I think the next several hundred years will be interesting historical times. If you think about it, it has only been five hundred years or so since Christopher Columbus found this country. In the next four hundred or five hundred years we may also have an entirely new understanding of our neighbors than we do now. It could be very interesting.

T. J. Streicher: Has your fear of death changed?

Marilynn: Completely. I have no fear of death, but I have to admit that, because I have had brushes with severe illness and being close to death, I have experienced fear not of death, but of the process of dying. What pain might I have to go through in that final battle of my life? The other thing I have to admit as being much clearer to me is my own sinfulness, and when I've been close to death, I've had profoundly enlightening life reviews. Salvation for myself and others is something that has become a premier concern on my mind, because I've learned through these experiences how much we need to accomplish here in these mortal realms in order to progress. I am not afraid of death, per se. I am afraid of the process, of the pain that I might undergo. I sometimes fear my own sinfulness, but then I remember to place my trust in the mercy of God. And I'm afraid of not being at peace with everyone and having truly forgiven everyone from the heart when I cross over. And hopefully, at the same time I will be forgiven myself by those I may have harmed in any way.

T. J. Streicher: Do you ever think of going back to these other planets, and if you do, for how long?

Marilynn: I have no doubt that I will go back after death. I believe that some of our afterlife resides on some of those planets and in general in the galactic heavens. I think that, in some of our heavenly realms and purgatorial places like Earth, we are here for purification, weeding out the good and the evil within ourselves and our societies. I do go back frequently now, but I do believe I will go back permanently when I die. But I also don't wish to be presumptuous, because I know that I must remain faithful to the end. And I hope I can do that. I find myself making more mistakes than I ought, but again, I have to turn to God's mercy and continue to learn and grow from them. In other words, I hope I will be ready to go there permanently; I hope I don't miss the point of the blessing of these experiences, which, in essence, is teaching me how to progress beyond these mortal realms into a higher existence.

T. J. Streicher: What is your reaction to those who think that your experiences are fantasy, illusion, or that you are crazy?

Marilynn: I usually tell them that it is perfectly reasonable for them to think that, because if I hadn't had these experiences myself, I would probably think the same thing. I think it is perfectly reasonable for people to think that, if they have never had this kind of experience. If you have had it, then you are in kind of a quandary, because the power of the experiences is so much that you cannot deny them, but you also know that, if you told some people, they would think you were insane. But, because of the work that I do, I have met quite a few people who have had some fascinating and similar experiences. There is much more study into near-death experiences, out-of-body experiences, after-death experiences, between life experiences, and now extraterrestrial experiences, as well. I think the hunger to know the truth is out there, and people are seeking it. And I think our extraterrestrial friends have a lot to do with that new kind of seeking that we see now. They have implanted it within our hearts to want to *really* know God . . . I mean really know Him.

T. J. Streicher: Do you ever consider yourself to be a person of two worlds?

Marilynn: Yes, I often do. Sometimes I tell my friends I ride the border between worlds. Part of this comes naturally because I have a serious illness. But it's more because of the experiences I have had. Sometimes you feel you're in both worlds at the same time, and you're trying to make them both fit into one world. Well, this one over here understands this one, but this one over here doesn't understand that one. So, you do feel like you're on the border between life and death and in between this world and the next. And because of the way it has been presented to me, I do believe that many of the extraterrestrial experiences that people are having are things that are part of the afterlife as well. I don't believe they are separate from the afterlife. It's like there's this world and the afterlife, and the afterlife contains the galactic heaven, and it contains all the other races, other existences. I see that when I cross over I will be able to go to an infinite variety of profoundly beautiful places. I may have to undergo some purification, but we all have to do this.

T. J. Streicher: How will you try to integrate these experiences into your consciousness?

Marilynn: I have integrated them by making it my lifework to disseminate it. The big part of this mission is peace. Peace within and peace without. Many of the things I've been instructed to write are meant to give understanding to things that are sometimes otherwise hard to comprehend. I've been called into an arena I didn't expect, many arenas, in fact. But one of these arenas is assisting others to understand one another. Many of my books combine quotations from all world religions, and in their comparison we find that, among the major world religions, we are more alike than different. In most cases, we share a moral code. And in the lives of the mystics in these varied religions, their experiences show a unity and oneness between them that would otherwise seem impossible if you only looked at the religion from whence the mystic emerged. But I believe this is so because there are certain universal truths that all true mystics, of any faith, touch into. That's why the mystics see more eye to eye, regardless of faith, than any other—because they all touch into God, who is unitive.

So somehow, despite different dogmas or varieties of faith, we have to begin with mutual understanding and respect. Doing so does not require us all to agree with one another, just to try harder to achieve peace despite whatever differences may remain. Ironically, all the world religions teach peace and respect. Not a single one does not. The fighting over doctrines and dogmas needs to stop. In the bigger scheme, when you have these experiences you realize they are irrelevant and that the dogmas cannot be fully defined. There is a place for dogmatic theology, but never forget mystical theology is just as critical to enable a fuller understanding. The religions of the world share so much. Moral codes, mystical theologies, standards of conduct . . . they are all really similar. If you read the mystics from all the different religions, that similarity increases even if their individual religions have some different beliefs. I think they are tuning in to that bigger picture.

I believe that the extraterrestrials that I have come in contact with are trying to create peace. By trying to create peace they create an opportunity to go to a much higher level of understanding. Raising consciousness and making some of those galactic connections is a part of what's required for the mystical to emerge, but this must also result in more mutual understanding and respect. Look at all the wars and genocide that have gone on in our world in the last hundred years: Native American, Russian Revolution, World Wars I and II, Kosovo, the Israelis and Palestinians, Africa and South America. There's more. . . . Many of these conflicts have religious undertones. Until we get people to actually have an interest in understanding what other people believe, respecting what they believe and why they believe it, being able to listen to what they believe—regardless of whether you agree or not—we aren't going to be able to stop this constant genocidal warring mentality, because it's always *us* and *them*. In reality, how stupid can we really be? It's not us and them—it's all *us*. We are all human, and there are probably several hundred other races out in the universe, and we have yet to deal with that factor. It is by listening that we learn to understand, and when we don't agree, which we often will not, it is by listening that we will actually become more able to help when there is misunderstanding or conflict.

The prophets, saints, mystics, and sages in all the world religions laid out paths in ancient sacred texts containing the keys that they left behind when they left this material world because they had found something more. Among these ancient sacred texts, regardless of religion, is one thing that is repeatedly told over and over again. We must follow the moral codes laid down by our forebears, purify our own thoughts, ideas, actions, and ideals . . . if we are to progress beyond this mortal realm. Our extraterrestrial counterparts are trying to help us to learn this same thing. But purification is as much an energetic shift in consciousness as it is a change in our way of thinking, a purer way of looking at our daily actions and what we revere as sacred and true. So as we progress through this process of purification, they come in along with the holy spirits of old to raise our vibrations to higher levels. When they do this, we see clearer and further and progress even more. But we must begin that process by beginning to understand. We continue that process by beginning to pay closer attention to what we are doing, thinking, and believing . . . and finally we have to accept that, by "entering into" this unconditionally loving state that God provides for those who reach beyond the mortal worlds and into the light worlds, we must become compatible with it. That means we must change, we must purify. To do this, we must reexamine the moral laws handed down to us as we've applied them in our lives. We must change the way in which we live to correspond to the basic commands that God has given us through every religion—the moral law.

If we can't even deal with our brothers in humanity, how are we going to deal with it when the extraterrestrials reveal themselves on a wide level? The extraterrestrials seem to be profoundly patient with us, as God is, too. We should reward that patience by taking a closer look at our lives, our purpose, and the reason we come to this world for such a short time, lest we miss the point of our coming.

[The question below is from a follow-up interview on August 31, 2010.]

T. J. Streicher: Can you include a description of the experience you had last night? (8/31/2010)

Marilynn: Absolutely, here it is. My spirit was taken to watch the workings of a very unusual star group of extraterrestrials. There were about five of them, very tall, grayish pinkish in their tone, and very serious in their facial expressions. Immediately, I experienced both awe and fear. But my fear was not of them, but a holy fear, a holy fear of God—the God that they served with such high distinction. I felt unworthy to be in their presence this night. Watching them, I was not allowed to speak to them. Their manner was one of being "matter of fact" and "to the point." No-nonsense creatures; their job was very clearly to get in, get the job done, and get back out—unnoticed, if at all possible.

As a profoundly high race of alien beings, they had been sent to the Earth many times to work with humankind to bring up their galactic receptivity. Their work was all done on an energetic level; it was to create in human beings a higher capacity for receptivity to higher realms and learning. The were allowing me to see that they were currently working with several members of the Catholic priesthood subconsciously; they were trying to assist them in bringing their Christian understandings to a higher and galactic level. But most of those priests are unaware of their contact, and in total there were at most ten to fifteen of them. The question was, why? They shared with me telepathically that they had approached the masses of humanity for a higher-end alignment and had found that they were only successful in doing this on a large scale with one group of people—the Tibetans.

I was shown one person who is involved in world events, a former politician, but I will not reveal the identity of this person, who is now also under the tutelage of these beings. Because of their unique solitude, seclusion, quiet lives, and meditation, these higher extraterrestrials had been able to effect this galactic hookup with most of them. There was also shown to me a former politician and world leader who was active in good works around the world whom they had also reached. In their presence, I was hiding around the corner, watching them do their work because they inspired such awe and holy fear. These were such high-level extraterrestrials that you knew they were given dominion to throw out any spirit who was present but not invited without a single thought.

They were utilizing a piece of equipment with a long metallic, bendable rod. At the tip of the rod was something that was shaped much like a traditional lampshade but rounded at the top and metallic. This was an instrument of some sort, which they utilized to make these alterations in their subjects.

These are not mid-level beings; these are some of the higher operators in the galactic heavens, and what they come to give is profoundly important. Although I could not adequately explain it, they were trying to bring some of humanity to a higher galactic attunement—an attunement with the Christ of the galactic heavens, because Christ is Christ in the galactic heavens just as He is on Earth, but He is much bigger in the galactic heavens than we know Him to be on Earth. . . . In the galactic heavens, there are beings from many different worlds. Heaven does not just consist of human souls, but souls from other spheres, other planets, and those we would consider extraterrestrial. But when you're in the galactic heavens, it couldn't feel more normal that we are all there together and that Christ is known to them all in a more explicit, advanced, profound, and galactic way.

As they were profoundly quiet, it seemed unlikely that these beings ever engaged in talk, but when they were present it was important to allow them to finish their work and leave in peace. Their work was difficult and required concentration. As I looked upon them in holy awe, I realized that their function of galactic attunement was something that humans could scarcely understand. The only way we could allow them to do their work successfully was to let them do it without our interference, our thoughts, our desires, our groundedness. It was essential that we become quiet in order to receive their gift.

9

DOMES OF MARS' ARCTIC CIRCLE

Gary Northcott

Conducted May 16, 2009

H. Gary Northcott, who has a master's degree in counseling psychology, taught junior and senior high school subjects and sociology, psychology, and public speaking at Brown Mackie College in Kansas City, Kansas. For many years he offered social services to manic depressives, severely emotionally disturbed teens, drug addicts, and members of street gangs.

Following graduation from the Monroe Institute's Gateway Program, which involved training in remote viewing and telepathy, he began being mentally contacted by spiritual beings from other worlds. Confused by these experiences, Gary followed advice to seek regressive hypnosis to learn about possible past lives. Although he was originally surprised to experience several past lives, he became more open to the experience as time went on. At this time, his spiritual guides began appearing to him in visions and training him for open contact with extraterrestrials. They began taking him physically aboard starships for trips around the galaxy; this has continued ever since. He is now assisting in conducting a support group for contactees to help them cope with this new reality, which is often frightening and painful to them at first.

For the past twenty-six years, Gary has performed in Kansas City's Renaissance Festival as a storyteller.

▼

T. J. Streicher: I want you to know that I really appreciate this opportunity to talk to you about something that might be important to people who are interested in learning more about other planets and similar types of experiences. I consider this information to be sacred, so thank you for working with us on this. Here's my first question: How large do you think this planet was?

Gary: I must tell you that the planet I visited is the planet Mars. I have a National Geographic map of Mars as well as a Mars globe. So I am familiar with the physical appearance of the planet. It is somewhat smaller than Earth.

T. J. Streicher: Where do you think this planet is?

Gary: It is the fourth planet in orbit around our sun. It comes before the asteroid belt, so it is quite some distance past the moon but before you get to Jupiter.

T. J. Streicher: And the name you mentioned for this planet is Mars, correct?

Gary: Yes, it's Mars.

T. J. Streicher: You sound very definite about that. Can you describe the civilization on this planet, if any?

Gary: There are currently three colonies on Mars. There is a large complex of domes and glass-like towers on the north rim of the Mariner Valley. There is another, smaller, complex of domes at the base of Olympus—the giant volcano—and then there is another complex of domes up on Mars' Arctic Circle. The group living up there is doing terra-farming. I am not aware of any other installations on Mars at the moment, nor do I know of any ancient civilizations or anything like that on the planet.

T. J. Streicher: Let's describe now how you actually viewed this planet.

Gary: My first attempt was remote viewing. I got just an image of those three installations and located them on the National Geographic map. Later, one of my space visitors—one of my friends—took me there physically.

T. J. Streicher: How did you go there physically?

Gary: Aboard a ship, which picked me up here and flew me there.

T. J. Streicher: When you say "a ship," do you mean a spacecraft?

Gary: Yes, a spaceship.

T. J. Streicher: So you took a spaceship to Mars?

Gary: Yes, this was my first actual trip there.

T. J. Streicher: So it sounds like you have been involved with this planet Mars for some time. Do you have any idea why?

Gary: I have been involved with visitors from space for many, many years. Part of that involvement is that they are educating me, so I am able to ask a lot of questions of them. I started asking questions about whether or not our own government here on Earth had any kind of secret space station on the planet Mars; at that point they told me yes, and that is when I started investigating this. The installations on Mars are mixed installations of human military people and a wide variety of different kinds of space visitors.

T. J. Streicher: Were there seasons on this planet? About how much time did you spend there?

Gary: I spent a little over a day visiting and traveling around. There are Martian seasons, which are detectable by our own science people. The colors change on the planet, and their ice caps both advance and recede. There are large sandstorms—we have huge pictures of the sandstorms on Mars. I myself have a picture of a Martian sandstorm that National Geographic put out; it's hanging on my wall here.

T. J. Streicher: What does the sky look like?

Gary: Actually, it has a slightly green tint to it—a little bit like a nice summer day here, but the color isn't blue, it's more of a greenish tint.

T. J. Streicher: How long is the light on there—that is, what is the light to darkness ratio?

Gary: Well, again, this is well known to our own scientists. I don't remember the details of it, but they have much longer days because the orbit is different.

T. J. Streicher: Did you see any vegetation?

Gary: I did not. The portions that I saw looked like sand and rock desert, maybe a little like the Gobi Desert.

T. J. Streicher: What was the color of the ground?

Gary: Reddish, there is a reddish tint.

T. J. Streicher: Could you compare it to anything here on Earth?

Gary: I have not seen sand and rocks that were exactly that color, but it looked like very normal sand and rock; there was nothing terribly unusual about it. It was exactly like the pictures that came back from Viking.

T. J. Streicher: Reddish color ground with a sandy texture?

Gary: Yes, sand and rocks.

T. J. Streicher: Could it be compared to the red brick that is used in buildings?

Gary: Not that deep a red.

T. J. Streicher: Did you see any animal life there?

Gary: Oh, nothing other than people in the buildings.

T. J. Streicher: And these people in the buildings—were they humanoid or something else?

Gary: It was a mix. There were some American and Russian military officers who were actually condemned to be there. They had been lied to—they were told they would be there for just a few months, but they are left there for the rest of their lives. Mixed in with them there were the gray Zetas that everybody talks about—you know, the short guys with big black eyes that you see in all the cartoons and stuff. But there were also humans from other planets; the one who was ferrying me around, for instance, is a tall human being with silver hair. He is from the fourth planet of Altar, absolutely human, and he is one of my chief mentors. He is one of the people who are teaching me. In addition, I saw some Mantas; these appeared to be, I guess, maybe seven feet tall, very, very, slender insects, with insect compound eyes and antennae. When I met one of them, I shook his claw and we had a conversation. There were others there too: there was a big shaggy-headed fellow who looked a little bit like a yeti; he was short and wide instead of tall and thin. So it was quite a wide variety of people.

T. J. Streicher: Could you be more precise about your actual physical trip to the planet or your remote viewing?

Gary: No, no, I was there. I was inside the building in the main complex.

T. J. Streicher: They have taken you there how many times?

Gary: Three times.

T. J. Streicher: Aboard spacecraft?

Gary: Yes.

T. J. Streicher: Did you see any natural resources available on this planet?

Gary: I did not personally see that. I was told that there is a variety of mineral resources, but I don't have personal observation of that.

T. J. Streicher: Did you experience any noises or lights?

Gary: Well, inside the building there were artificial lights—nothing that was not artificial. I was not out on the surface of the planet; I was only inside buildings. I was also inside a flying craft, an expedition craft; they took me in it to fly over the other two sites, but I never landed on those two sites or got into them.

T. J. Streicher: So do you mean you were not physically exposed to the environment?

Gary: I only saw the environment through the windows; I was not out there. It would take an environmentally protective suit to do that, and I was mainly interested in meeting the people.

T. J. Streicher: Were there any kinds of buildings, vehicles, or underground tunnels on this planet?

Gary: I am told there are underground tunnels, but I was never shown that. I was in two very large buildings. One of them was a white dome-shaped building, much larger than a football stadium here. The other building was a glass tower—or at least it looked like glass. It was a smooth rounded tower; it did not have square corners or anything like that. I was taken to that building in a ground vehicle, but it didn't have wheels; it floated from the dome over to this tower. The tower was about the size of our power and light building in Kansas City; it was about the size and shape, but it was all rounded and shiny glass, or appeared like shiny glass. I was taken inside that and was given a tour of that building.

T. J. Streicher: Did you see any other buildings around?

Gary: This complex was a cluster of buildings, but they were all connected in what was almost one large building.

T. J. Streicher: Do you mean kind of like the Pentagon building in Washington?

Gary: Nothing with hard edges; everything here was smooth and rounded.

T. J. Streicher: No, I mean in being connected together.

Gary: Yes, in that sense, yes.

T. J. Streicher: You say they were shiny—could they be transparent?

Gary: It wasn't transparent—it was almost mirrored, but it was a white mirrored appearance. These buildings ought to be very clearly visible from space, but our own satellites that are around Mars are not taking pictures in the areas where these things are located.

T. J. Streicher: So do you think the U.S. government or NASA might be aware of some of these things?

Gary: Oh, yes, they have shipped up officers there, and the original intent, I was told, was an agreement with space visitors for an exchange of technology. They were going to have a major super base there, but the people there essentially declared their independence and broke off from the Earth government. This is all part of the Cheney-Bush junk. Then our government people stopped sending ships there and left those people stranded. The humans, Americans and Russians, who are there joined in what you might call a revolution and simply declared their independence for reasons of morality. Did any of that make sense?

T. J. Streicher: Yes, sure it does. Do you have any other descriptions of the planet that struck you or stood out?

Gary: It looked to me at the moment that it was not a very habitable planet. I have studied a lot of astronomy; it's in the habitable range, it's one of those planets that could support life at some point in its evolution, but it doesn't look like it's quite there. However, it looks like the people who are there are changing that and terra-farming it into a habitable planet. I asked them why they were doing that, and I was told that long-term, over a thousand years, they see it as a major planet for both species, for the human species and the ones from outer space, to share, and that was their goal. At the moment, the atmosphere is too thin, the water is all underground, and it's just not ready to do that yet. From space, it looks a lot more like the moon than like Earth. This is rock and sand with little white caps, and you see changing seasons because parts of the planet change color over the year. That was my first impression.

T. J. Streicher: Would you describe the moon as a planet?

Gary: No, no, the moon is much too small, but more importantly it doesn't have atmosphere, and it doesn't have water that we know of. Mars does have an atmosphere, but it is a thin atmosphere. Our scientists have not found water, but the people who are there tell me that the water is all underground.

T. J. Streicher: Do you think that in the future the terminology we use to define planets might change?

Gary: It has already changed with regard to Pluto, which half the world no longer considers to be a planet and the other half of the astronomers in the world say it is. So the definitions are shifting even now.

T. J. Streicher: Is there anything else that stood out for you on this planet?

Gary: No, I don't think so. Again I knew the physical appearance of the planet before I got into all of this, like the big valley, the volcanoes, and those kinds of things. So I wasn't surprised by any of that at all.

T. J. Streicher: Well, you never really described that. So I am imagining that I am there right now and looking out over the landscape and horizon, and I want you to fill me in on what I see.

Gary: Most striking of all is what our scientists call Mariner Valley. This is a giant, giant Grand Canyon as described by Carl Sagan in *Cosmos*. This thing stretches for something like four thousand miles. The city that I'm talking about is built on the northern edge of it, about in the middle of its length. Nothing on Earth can even remotely compare to this valley; the entire Grand Canyon, according to Carl Sagan, could easily be fitted into one of its tiny branches, it is so massive. The other big physical feature that I was not present at but flew over later is Olympus Mons, which is another giant feature. It is a huge volcano. Apparently, Mars has at times had active volcanoes. These are very clearly seen on the pictures and maps of the surface of the planet.

T. J. Streicher: You mentioned a city?

Gary: The first complex that I described to you—the one with the domes and the towers—that amounts to a small city. There was a greenish tint to the sky; there were no clouds at all; the two Martian moons were too small for me to see from the surface of the planet.

T. J. Streicher: Was anything else visible?

Gary: No.

T. J. Streicher: Do you feel satisfied with your description?

Gary: Yes.

T. J. Streicher: What was your reaction to your experience on another planet?

Gary: There was a sense of awe just from the reality of being there. Also, there was intense questioning. I was surrounded by all this really marvelous stuff. I was in a building with a wide variety of people, some of whom were not even human. I was talking to people about the nature of their political structure and what was happening in the galaxy at large. This is just amazing, absolutely amazing. I should tell you immediately that these are all good people; these are friendly people; there are no nasty, evil monsters in this group of people. They are not here to conquer the world or anything like that. They are mainly here as a kind of Peace Corps, hoping to help us through a step in evolution that is very difficult for us. So they regard themselves primarily as teachers, and that's how I received them—they are teachers. So it was a marvelous experience; I mean, it was just glorious.

T. J. Streicher: How do you think this experience affected you, or is affecting you now?

Gary: Oh, well, it is still affecting me. It is opening doors, changing my view of the world; it's changing my philosophy and view of life into something that is much nicer, more peaceful, and more hopeful. I believe at the moment that we are in extremely desperate times and they are going to get much, much worse. There are an awful lot of people in our world who are going to die in the next ten to fifteen years, primarily of starvation; it's all really bad here. It's going to get worse before it gets better, but when it does get better then they are going to need people like me to help the rest of the folks cope and adjust and move into something that might approach a golden age.

T. J. Streicher: Would you describe what changes took place in you?

Gary: My background is in psychology. I have a lot less anger inside of me than I used to have. I have less interest in some of the more traditional things in our world. Like many people my age who grew up in the 1950s and '60s, I had a lot of interest in military stuff; I read a lot of military history and books about the Army and all that kind of thing. I have no patience with that anymore. I have no patience with war at all; instead I am much more interested in trying to seek ways to educate people out of their fears. It has been my conclusion after these experiences that almost all the people on our planet are living in fear and superstition. We have got to find a way to move them out of this fear and superstition. So that's where I am at right now, and I didn't use to be there. I used to be at that place where I would look at the corruption in our politics and think we really ought to kill those guys, and I am not there at all. I have had a basic philosophical change.

T. J. Streicher: For instance, let's say, with the staggering economy and what is going on inside our country, what do you say to people who have lost their job?

Gary: I am one of those people who have lost their job. I pick and choose: there are people who are not yet ready to grow, and they won't listen; they don't want to hear it—they just shut it out, and I try not to waste my time with those folks. I try to find the people who still have an open mind and do want to listen, and then I start talking about how things are bad, they're going to get worse, but they are eventually going to get better. I typically do not talk very much at all about psychic phenomena, UFOs, or experience in space, because I don't meet a whole lot of people who want to hear that or are willing to listen to that. So again, I pick and choose. I have made speeches to UFO meetings and those kinds of groups, but I don't talk about this publicly. I certainly didn't talk about it to students or faculty when I was teaching college. These days I talk about survival, planning ahead, coping skills . . . how we are going to get through this mess, and that kind of stuff.

T. J. Streicher: When you were on this other planet, what were you thinking and feeling?

Gary: I was thinking, "My God, I am actually here," and I was also thinking there is a universal problem called the confabulation concept in psychology, and it generally refers to the mind's absolutely infinite capacity to simply make up thoughts, images, and memories. The human mind can create a scene of events that is so absolutely realistic that you can't tell that it is a false memory. In all my experiences with this kind of thing, I kept confabulation in mind, and all you can do with that is you can ask the doubting question, "Is this real, or am I making it up because it is such a thrilling idea," and know that you can't really tell at the time if it is real or not. What you can do is try to seek confirmation of it. You can get confirmation from other people; then you have a good idea that this is really happening. I was aware at the time that this could be some kind of incredibly long, detailed, fantasy dream that my own mind was making up. I assume you have encountered this kind of idea before.

T. J. Streicher: Certainly, but I also think it could be important.

Gary: So what I do after I have one of these really bizarre experiences is I look for confirmation. There are several kinds of confirmation; one of them is that there are many, many reports from many other people who have had these kinds of experiences describing exactly the same thing. They have seen buildings on Mars; they have talked to people from outer space who basically told them the same thing. I didn't know these at the time I had my experiences; I only learned about these other episodes with other people after I had my experiences, so it's not like I saw something on television and filed it away in my memory and dragged it up again. So that's what I call confirmation, and I have had that.

I have had very, very strong confirmation about my earlier psychic experiences that are not relevant to your study, so I am extremely confident that I had real psychic experiences, because those have certainly been proven out by actual fact and historical facts. So I am very comfortable with that now. But you do have the doubt that you have to file away and try to check out when you can. I have not met another person in the world who has visited the place that I visited on Mars. I have met quite a few people who have remote viewed the same place that I have visited on Mars, describing the exact same buildings, so there is something to it—it's not just a dream.

Mainly, though, I was just amazed at the experience and the people I was meeting, especially the nonhuman people. In other reports most people tend to be talking about the little gray Zetas, and there were some of those there, but frankly they seemed to me to be not terribly important, that is, not leadership people. The leadership people were the humans, from what they reported to be the Altar system and stars in the Orion system, and the nonhumans. I was mainly fascinated by the nonhumans. This Manta character has been with me my whole life; I didn't know that at the time—I only learned that later, but he has popped in and out of my life routinely ever since I was born. He is genial, he has a dry wit, he will tease a little bit, he enjoys calling me Earthling, but he says it in a kind of funny way. He will turn and talk to another one of his species in a high, chattering, almost an electronic kind of language that makes no sense, but then he turns to me and speaks to me in a resonating baritone voice. In getting familiar with our customs, he put his claw out for me to shake in a handshake, which I did. I could feel the hard surface of that claw, and I could smell him— he has a detectable smell, not very pleasant, almost musty smelling. I perceived him through the major human senses and I couldn't help but feel amazed that I was standing in front of this guy and he was actually talking to me and telling me about the universe . . . this was just amazing. So that is my general impression of the whole trip.

T. J. Streicher: When you were on this other planet, do you recall any emotions or feelings you can identify with?

Gary: Well, if you're talking about the other people there, they were all excited. These are people who are involved in what they believe to be extremely important work.

T. J. Streicher: I was thinking more about what *you* were feeling.

Gary: My feeling continued to be just "Oh, wow!" for the most part. I never had any sense of fear at all, not even remotely, no hint of unease of any kind. In fact, it was much more joy; it was more "I want to be with these people, this is wonderful"—it was an ecstatic kind of feeling.

T. J. Streicher: What do you think was the most meaningful part of this experience on another planet?

Gary: Becoming aware of their sense of really wanting to help us, that they are there to help. They're not going to bail us out; they're not going to come in and fix all our problems. They have the capability to do all that, but they're not going to do that. They are a tough-love kind of people. They say that, if they came in and landed on the White House lawn and corrected all the crimes and showed us a new economic system and all that kind of stuff, it would weaken us too much, it would make us dependent upon outside help. We have to learn our own strengths, and they are going to help us do that. This is to help individual people become enlightened people, so that we can then solve those problems. I suppose the main thing would be a sense of hope. It's not all dead; we are not going to completely wipe out our whole species. There is a chance that we can learn to change things, with the help of these people teaching us as individuals. So I would sum it up as hope.

T. J. Streicher: When did this experience occur?

Gary: I could actually look that up if I had time to find it.

T. J. Streicher: Approximately?

Gary: Approximately seven years ago.

T. J. Streicher: Was that your first experience of being taken in space-craft to another planet?

Gary: Yes. I have only had three or four experiences of actual physical travel. Most of my experiences have been remote viewing experiences. Yes, that was the very first experience I had of actual travel.

T. J. Streicher: How often did this happen?

Gary: Let me see now—we want to be precise. This was my only journey to the planet Mars. The other trips that I took were way across the galaxy, and they were not to a planet.

T. J. Streicher: Why do you think you only went there that one time?

Gary: I learned what I wanted to learn from them, and I also learned that I didn't need to go back—that where I needed to go to learn more was not on the planet Mars. They were doing their thing. They were fulfilling their mission, but for my education I needed to go elsewhere.

T. J. Streicher: Has this experience given you a different connection with humanity?

Gary: Yes, I think so. On the negative side, it has made me much more cynical about humanity. I have the conclusion now that the vast majority of people on this planet are ignorant dumb animals living in superstition and fear. I need not give my attention to the majority of the people I meet, and I must be highly selective for open minds and people who are seeking genuine awareness. Now that moves into the question of religion, because I have reached the conclusion that religion on our world is a vastly negative force for the human species, so I am hardly paying any attention at all to people who are involved in the traditional religions. The one exception to that is the Tibetan form of Buddhism and some of the forms of Hinduism, which are totally different from what we regard as the three main religions of the Book. I have just dropped them off my list completely. Every time something happens, I turn around and look at it, and it has happened because of extremely ignorant and bigoted people. So in that sense I have become very, very cynical about the human species as it stands right now. I feel my job is to change that, and to work with people to change that.

On the positive side though, when you meet people who have an open mind, who are questioning, daring to question everything—God, they are wonderful people! These are the people like da Vinci, Galileo, and Newton—those you want to nurture, those for whom you want to do as much as you can. So that's where the bright spots are. There is a line in the musical *Camelot* about people being an ocean of drops, but only a few of those drops of water actually sparkle, so we are looking for the sparkling ones.

T. J. Streicher: Has your concern with the material things of life changed?

Gary: Well, I have been through a lot of very hard times, and I have lost most of those material things, and they don't matter much anymore. As long as you have subsistence, that's okay. I don't pay any attention at all to commercials on television or to ads anywhere. I don't need any of that stuff; that stuff is just frivolous stuff and it's waste. Even if I had money, I wouldn't be spending it on that kind of stuff. I have a closet full of clothes; I have no need to buy any more clothes, so I just have no interest in clothes, and on and on and on. I suppose I have grown to a much simpler existence; it's not something I would have chosen—it was basically forced into me. But now that I have been there for a few years, I'm quite content with it, and I do just fine.

T. J. Streicher: Has your concern for the welfare of planet Earth changed?

Gary: I am convinced that in the long run it will all work out and be all right. Right now we are in the midst of a sinking disaster, and I believe it will get much worse before it gets better. The planet will survive in the long run, but it will be quite awhile before we start turning things around. It's going to be quite awhile, because we have to change enough people to actually vote for good things instead of things based on fear. At the moment, we do not have a government capable of solving those problems, so we are just going to have to tough it out. But in the long run, it is going to be all right.

T. J. Streicher: Has your desire to help others changed since your initial experience?

Gary: Most of my career was in the helping profession of psychology; I was very sincere about that, and I did a lot of good. I saved a few lives here and there, but now I am more targeted, I am more specific. So I am looking for those special people and I am not terribly concerned about the masses in general anymore. A lot of those people don't want to learn, they don't want to live; they are going to die, and we need to let them die, so that we can gain control of the forces of good in our world. So, yes, this is part of that cynicism thing. Some of the experts in our century are predicting that as much as 50 percent of our population is going to starve to death in the next twenty years. I don't know if that is accurate or not, but I think it is a general truth: we are going to have an awful lot of people doing that. It will be the ones who don't want an education—they want to watch football on television instead. They are wasting their life away; they cannot be saved, and I am just not going to worry about it.

T. J. Streicher: So what will you do to keep yourself from starving?

Gary: That's a daily problem. I am living in extreme poverty, and I have to be very, very careful about every single penny to keep my subsistence lifestyle going. So far I have been able to do that. I was a college teacher, but many colleges now have hiring freezes. It is my hope that at some point they will finally drop those hiring freezes and start to hire again. In the meantime, I am just plain scrambling to stay alive, and that is just the reality I am in.

T. J. Streicher: How do you feel about being back on Earth now?

Gary: I did not want to be anywhere else. I loved the people that I met on Mars, but Mars is not where I am supposed to be. I am supposed to be here. This is where my journey needs to be, in terms of finding and helping those selected people. That is my duty. I had nothing to do on Mars. I had nothing to do on the other places that I had visited; this is where I am supposed to be.

T. J. Streicher: Would you consider this to be a spiritual or religious experience?

Gary: Certainly spiritual, yes, this has been a very enlightening experience; it has opened doors for me into the entire universe that I did not know existed before. I believe the purpose in life for human beings is to move toward enlightenment, to become more and more aware, to know a larger and larger universe, and this is why we are here, to do this. Both the Buddhists and the Hindus have a grasp of this in their teachings; the Buddhists, especially, are very good about teaching about this in books like the *Tibetan Book of the Dead*. I do not believe, like the major religions, that our purpose in life is to be obedient to a set of rules that has been sent down by some magical being. This hinders the growth of the human spirit. The experiences that I have been through have all been aimed very specifically, very directly, at further enlightenment. So, yes, it is a very strongly spiritual experience, but it is not a traditional one in terms of our culture.

T. J. Streicher: Will you define the difference between spiritual and religious?

Gary: The three main religions in our world—I taught sociology, so I know this stuff—the three main religions in our world are obedience religions, they are dominant religions, they are "Obey the rules that are written in the book," whether the book is the Koran or the Christian Bible or whatever. This has the tendency of keeping people in their place; it is a slave/master mentality. Enlightenment—whether you're talking about the enlightenment of the rationalists in the early 1800s or the teachings of Buddha or whatever—enlightenment has to do not with obedience to rules, but with learning more and understanding more, becoming more sensitive, becoming more helpful to other people. It is an entirely different basis for thought and experience, and I think it is much healthier than an obedience kind of religion; that is where I am at right now.

T. J. Streicher: What are the three main religions on our planet?

Gary: Christianity, Islam, and Judaism. These are the ones that are controlling the politics of the majority of our world. Christianity has had a stranglehold on the United States all along and will continue to have it, as does Judaism, and in the other half of the world, Islam. It has become my opinion that they are just plain wrong.

T. J. Streicher: Have any of your personal goals in life changed since your initial experience?

Gary: Yes, I think so. I can remember going back now that I used to have goals of personal recognition, popularity, wealth, that sort of more traditional thing. Back then I wanted people to admire me, look up to me, praise me; I wanted to find some sort of way to get a lot of money so I could have all of the wonderful toys that I wanted to play with and that kind of stuff, but that all changed. I am at the point right now where I have no interest at all in whether people believe in what I say or not; I just don't care. Most of them will say I'm a crackpot; in fact, I have been called a crackpot and other such names most of my life, and I used to resent it and get all upset about it, but I just don't care anymore. They either believe or they don't; the ones that don't believe aren't worth my time—it's the ones that do believe I want to pay attention to. It's no longer a matter of prestige or being admired or being thought of as a special person; I have lost all of that. I ran into hard times with a long illness and then the budget crunch, so I was kind of forced out of the whole idea of money and whether I would have that wonderful car that I wanted to buy. I drive an old junker now, and it gets me around town—that's all I need it for, so that's okay. So I am no longer into the money trap and glory—it was a fantasy view and it just doesn't happen. My whole perspective on life, my whole paradigm of the world, has really been changed, largely, I think, from these experiences—from learning about a wider universe and being exposed to greater ideas than what I had been living with, and from having the fears diminish and go away. I am not much afraid of things anymore, the way I was in my earlier life.

T. J. Streicher: Has your fear of death changed?

Gary: I have no fear of death. I will admit to a fear of pain, but not of death, and in that the Buddhists, especially in the *Tibetan Book of the Dead,* have been extremely helpful to me. We are all going to die and transition into another existence after we die; although the Christians, Jews, and Muslims all have that teaching, they have the description of that other existence after we die that is very, very different from what the Tibetans offer. I have reluctantly been forced to conclude that there is such a thing as reincarnation. So death just isn't that big of deal; it's a door into a new room, so to speak. So, no, I don't fear death at all. I think there is an obsession with death in our culture that is extremely unhealthy, but that is a whole other conversation.

T. J. Streicher: Do you think of going back to this other planet, and if so, for how long?

Gary: This is not a necessity for me. It may be fun to go back and see the people again and check in on their progress and that sort of thing, simply out of curiosity, but another visit is not on my agenda. If I wished, I could remote view them again, but in a remote viewing I, at least, am not able to have a conversation with them, so I don't see where there would be much purpose in that other than just going and lounging around. So, no, I don't think so. The other place that I visit, which is not a planet but a space station, I do return to it and I will continue to return to it, but it is not part of your study.

T. J. Streicher: What is your response to people who think that your experience is fantasy, illusion, or something like that?

Gary: Well, that's all right. I don't get upset about that; they are not ready to learn these things, and there is nothing I could say to make them ready to learn them. They have to go on their own trip. But bear in mind that people who begin to have these psychic experiences do so because they have reached a certain point in their lifelong evolution that makes them ready for them. This goes back to the reincarnation take, too. Sometimes those steps take many, many lives, and they simply have to live them out till they reach a point where they are able to wake up their mind and begin to understand these larger issues. So they're just not ready yet, and that's fine. They're nice—I have a lot of friends like that, and they're good friends. It's not important to me that they don't accept the things that I say.

T. J. Streicher: How long did it take for your experience to sink in?

Gary: Years—oh, Lord—years.

T. J. Streicher: What about your first experience, about seven years ago?

Gary: No, once I made that trip, it sunk in; I was absolutely certain.

T. J. Streicher: Was it immediate?

Gary: Yes; that's because I had telepathic conversations about these issues with some of the space visitors before I made that trip. They had been teaching me this stuff.

T. J. Streicher: What is your earliest recollection of having contact with extraterrestrials?

Gary: Oh, that's like twenty years ago, probably more than that, let me think. . . . I have had psychic experiences all my life and I know when the first one of these occurred. I think it was somewhere in the late eighties. They did not tell me specific things about Mars—I never got that. What I got was, yes, there are intelligent species; yes, we are doing this; yes, we are doing that. I was introduced to a number of them on a telepathic level, but this has nothing to do with the trip to Mars. That just came about in response to questions that I started asking. So it wasn't like I was primed for what I experienced on Mars—I wasn't. That was all a new experience for me; it had not been described to me in any way. I had had extensive telepathic conversations before I made that trip, so I was not shocked or surprised about what I finally experienced there.

T. J. Streicher: Do you ever consider yourself to be a person of two worlds?

Gary: It would be more accurate to say, "a person of a larger world." I consider myself now to be a person of the galaxy who is currently residing on this one obscure little planet. Because I have been out there, I have met people from out there, so I am no longer limited to the environment of, say, Kansas City, where I live.

T. J. Streicher: How will you integrate this experience into your consciousness?

Gary: "Integrate"? I am not sure what you mean by that.

T. J. Streicher: Okay, how will you include this experience into your realm of reality?

Gary: Oh, well, it's a major part of my reality.

T. J. Streicher: Would you be more specific, please?

Gary: It's like somebody who is living on Samoa, and their whole life has been on the island of Samoa, but they know about all of the rest of the world that they have never been to and it's part of their reality, they know it exists, and all of that kind of stuff, but the main part of their attention has to do with living on Samoa—it's like that. All of this other stuff, for me at least, is absolutely real, and I have no doubts about it at all. It is a major part of my understanding of life. Day by day, I am living in a tiny little apartment in the city, and taking care of my subsistence needs, and that is where a lot of my attention has to go, but all of my attention is not limited to that. I can read books; I can have contact with people who live very far away from me in a lot of different ways, and that, too, is part of my reality, and that keeps me from backsliding into fear and superstition and that dull old world that I used to live in.

T. J. Streicher: If you consider this an extraordinary experience, sometimes people have a difficult time bringing this back into their reality.

Gary: Yes, it is. Now there are special counseling programs that exist in this country to specifically help people with that kind of problem. I have done counseling and therapeutic sessions with a couple of people here who have that kind of problem, and I am trying to help them keep from being lost in their experience and keep them grounded in the world here, as well as letting them enjoy that larger world that is out there. So the therapeutic process already exists for people having that problem.

T. J. Streicher: Will you continue contact with the extraterrestrials that you have been involved with, and, if so, how do you integrate that?

Gary: I am going to continue to have contact with these people for the rest of my life—I have no doubt about that at all. I can reach them telepathically almost any time I feel like it. What I am finding is, although much of what they tell me is not terribly relevant to the world I am living in right now, it's relevant to me. I have an understanding of major events that are now occurring in the rest of the galaxy—that have no effect on me personally, but like anyone who enjoys reading a lot of history it's just fun to know. So I can describe to you where the major civilizations are out in our galaxy, where they are located in the galaxy, and what is happening in that region, and so on. So I follow that along, the way any historian would follow it along, just because of the fun of knowing these things. They have no relevance at all to my day-to-day life here, and that's okay. I don't see any way to connect those giant events out there to my day-to-day life here. But it helps me keep in perspective watching what is happening on this planet; it helps me to not be overwhelmed by the major disasters that are occurring here, and that is a useful thing for me. Did that answer your question?

T. J. Streicher: Yes. In retrospect, when you look back now, where was your tipping point that led you into this phenomenon that you're into now?

Gary: Oh, that's a neat question. I had several steps that led up to this point—are you looking for the major steps?

T. J. Streicher: Yes, when it really switched your thinking.

Gary: The major step that led to open and direct contact with these people occurred during a healing session that I was undergoing. I had a major health collapse that traditional medicine could not address; they just couldn't find what it was and had no clue to what to do about it. My family physician recommended I go to an energy healer—are you familiar with energy healers?

T. J. Streicher: Yes. At what age is this?

Gary: In the early '70s, I think.

T. J. Streicher: How old were you?

Gary: I think thirty-one. I would have to look it up on the computer. I went to this energy healer, and she is doing her thing, basically moving energy around in different parts of the body; she poured extra energy into my heart, for instance, and she was doing those kinds of things that energy healers do. Then she suddenly spoke up and said that there was somebody else present in the room. She said there was a spiritual being here with a message for me, and that message was that I should look into past lives and my health would improve if I did that. I took that down; it suggested reincarnation, and I was not thrilled with that, but I went to a clinical psychologist here in town, a licensed clinical hypnotherapist, and had him do regressive hypnosis on me into past lives. I found some, and really strange things came out of that; for one, I started having visions of a person—his face appeared to me. I took a chance and said "Hello," and he started talking to me telepathically, and that was my first contact with a star visitor. I later learned he came to me because what I was doing through regressive hypnosis was an indication that I was now ready to be contacted, and that is how it all started.

T. J. Streicher: Are you still engaged with hypnosis?

Gary: No, after a long series of hypnosis, which I documented in my journal, we found that I didn't need the hypnosis in order to make contact. I felt I could establish that contact without being hypnotized, which I have done ever since.

T. J. Streicher: Is there anything else you would like to say before we close?

Gary: In the book that I am trying to write, I never say I wanted any of this stuff to happen. I never sought it out—these are things that happened to me. I have come to a point in my life where I am now grateful that they have happened, and I am completely comfortable with it and living essentially a happy life, even though it might be in poor economic circumstances. I am delighted with the direction that my life has turned.

10

ANOTHER TIME, ANOTHER PLACE

Alexandra Stark

Conducted June 18, 2009

Alexandra Stark, a former social worker, was born in Massachusetts in 1954. As a child, she experienced out-of-body experiences (OBEs), seeing and communicating with the spirit world and having contact with Beings not from Earth. In the late 1980s she participated in paranormal experiments at the Rhine Center at Duke University.

During the 1990s, Alex wrote articles on paranormal activities and assisted in producing several TV shows on the subject. Now working on a book narrating her lifelong experiences, Alex is a member of an international organization that helps law enforcement agencies locate lost people.

▼

T. J. Streicher: I feel privileged to have this opportunity to talk with you about a topic that may be considered important, especially to people who have had similar types of experiences. Basically, the interview is divided into three sections. The first has to do with descriptions of the other planet and how you perceived it; the second concerns questions about your reactions to your experience on another planet; and the last is basically about your reflections on all this information that you received. If you have any questions for me during this interview, just stop me and ask. I am recording it; later I will transcribe it; and then I will send it back to you for your approval.

So, how large is this planet, where is it, and what is its name?

Alex: The planet has a 22-million-mile diameter compared to Earth's 7,926 miles. It is located in the Boötes constellation. The planet is Arcturus.

T. J. Streicher: So, it sounds like it is quite a bit bigger than Earth?

Alex: MUCH!

T. J. Streicher: Where is this planet?

Alex: It is the brightest star in the Boötes constellation.

T. J. Streicher: Could there be any way to measure it from Earth?

Alex: It is thirty-six light-years from Earth.

T. J. Streicher: Can you describe the civilization on this other planet, if any?

Alex: The people I remember are light blue, tall, thin with large bald heads and small facial features that are very human. Their eyes are like cat eyes, having elongated pupils. Most wear long blue gowns. They are very advanced spiritually. They live with unconditional love for everyone. They interact as one consciousness, yet still are individuals.

T. J. Streicher: Would you describe the civilization a little bit more?

Alex: They practice communal living; everybody works together, and there is no monetary system, no class structure, everyone is equal.

T. J. Streicher: Is there any form of government?

Alex: It's not like the government of Earth. Those of a higher frequency, more advanced and more knowledgeable, mentor the others. They don't dictate what you have to do. The words on Earth are very archaic to describe such a system. [Alex begins speaking in a different language, which I understand through the practice of resonance, in which I am in tune with her meaning.]

T. J. Streicher: What language were you speaking just now?

Alex: It's the Light Language, a universal language used as is English on this planet, so Beings from many different cultures can understand each other.

T. J. Streicher: It almost sounded like Lakota.

Alex: Yes, my understanding is that many of the indigenous languages on this planet still have words from the Star languages. The Lakota, along with other indigenous peoples, are the Keepers of the Star information.

T. J. Streicher: Are there seasons on this planet, Arcturus?

Alex: No, it's warm all the time, but I only remember one section of Arcturus, so I am describing that one section. We have many species on our planet, and many Beings.

T. J. Streicher: Since you said how gigantic Arcturus is, there could be many different temperature zones there?

Alex: Correct. I remember it was beautiful and warm where I was.

T. J. Streicher: Do you recall what the sky looked like?

Alex: I know that there were two suns—like your sun, only two.

T. J. Streicher: Were they close together, or far apart?

Alex: They are side by side.

T. J. Streicher: Was there vegetation there?

Alex: Yes, there was; it looked tropical. Ferns and palm trees were similar.

T. J. Streicher: Did you see any type of animal life?

Alex: I don't recall any.

T. J. Streicher: Did you see any type of mining, or taking things from the ground?

Alex: No, they do not believe in killing the planet they live on.

T. J. Streicher: Were there any types of natural resources such as solar energy, wind energy? How was the power generated, if they were using any?

Alex: At 147 years I was yet a child. I don't know. Solar power is an archaic technology on the planet.

T. J. Streicher: Did you experience any noises or lights on your home planet of Arcturus?

Alex: No.

T. J. Streicher: Are there any buildings?

Alex: Yes, they look like stucco; they are very low, they are not over-whelming, they blend in with the landscape. Everything is done so that it's in harmony with the spirit and energy of the planet.

T. J. Streicher: What is the shape of these buildings?

Alex: They are all shapes, depending on the person's preference.

T. J. Streicher: Have you seen the whole planet?

Alex: I have not.

T. J. Streicher: Did you experience any vehicles there?

Alex: Yes. I remember there were transports like small round vehicles that were used for over-planet travel. I remember asking my Earth mother why the cars were on the ground, because I remembered them flying on Arcturus.

T. J. Streicher: Did these round vehicles hover above the ground a little bit?

Alex: Yes, a little bit; you could fly anyplace. We didn't drive on the ground like here.

T. J. Streicher: Did you experience any underground tunnels of any kind, or caves that go inside the planet?

Alex: No.

T. J. Streicher: Is there anything else you would like to add to the description of your home planet Arcturus?

Alex: The mountains are bare, like Arizona, yet in the valleys it was very tropical and very green with clear water.

T. J. Streicher: So there was water? Do you mean like lakes, seas, or oceans?

Alex: I remember lakes.

T. J. Streicher: What color was the water?

Alex: It was a green color.

T. J. Streicher: If you were walking on the ground there, what did the actual composition of the ground look like?

Alex: It looks like sand.

T. J. Streicher: When was the last time you were there?

Alex: I was there before I came to this planet fifty-six years ago.

T. J. Streicher: Before we move into section two, is there anything else you would like to say regarding the descriptions of your home planet?

Alex: The nighttime sky is like this one, except there are many more stars, many more planets.

T. J. Streicher: What did the other planets look like in the sky?

Alex: They look very similar to the way they do here.

T. J. Streicher: Do you recall anything out of the ordinary?

Alex: Well, you see ships flying around, and everybody knows they are ships. Here people freak out and call the ships "UFOs." I was amazed that people here didn't know that there are other Beings living outside their planet.

T. J. Streicher: What was your experience on this other planet like?

Alex: Does anyone on this planet know what unconditional love is?

T. J. Streicher: Yes, maybe not that many, but I think that some people have experienced it.

Alex: Living in a civilization that does not judge but only supports you, that cares for you, everybody working together for the betterment of the one. Coming here was a very big disappointment and a sad experience to see how human beings treat each other, other species, and their planet.

T. J. Streicher: So how do you think this experience affects you?

Alex: I found it very difficult and challenging to be in this world. When I was very young, I was appalled at the violence on this planet and that the same species kill each other. My Earth mother would talk about cutting into the body for surgery; they did not do this on Arcturus. At age four I was scared, knowing I was on an archaic planet. I remember going outside, looking up at the night sky crying, "Please take me home; I hate it here." It was very difficult, because I was different and made fun of most of the time. I remembered before I came here being able to walk through things; I remembered being able to fly. I remembered being able to move things and talk with my mind. I tried doing that here with my siblings as my witnesses. I can understand why they thought I was "not quite right."

T. J. Streicher: Could you do it?

Alex: I could not.

T. J. Streicher: What changes took place in you?

Alex: When my Guardian could not take me back to Arcturus, I became angry; I was an angry, introverted child. I didn't fit in with what I knew and I didn't even look like the rest of my family, and people would point that out.

T. J. Streicher: What do you mean by different-looking?

Alex: I did not look like my Earth family. I had six siblings and two parents, and I didn't look very much like any of them.

T. J. Streicher: Were there other changes that took place in you? You mentioned, for example, your innate powers that you were not able to utilize here.

Alex: It was probably around the age of six or seven that I was trying to convince everybody I could do that—walk through walls and fly. I went on the rooftop of the garage, jumped, and ended up getting hurt, so I stopped trying.

T. J. Streicher: When did you ask to go back to your home planet?

Alex: Throughout my entire childhood, and sometimes even now, feeling like I have had enough and want to get back to the peace and joy I knew before Earth.

T. J. Streicher: Do you realize now why you are here?

Alex: Yes.

T. J. Streicher: Do you have a mission here?

Alex: I know I have a mission. I was told when I was five years old that there would be an awakening; I had no clue what that meant at the time. I was given information that the world, as we know it, will end, and somehow my being here (along with many others) was to help others through this event.

T. J. Streicher: When?

Alex: I wish I had dates, because I would be a multimillionaire today.

T. J. Streicher: Anybody's world could change tomorrow; we can change our realities whenever we want, right?

Alex: Absolutely, but this is going to be a major change for this world; there is going to be something that will startle this world into knowledge of what we really are and where we really came from.

T. J. Streicher: It seems like that has been going on for some time now already, but maybe this will be at a greater scale.

Alex: I believe it is going to be larger; it's going to affect all of the population.

T. J. Streicher: While you were on your home planet of Arcturus, could you recall what you were thinking and feeling?

Alex: I remember being extremely happy and free. Arcturus doesn't have what Earth has; you don't have guilt, and there wasn't any negativity. Everyone worked together just unconditionally loving each other.

T. J. Streicher: Can you recall what you were working together on, such as a goal?

Alex: We were helping each other increase our frequencies to improve ourselves and share it with everybody.

T. J. Streicher: Do you recall eating or consuming anything on this other planet? Would you give me an idea of what?

Alex: I remember a green drink—we just had to take it once a day, and I also remember receiving nutrition from the suns.

T. J. Streicher: You mentioned the green water—is there any connection to the green drink?

Alex: I don't know. I just remember that we had the ability to drink and eat, but there was no meat, and we didn't eat anything that would bleed.

T. J. Streicher: Do I recall you saying that you didn't think there were any animals there?

Alex: I do not recall seeing any.

T. J. Streicher: What do you think was the most meaningful part of this experience on Arcturus?

Alex: That I have a goal to reach and that is to be an example of unconditional love on this planet and hold the energies for those around me.

T. J. Streicher: Can that be challenging?

Alex: With this world and what we are programmed with, it's the most challenging thing anyone will ever do on this planet. Unconditional love simply means accepting everyone for who they are and where they are in their development.

T. J. Streicher: Is it difficult for you to accept people who slaughter animals? How do you get to the point of accepting that?

Alex: That is their journey. If I can intervene in any way, I will, and I have.

T. J. Streicher: How do you intervene? Have you ever used force?

Alex: I have gone to court for an abused animal.

T. J. Streicher: When do you think this experience of living on Arcturus occurred?

Alex: It was my life before this life.

T. J. Streicher: Have you ever listened to very young children talk?

Alex: Yes, they talk about the life experiences they had before coming here.

T. J. Streicher: Absolutely. Many adults just shut the children down, saying, "No, that couldn't be possible."

Alex: The children are talking their truth.

T. J. Streicher: Certainly, but then they have to go to school and it becomes more difficult for them.

Alex: This is the programming; we don't want you to acknowledge that you are something else other than flesh and bone.

T. J. Streicher: Or what we want you to be?

Alex: Correct: the cog in the machine.

T. J. Streicher: So you know that this experience occurred in your former incarnation. Has it happened more than once, say, on this planet?

Alex: I do have memories of other lives on other planets as well as on Earth.

T. J. Streicher: As far as you know you only had one lifetime on Arcturus?

Alex: I do not know.

T. J. Streicher: Do you think this experience has given you a different connection with humanity?

Alex: It has given me different knowledge. I came in with a strong connection to spirit, which I have never lost.

T. J. Streicher: Are you able to accept humans where they are?

Alex: Yes, I pretty much can say that I can accept everybody; that doesn't mean I like them, but I can accept them.

T. J. Streicher: So, through the years have you developed a different connection with humanity?

Alex: Yes.

T. J. Streicher: Have your concerns for the material things of life changed?

Alex: Absolutely. When my ex-husband and I reached the American dream, the big house, money, and most everything we wanted, I was the unhappiest.

T. J. Streicher: Do you live a different lifestyle now?

Alex: I like me as a person a whole lot better with a different attitude and consciousness about this existence. As far as material things go, a lot of people come into my apartment and mention it is sparse. I have what I need, and I feel happy with that.

T. J. Streicher: So as long as you're just comfortable and getting your needs met, nothing more than that?

Alex: I take care of my needs first; then I assist others.

Alex: Has your concern for the welfare of planet Earth changed at all?

Alex: I am concerned for the people. I know Mother Earth is an entity within herself and will take care of herself. I have empathy for those people who cannot embrace different ideas and are stuck in "Earth mode." I don't want to see anybody hurt, shocked, or in such fear that they lose all rationality. I want people to understand that this is not the only reality.

T. J. Streicher: So you are not too concerned about planet Earth itself, but you are concerned about the people living on it—are you concerned at all about the Earth destroying itself?

Alex: I feel Mother Earth changing now, and I know it is due to what humans have done to her, so I don't blame her one bit. Medicine man Morning Sky says, "Mother is about to shake the fleas off her back, and we are the fleas."

T. J. Streicher: Do you foresee any cataclysmic collisions of celestial bodies or anything like that?

Alex: I don't.

T. J. Streicher: Has your desire to help others changed since your initial experience?

Alex: No, because I have always wanted to help people.

T. J. Streicher: In what ways do you like to help people?

Alex: Well, that has changed. I tried to help people by doing things for them. Now I understand no one can do anyone's work for them. I share my information about spirit with anyone who will listen. Those who cross my path, I consciously surround them with love.

T. J. Streicher: When was the last time you went to Arcturus?

Alex: I have not been there since I left.

T. J. Streicher: Have you dreamed or imagined being back on Arcturus?

Alex: No. I have visitors from Arcturus, but I have not been able to go there.

T. J. Streicher: So you're basically coming into this from a past life?

Alex: Yes. The same energy, but in a different container.

T. J. Streicher: How do you feel about being back on Earth now?

Alex: This is probably the most interesting time to be here. Not only am I seeing people waking up but interesting Earth changes. Many people I speak with are very well aware that something different is happening.

T. J. Streicher: Tell me about your sense that something is going to happen . . . would you be more specific about that?

Alex: I can tell you what my Guardian showed me: that Earth is heading for what looks like swirling gray energy around the black hole. He tells me that Earth is going to hit this swirling gray mass of energy and she is going to flip, and when she flips she will begin her transformation. He said there are many Beings here to help. He showed me oceans of lava—mountain tops blowing off with lava flying through the air. He also showed me many ships coming to take people off.

T. J. Streicher: Has he mentioned that he would come and get you?

Alex: He doesn't have to. I know there are ships on this planet already.

T. J. Streicher: Before you were saying you didn't have the power to get yourself off, right?

Alex: Arcturus is a different frequency level, and I'm unable to take this body because it is too dense.

T. J. Streicher: Could you leave your body here?

Alex: I could, but why leave now when the party is almost over and the best part is yet to come?

T. J. Streicher: Are you experiencing any type of planetary travel now, in this body?

Alex: Not in this body, but in the etheric body I do. I can leave this body and I have traveled to different places. Everyone visits other places in Dream Time. The fun part is that our etheric bodies are our natural form. Every time I meditate, or have hypnotherapy, the first place I start is in space among the stars.

T. J. Streicher: Are you receiving hypnotherapy?

Alex: I did a couple of sessions.

T. J. Streicher: Is it helping you retrieve memories about what we are talking about?

Alex: No.

T. J. Streicher: Hypnotherapy concerns me, so I had to ask a couple of questions.

Alex: The information retrieved is an expansion of the information I already have.

T. J. Streicher: Would you consider this to be a spiritual or religious experience?

Alex: I don't believe in religion. It is a frequency booster, yes!

T. J. Streicher: Earlier you mentioned connecting to the greater source— would you please explain?

Alex: We call it the Source Energy.

T. J. Streicher: Could that be a "Higher Power" concept, in a sense? Is it ever considered to be like God or a form of God?

Alex: Yes, it is a higher frequency, but we don't believe in the old man in the sky. God is a much-abused term on this planet, because everybody uses him for their own purposes. They call God a "him," but there is no sex to it. We call it the Source Energy, the energy of all.

T. J. Streicher: So there is a "Higher Power" concept, if I understand you correctly. Would it also be correct to say that you are trying to improve your relationship with your Higher Power?

Alex: I don't have to improve a relationship with a Higher Power because I am part of it; what I am trying to do is get my frequencies to the point where I no longer have to live in a lower-frequency level like this dimension.

T. J. Streicher: Is that your desire or goal, then, as you have to deal with human life forms?

Alex: We are all the same; we are universal energies in a human body, from many places with many different experiences, including being in different containers on many different planets.

T. J. Streicher: But we also know that people are at different levels of consciousness.

Alex: Absolutely.

T. J. Streicher: Have any of your personal goals in life changed?

Alex: My goal has always been to be the best person I possibly can be. I have a different definition of what that is now and have the courage to live my Truth.

T. J. Streicher: Would you be more specific about that?

Alex: The goal is to become an unconditional loving Being who can accept everyone for who they are, where they are, what they are doing. To do this we need to step out of the programs given us and follow our authentic truthful selves.

T. J. Streicher: Has your fear of death changed?

Alex: There is no death. This life is only a very small portion of our experiences.

T. J. Streicher: Do you ever fear the pain that can be associated with death?

Alex: Fear is a lower frequency. I live in the moment, not in the past or the future.

T. J. Streicher: You mentioned the time as a child when you got on the roof and wanted to fly, so you jumped off and hit the ground—wasn't that painful?

Alex: Yes, it was.

T. J. Streicher: So do you still have painful experiences?

Alex: This is part of the human experience. But why dwell on such matters?

T. J. Streicher: Have you ever had a near-death experience?

Alex: I have.

T. J. Streicher: Was it painful?

Alex: No, it wasn't.

T. J. Streicher: So you only remember a few times in your life dealing with severe pain?

Alex: There were several times I had severe pain.

T. J. Streicher: But you're not fearful of that—you just take it as it comes?

Alex: Correct.

T. J. Streicher: Are you involved in any type of experiences that could be painful, but you know that through the pain you will get to a new realization?

Alex: Pain may be a way for some to have "new realizations." Pain doesn't need to be the catalyst for new realizations. Why not think of joy as the catalyst for change?

T. J. Streicher: Do you put yourself in uncomfortable positions? Let's say you want to go into a sweat lodge and you know it is very hot in a sweat lodge, so it could be a very uncomfortable situation.

Alex: Actually, I find it very soothing.

T. J. Streicher: Have you experienced the sun dances? Some of the people choose to pierce, and some are women, and they say it is painful but through the pain there is a new realization.

Alex: You are talking to somebody who passed out when she had her ears pierced, so that probably would not work for me.

T. J. Streicher: Is there anything else you want to add concerning your reactions to the experience of being on another planet?

Alex: Right now I am in such gratitude that I came in with the information and retained it, because it gives me an understanding that there is so much more "out there" than just this world.

T. J. Streicher: Do you think of going back to this other planet, and, if so, for how long?

Alex: I think about going back, and I don't really know for how long.

T. J. Streicher: How often do you think about it?

Alex: At least once a day.

T. J. Streicher: How long would you like to stay?

Alex: If I had a choice not to come back, would that be a choice?

T. J. Streicher: Yes.

Alex: Absolutely. I would go in a second.

T. J. Streicher: What is your response to people who think your experience of going to another planet is fantasy, illusion, or just crazy?

Alex: I had an experience when I was seven, and my neighbor saw me being pulled into the ship. I went home and proudly told my mother I had a nice ride with a really nice blue man in his spaceship. My mother looked at me in shock, and then ugly words were thrown at me. My Guardian told me she was coming from fear, so early on I learned it is fear that evokes that type of response. I don't challenge anyone's beliefs, and I rarely share my experiences with just anyone.

T. J. Streicher: So your response is that you try to approach it in a kind and loving way, and if that's not accepted, then what?

Alex: Everybody has their own comfortable conscious reality, but I will broaden that reality if the opportunity arises. I have scared off many dates this way, LOL!

T. J. Streicher: If you let people know that you're from another world and they respond, "That's really crazy, you must be on drugs, or you're hallucinating," how would you respond to that?

Alex: I usually make a joke out of it and make a light comment like, "You could be from another planet too."

T. J. Streicher: So you try to engage in more communication?

Alex: No, not if the person is not receptive. The thing is, I don't go around telling everybody that information.

T. J. Streicher: That's correct, but you have told a few people. Have you always gotten positive comments from those people?

Alex: The people around me understand, because they have similar information and experiences. Others who don't understand still look at me like I have something seriously wrong with me. I am no longer ashamed of what I know.

T. J. Streicher: So there was a time in your life when you may have been ashamed of it?

Alex: Ashamed only because the information was so different it scared people, and I was sad about this.

T. J. Streicher: I think you mentioned that your own mother had a hard time with it.

Alex: My own mother had a hard time with it, but my whole family and neighborhood saw ships all the time.

T. J. Streicher: Where was this?

Alex: In Berkshire County, Massachusetts; we watched them all the time. What really astounds me is no one ever talked about it—what was that about? How can you see something that's just so different and not talk about it?

T. J. Streicher: Does that mean you had group sightings at an early age?

Alex: A dozen people most times.

T. J. Streicher: Can you remember the earliest age you had a group sighting?

Alex: Yes, when I was five years old.

T. J. Streicher: You were there with a group of people, and they were all commenting on what they were seeing, and they're seeing the same thing you're seeing?

Alex: No, the only comment would be, "There is another one"; they watched mostly in silence. Wouldn't you think that people would be talking about it?

T. J. Streicher: Well, they might be seeing it in a different way, just like when the natives saw Cortez's ships in the ocean; it was like an ontological shock. Everyone is in a different reality; many of those natives didn't see those ships, literally didn't see them. In their reality, that didn't exist, and I think that, in many people's reality, UFOs do not exist, even if they're right in front of them. But you saw them?

Alex: I have been in them.

T. J. Streicher: How long do you think it took for this experience to sink in?

Alex: I had experiences my whole life, but it seemed I was living two lives in two worlds. My two worlds did not integrate until I was almost fifty years old.

T. J. Streicher: So it took a while for you to come to a conscious understanding of what was going on for you?

Alex: Yes, almost fifty years.

T. J. Streicher: At four, five, and six years old, you reported having experiences, and you felt there was something different about you, but you mean it didn't sink in yet, is that what you are saying?

Alex: Seriously, it did not sink in. When my ex and I saw a Being from another place, my ex realized it right away. He looked at the Being and turned to me, scared, saying the male before us was "not from here." I in turn agreed, and said I thought he was "from California."

T. J. Streicher: You did mention that the Beings on Arcturus were very similar-looking to humans, right?

Alex: They have eyes, nose, and a mouth, but they have larger bald heads and are blue.

T. J. Streicher: Would you be able to distinguish that immediately?

Alex: Yes, but this Being that my ex and I saw was not Arcturian.

T. J. Streicher: A male from where?

Alex: The Pleiades.

T. J. Streicher: Did he look like an Earthling?

Alex: A beautiful Earthling; the perfection was amazing.

T. J. Streicher: Are you in contact with the Pleiades?

Alex: No, the Arcturians are the ones I have contact with.

T. J. Streicher: How did you know that this male that you and your ex-husband saw was a Pleiadian?

Alex: He told me.

T. J. Streicher: Did he go on to talk about his planet or anything?

Alex: No.

T. J. Streicher: Do you ever consider yourself to be a person of two worlds?

Alex: I am a person of two worlds.

T. J. Streicher: Are you a person of more than two worlds?

Alex: I consciously know two worlds, but I think we all are from many worlds.

T. J. Streicher: Is there anything else you want to say about that?

Alex: I think we have a spirit world and we have a physical world, and people here are trying to balance the two.

T. J. Streicher: So, with all this information, how will you integrate this experience into your consciousness?

Alex: I don't mean to sound redundant, but unconditional love for all Beings on this planet is my goal, and to continue to hold my energy for those around me. I see myself as one of many messengers.

T. J. Streicher: We also know that there are shifts in consciousness, and that is what this question is leading to, basically. Before, I was asking about how long it took for these experiences to sink in, as there are ways to integrate these experiences into consciousness, and you know because you have done it. I want to know about the techniques that you are using to bring your experiences into consciousness. For instance, when you were a young child and you thought you were different but really didn't believe it, obviously something happened so that you didn't let go of that impression. Eventually, it sank in, you said, at about fifty years old. So help me understand how you got to where you are today: how did you arrive at your present reality?

Alex: It was April first. My dog had to take a pee. I was outside at 3 a.m. when I saw a craft coming through the woods. It was square with three headlights. I was scared. After bringing my dog in, I ran upstairs to try to wake up my ex. He wouldn't wake up. I had an investigation done by MUFON [the Mutual UFO Network], because I demanded an answer to what was flying around in my backyard at this time. I was assured that 98 percent of experiences had a logical explanation. Unfortunately, mine was in the 2 percent that didn't. Both worlds collided that early morning, and I began to integrate.

T. J. Streicher: Was that in 2000?

Alex: It was in 2003.

T. J. Streicher: You mentioned feeling low in 2000: was that because of a divorce or something?

Alex: No, after accomplishing the American Dream—large house, nice clothes, cars—well, you get it, I felt the most miserable.

T. J. Streicher: You reached your goal and there was no rainbow at the end of the tunnel.

Alex: Correct.

T. J. Streicher: I didn't mean to interrupt you; you were talking about integrating these experiences.

Alex: It was an integration but also a connection to something much larger—becoming awake and conscious.

T. J. Streicher: Was this a wake-up call?

Alex: It was a wake-up call.

T. J. Streicher: Have you had a lot of schooling?

Alex: I have six years of college education.

T. J. Streicher: That was the last question of the interview. Is there anything else you would like to say?

Alex:. We can label ourselves anything—Arcturians, Pleiadians, humans, whatever—we are all part of the One, every single one of us a part of each other. Why can't we live together in peace and harmony and work for the betterment of all?

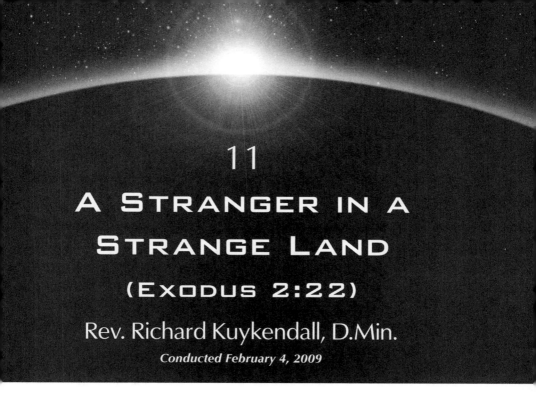

11

A Stranger in a Strange Land

(Exodus 2:22)

Rev. Richard Kuykendall, D.Min.

Conducted February 4, 2009

Rev. Richard Kuykendall, D.Min., who began his ministry in 1977, is currently the minister of the First Congregational Church in Auburn, California. He is also the founder of Spiritwind, a study group for spiritual adventurers that has been meeting for over twenty years in Tehachapi, California. Rev. Kuykendall and his wife Nancy have worked hard to make their faith relevant to the unchurched. Through Spiritwind, they have also espoused a "deep ecumenism," which has sought to embrace God's people of all faiths.

Rev. Kuykendall has worked with a psychotherapist based in Claremont, California, who is a specialist in treatment of participants in alien abduction, also known as "experiencers." Rev. Kuykendall was an active member of an experiencers' support group for a number of years. He is the author of *Prophetess of the Earth,* a rewriting of the Gospels and the Apocalypse, featuring a feminine Christ-figure who teaches "the gospel of the way of the Earth," in contrast to Jesus's "gospel of the kingdom of heaven." Rev. Kuykendall holds bachelor of arts, master of divinity, and doctor of ministry degrees.

▼

T. J. Streicher: Hi, Richard, how are you doing today?

Richard: I'm just fine.

T. J. Streicher: Good. I'm grateful that we can meet today and talk about something really important, I think, for both of us. I would like to give you some sacred space at this time to let you know that we are keeping this confidential, and that I honor this space that we are in, so thank you for being here today.

Richard: Okay. My experience began back in June of 1997. I was in my bed and lost consciousness for a number of hours. When I woke up, I was just sitting up in my bed; I never lay down or anything. I saw four beings that looked like they were wearing blue, dark blue, jump suits. They were not facing me; they were at my feet. They appeared like they came through the wall. They floated me out of the room. I was still lying on my back with my feet toward them. It seemed like we were going through a tunnel of light, although I could see no edges. And there were just all kinds of colors going by. Then, at a certain point, I felt a sense that I was going up. When I finally stopped, I found myself on the top of a mesa. I thought it reminded me of Monument Valley, but my wife and I went to Monument Valley after that experience to see if I was just seeing that, and it was not that. There was no plant life on this planet. It was reddish brown dirt, and I was on top of a very high mesa, and I could see another mesa on the horizon. It seemed to me that it was sunset, and the sky had purple with red and all that, and the temperature felt very moderate. As I was there, I noticed this alien being that I had seemingly had a relationship with since I was a child, with him visiting me at different points. He was telling me, which was very interesting, that early in my experience as a child I had been abducted against my will.

T. J. Streicher: Do you have any memory of this, or through hypnosis have you regained memory?

Richard: Yes, it was through hypnosis, but I did have one waking memory, when I was in my teens. What this means is that he had been following me through my life, kind of like a biologist who tags an animal so he can follow its habitat and eating habits and all those kinds of things. He had been studying me throughout my life, and this was kind of a gift to let me see where he came from.

T. J. Streicher: Now is this the earlier experience, when you were a teenager, or is this the most recent experience of 1997?

Richard: Right, he had brought me there to show me where he lived. Normally, I am afraid of heights, and yet I was on this very high mesa and without fear. I felt completely secure. I had no fear of the situation at all. I thought, if this is your home, where do you live? There is nothing here, it's just mesas. It looks like you're out in the desert or something. So then he took me underground and showed me that they lived under the ground. There was a small river of water going down; it was kind of cavernlike on the inside. So they apparently—the beings that lived there, they lived under the ground. I did not go into any one dwelling place, so I never really saw any other beings down there. But that's basically what he showed me. Another thing was very strange; I couldn't figure this out, but they had their crafts, which were saucer-shaped. Somehow they were able to go up through the center of the mesa. It would be like if you thought of an elevator going up and took it to the top of the mesa, and they would take off from there. The thing that was strange about it was it didn't seem like there was anything mechanical; it seemed almost like it was an organic thing, and I don't understand how that can be.

The other thing I got from the experience, which I think is the most important, is that people talk about how, since other planets are so many light-years away that it is impossible that we can ever go there, we would be dead before we got there, because it takes so long. What I found through this experience is that there are different dimensions—like when I saw the four beings in the beginning walking through the wall, they were just stepping across from one dimension into another, so it's almost like there being a parallel universe, or a parallel world, so that they can be here in just a matter of moments rather than traveling through years. That is the main thing that I got from it. After the experience was over, which I was thrilled about, I thought it was wonderful: those four other beings brought me back into my room and put me back into bed. That is when I woke up and realized that a number of hours had gone by. So that's basically the experience I had.

T. J. Streicher: Okay. Richard, you mentioned earlier that you may have been abducted at an earlier age—would you give me a little more insight on that?

Richard: Well, when I was a young child—I don't remember exactly what age I was, but probably younger than ten years old, I had an abduction experience, where I was taken onto a ship that was saucerlike in shape. I only knew that because from the inside it looked like the ceiling and wall curved down like it was a saucer. There was an examination table, and they did some body probes and things like that. I was very scared about what had happened, so that was my first experience. Then when I was in my late teens—I was probably seventeen years old—I had an experience when I woke up in the middle of the night and I sensed there was some presence in the room. I sensed there was someone there. I didn't want to look, but then I felt like someone sat on my legs, which were outstretched in the bed. When that happened, I sat up, and when I looked, I could not see anything. I reached my hand out and felt that a face was there; even though I couldn't see a thing, I could feel this face.

This is where it gets weird. I said, "Who are you?"

He said, "I'm Satan."

"What do you want?" I asked.

He said, "I want to ask you a question: If God forgives you and you can be saved, why can't God forgive me?"

Then I heard God say (that is, the spirit speaking in me), "because he is not sorry."

And then all of a sudden he started laughing. I ran out of the room and locked myself in the bathroom. Then I totally lost consciousness; when I awoke, I was back in the bed. What happened is this: my therapist did a regression on that experience so I could go through it again. It turns out that it wasn't Satan—that it was this being that had taken me into the ship for an examination when I was younger. This was the same being that took me to where the mesa was. What I got from it was that he was doing this just like what was done when I was a child and had a physical examination; this was some kind of psychological examination to see what I would do if I was confronted by Satan, but it wasn't really Satan. So those are the experiences I remember.

T. J. Streicher: Can you recall what this being looked like, and how he may have changed through your experiences with him—I'm assuming it was a male?

Richard: I think it was a male; he looked exactly like what people call "greys," with a large head and small body, huge eyes . . . but he looked more blue than gray, he was a bluish color, bluish gray, you might say. He looked the same every time I had an interaction with him in this life.

T. J. Streicher: Now let's go back to your experience on the other planet. You mentioned earlier that you thought there was red dirt, with mesas, somewhat barren. As you're looking out across this planet, can you possibly describe its size or its curvature?

Richard: As to the curvature I would expect that it was probably the same size as our planet. I had said that my wife and I had gone to Monument Valley to see if that is what I had seen, and the mesas were different where I was, but if you've ever been to Monument Valley and you see that big expanse that is there, that is the same kind of sense that I got on this planet.

T. J. Streicher: Would you please tell me what it looked like? Do you recall any type of vegetation?

Richard: No vegetation whatsoever.

T. J. Streicher: Any animal life?

Richard: No, no type of animal life.

T. J. Streicher: Any type of resources there?

Richard: There was water under the ground. One of the interesting things that occurred to me afterward was that this is something our own planet could learn from, that is, that even though they are technologically far more advanced than we are, in that they have these crafts and are able to go through different dimensions and everything, yet they lived very simple lives in harmony with their environment. They had water under the ground and they drank—I don't know where their food came from, but maybe there were plants that grew somewhere. I don't know, but it seemed they were in harmony with their environment.

T. J. Streicher: Did you actually ever see them eat?

Richard: No.

T. J. Streicher: Did you get to see their faces and observe how large their mouths were?

Richard: Their mouths were very small, just like a slit almost, not even lips.

T. J. Streicher: Going back to your experience on the other planet, was there any kind of light or noises?

Richard: There was the sky that was like a beautiful sunset. There were purples and reds and blues. I had the sense that there may be more than one sun, like they may have had two suns.

T. J. Streicher: What gave you that impression?

Richard: It was just an inner sense.

T. J. Streicher: What was the temperature like?

Richard: It was very comfortable, but I thought it must get pretty hot during the day because of the lack of vegetation.

T. J. Streicher: What gave you the impression that it was sunset?

Richard: I don't really know; it could have been sunrise, but it is at that time of day when the sun is not up or down yet.

T. J. Streicher: I am really interested in the red dirt that you mentioned. Did you kick it around, or was it like clay?

Richard: It was just reddish brown dirt. I can remember that, when I was under the ground, I could distinctly smell the dirt; it smelled like dirt that we have—it had that smell.

T. J. Streicher: "It smelt like dirt that we have." Let's say, if we were to go in the back here and pick up a handful of darkish brown or blackish dirt, would it smell similar to that?

Richard: Yes.

T. J. Streicher: Did you see any kind of civilization on top of the planet, on the exterior?

Richard: Yes, just the spacecraft on top of the mesa; that is where they would take off from.

T. J. Streicher: Was there a particular mesa that was a bit higher or something that a spacecraft could land on, or any distinguishing marks on the mesa?

Richard: I don't know, but the mesas . . . [Richard draws a picture of what they looked like].

T. J. Streicher: About how many feet long are this mesa and the spacecraft on it?

Richard: It wasn't really big—like twice the size of this room.

T. J. Streicher: Was there any sign of civilization under the ground, when you were underneath and seeing the water?

Richard: There were footpaths and bridges that went over the water that was running down through the center; that's the only thing. Then another thing was that there was some kind of overhead lighting, but I couldn't determine the source of it. What it reminded me of is how some places have a fluorescent light around the top of a bookcase and it lights up the ceiling. It was like that. I didn't actually see any bulbs or anything, but that is how it was lit.

T. J. Streicher: Was it a whitish color light?

Richard: Yes, pretty much, but it wasn't very bright. It was kind of a soft light.

T. J. Streicher: As you were in this underground facility, did it seem like it was dug out or something more natural looking?

Richard: I haven't thought about that.

T. J. Streicher: Did it look natural?

Richard: It probably started off natural, but it looked like it had been modified, like it was made, like the walls on the side were smooth. I have been in caverns before, but this wasn't like that; it was all uniform. I guess it was all made; they made it that way.

T. J. Streicher: While you were in this facility, did you see anything out of the ordinary—machines, tables?

Richard: Just open space. That's what impressed me, because it was so natural. I wasn't seeing mechanical things or anything like that, and even the way they transported the saucer to the top of the mesa—I don't understand how they can do it, but it did not look like it was mechanical, it looked like it's almost organic.

T. J. Streicher: Did you recall seeing a spaceship in the underground facility?

Richard: No, I just saw it come up.

T. J. Streicher: Could the spacecraft have actually been concealed in the mesa?

Richard: I recall it coming up.

T. J. Streicher: Did you take off from the same place?

Richard: Yes, I think it was the same place, but I did not see it when I was down inside there.

T. J. Streicher: Do these mesas have any kind of ridge markings on the outside of them?

Richard: Yes, they had ridge markings [Richard begins to draw the markings on paper]; they weren't perfectly smooth.

T. J. Streicher: If the craft was about thirty feet long, would you say the top of the mesa was about thirty feet long as well?

Richard: Yes, they were. To me they were fairly small mesas as compared to Monument Valley.

T. J. Streicher: As you recall this scenario one more time, do you recall anything on Earth looking like this?

Richard: I have seen pictures of Devil's Tower, but that is much taller. We had planned to take another trip to Mesa, Arizona, to see if the mesas were like what I saw, but we never made the trip. So I haven't ever seen a place on Earth that looks like that.

T. J. Streicher: Can you think of anything else you saw on this planet?

Richard: No, that is about it.

T. J. Streicher: So all together, how long do you think you were there?

Richard: Probably just a couple of hours, maybe.

T. J. Streicher: When you were in this underground facility, did you walk around a little?

Richard: Where I walked I didn't see any other beings, and I didn't see any dwelling places or anything like that, so I probably would have had to walk farther in than I did to see it.

T. J. Streicher: Do you recall what you were walking on?

Richard: Yes, it was a dirt footpath.

T. J. Streicher: Do you recall what color the dirt was?

Richard: I don't recall, but I expect it was like what was outside; it was a little darker in there, because the lighting was up above and not on the ground.

T. J. Streicher: Now we are going to shift gears a little bit and go into what your reactions were to this experience.

Richard: I felt euphoric. I felt I couldn't believe it.

T. J. Streicher: At the moment? Or upon your recall?

Richard: At both the moment and the recall.

T. J. Streicher: At that time, were you able to put some of the pieces together—that you could have been with the same being at that point that you had early experiences with?

Richard: Yes.

T. J. Streicher: This being that we are talking about—did you have a name for him?

Richard: It was all mental telepathy.

T. J. Streicher: You mentioned the word "euphoric"—what do you mean by that? Was it something you have experienced before?

Richard: Yes, it was a mixture of joy and peace at the same time, feeling secure without any fear—that's how I experienced it.

T. J. Streicher: Were you always feeling like this being was treating you with respect, and the rapport was all right?

Richard: Yes.

T. J. Streicher: How has this experience affected you now? This happened ten years ago, and you haven't mentioned if you have had similar experiences since then.

Richard: Not that I know of. There was one time since then when I had gone to bed at night and woke up in the morning on the living room couch, and I had no idea how I got there. If I were still doing regression work, I'm sure my therapist would have wanted to explore what happened at that point, but I haven't been doing it, so I kind of think of that last experience as being his way of saying thank you. I sensed that would be the last time I would see him.

T. J. Streicher: How are you feeling about it now? This was a euphoric experience that happened to you over ten years ago: is there a part of you that wants to go back there or maybe get more involved?

Richard: Yes.

T. J. Streicher: Do you ask for that?

Richard: No, I haven't really asked for that.

T. J. Streicher: Or maybe you feel it's finished?

Richard: I kind of felt like it was finished.

T. J. Streicher: For you or for him—you're assuming that he is finished?

Richard: Yes, that is correct.

T. J. Streicher: Have there been any changes in how you look at your world, the universe, the cosmos—do you look at things differently now?

Richard: Yes, I do, but the main thing that changed my way of looking at things was this inner-dimensional travel. Because, since I am a minister, it made me think completely differently about the idea of angels. I started thinking about the angels that appear in stories in the Bible; they don't describe them as having wings anywhere in the Bible, and yet people put wings on them as if they flew. Where are they flying from? If they were even as close to us as Mars, that is still a long way to fly. People think that heaven is out there beyond the horizon—and then all of a sudden I thought, no, they're here right now, it is just another dimension. When people see an angel, the angel has just stepped across from one dimension to another; it's not like they are flying for hours or days from somewhere far away. This made me think differently about angels, on the one hand, but it also made me think differently about space travel. People think that it would be impossible to go that many light-years away, but there are inner-dimensional worlds. Somehow they are just able to step across. I don't fully understand it.

T. J. Streicher: Some people refer to this as a transdimensional gate—does that symbolism work for you?

Richard: Yes.

T. J. Streicher: Would you describe some of the changes that took place in you since that experience?

Richard: Well, the main change that took place was that I did not fear it anymore. With the experience I had when I was younger, I was afraid.

T. J. Streicher: Afraid of what?

Richard: Afraid of what the beings might do.

T. J. Streicher: When you were on the other planet and looking out over the horizon, what were you thinking?

Richard: I was thinking that it's beautiful.

T. J. Streicher: It seems like this planet was dry on the outside, with no vegetation or animal life, but underground there was water. Did it seem near enough to get to if needed?

Richard: Yes.

T. J. Streicher: Did you get to try the water?

Richard: No, I did not try it.

T. J. Streicher: Did the water look like our water?

Richard: Yes.

T. J. Streicher: As you look back now, what do you think was the most meaningful part of this experience?

Richard: Just to be there.

T. J. Streicher: As far as you recall, this experience happened in 1997; how many times have you gone to another planet?

Richard: This experience only happened once.

T. J. Streicher: Why do you think that is?

Richard: I think that this was a way of thanking me. It's funny that he never asked my permission in the first place to do what he was doing, but it seemed like he wanted to show me his world.

T. J. Streicher: How has this experience affected your connection with humanity?

Richard: How it has affected my work is this: There is a guy named Barry Downing [a minister who wrote the book, *The Bible and Flying Saucers*], so I use things that he has said in a number of my sermons. When I was talking about the transfiguration of Jesus on the mountain, it says that Moses and Elijah appeared with him; he's shining bright, a cloud comes over, and a voice comes out of the clouds saying, "This is my beloved son here." So in my sermon I said there is a Presbyterian minister named Barry Downing who speculates that the cloud was actually a UFO. I said, you're probably thinking that's really far out and it's strange to think that, and yet you feel perfectly comfortable hearing about a voice coming out of a cloud, a cloud that talks. Why is it impossible for it to be a spacecraft, and not impossible for a cloud to talk? I have also done it with the star in the sky that led the wise men; the Bible says it stopped and started again, but stars don't start and stop. So I bring this up in my sermons.

T. J. Streicher: How long have you been a minister?

Richard: About twenty-three years.

T. J. Streicher: I noticed from your questionnaire that you have a doctoral degree—is this in theology?

Richard: It's a doctorate in ministry degree, from the University of Creation Spirituality, at the Mathew Fox School in Oakland.

T. J. Streicher: Has there been any change in how you look at the material things in life?

Richard: I don't think I changed in that way.

T. J. Streicher: Have things changed in your service area?

Richard: Well, as a minister I talk with people who have had all different sorts of problems. If people knew about my experiences, they would probably think I am nuts. So, having had these experiences makes me more compassionate and more understanding of people who are going through different things, because I have gone through my own stuff.

T. J. Streicher: So maybe it has given you more compassion and empathy?

Richard: Yes.

T. J. Streicher: Have your concerns for this planet changed at all?

Richard: Obviously, I am concerned about the environment and all that. But I know from astronomy that eventually the sun is going to get bigger, and the Earth is eventually going to be vaporized, so we need to be working toward a way to go somewhere else. I know it is not going to happen in my lifetime or my kids' lifetime, but eventually it is going to happen.

T. J. Streicher: Are you saying that this experience may have opened your mind to another reality, one with the possibility of there being other worlds that we could live on?

Richard: Right.

T. J. Streicher: And that this planet may be destroyed someday?

Richard: Yes.

T. J. Streicher: Are you trying to raise other people's awareness of that fact?

Richard: Yes. I do it in my sermons, and I also have a study group that meets here on Tuesday evenings and we study all sorts of alternative things—like this next month will be on Sufism, the month after that is on Tarot, and last year I did a whole month on UFOs. We watched a couple of documentaries, and I talked about the Bible and UFOs, and basically presented what Barry Downing did in *The Bible and Flying Saucers*. I have tried to raise consciousness and give some validation to it, so it's not looked at as just some French movie stuff.

T. J. Streicher: How do you feel about being back on Earth now?

Richard: I feel okay.

T. J. Streicher: Do you ever feel like a part of you is still there, on the other planet?

Richard: Well, it is there in my memory, and at times I wish to have that same euphoria that I had when I was there.

T. J. Streicher: Would you consider this to be a religious or spiritual experience for you?

Richard: Yes, I would.

T. J. Streicher: In what regard?

Richard: The whole idea of being on another planet, communicating with a being from another world—to me, that is spiritual.

T. J. Streicher: Would you consider this being to have an angelic presence?

Richard: I have speculated about that, mainly because I have stereotyped what an angel is supposed to look like, such as big white wings, and he definitely didn't look like that. But that has made me rethink what the angels were in the Bible.

T. J. Streicher: Have any of your personal goals changed since this experience?

Richard: I don't think so.

T. J. Streicher: How about your fear of death?

Richard: No, I have no fear of death. I think that since that experience there has been less fear—I just don't fear death. I take it as just traveling through another dimension.

T. J. Streicher: You did mention that you were very scared in the first experience.

Richard: Yes.

T. J. Streicher: Before the age of ten, did you ever read any UFO books or see any movies about UFOs?

Richard: I saw the old movies *The Day the Earth Stood Still* and *Invasion of the Body Snatchers*. I saw a lot of science fiction things.

T. J. Streicher: Do you think of going back to this other planet, and if so for how long?

Richard: I would like to go and take my wife. I don't know if that would work, but I would like her to see what I saw.

T. J. Streicher: How does she feel about that?

Richard: She definitely acknowledges that I had that experience, but I don't know if she acknowledges it literally.

T. J. Streicher: If you went back to this planet with your wife, how long would you like to stay?

Richard: Maybe a couple of days, to see what it's like when the sun comes out, and see what I didn't see.

T. J. Streicher: What if you saw the Earth in a state of irreconcilable differences and you knew there was going to be great destruction on the planet, would you consider living on this other planet?

Richard: Yes, definitely.

T. J. Streicher: What is your response to people who think your experience is fantasy or illusion, or that you're crazy?

Richard: This has given me more empathy and compassion when talking to people who have had unusual experiences of one kind or another. This is also why I am guarded and don't put it out there that I have done this.

T. J. Streicher: So you don't talk to people about this?

Richard: No, not at all.

T. J. Streicher: Because you're not sure of the reactions?

Richard: I had a bad experience about six or seven years ago, when I was at my therapist's house and they were filming our experiencers' group meeting for a documentary that was supposed to come out, on abduction and that sort of thing. But what ended up happening, after we signed waivers and everything for this, was a show that Penn and Teller were doing, and they were making fun of people like me, suggesting that we were a bunch of nut cases, and that there were few people who actually had seen this.

T. J. Streicher: How did you get together with your therapist?

Richard: Strangely enough, my wife had gone to her as a therapist years before we met. I think I first came to her at the time when I was going through a divorce; I was going to her for counseling. She asked me if I had done any regression work; I had, actually, with a therapist friend of hers, long before. Somehow we got to talking about my childhood and so forth, and I wanted to explain some problems that I had. She was bringing me back to this time in my childhood, and she was having me imagine I was going down an escalator as she was putting me under hypnosis. When it stopped, I sensed someone looking at me, and she said, "What does he look like?" I burst out crying, saying that he was not human. That was the first breakthrough with regard to meeting this being. It was very scary at that point.

T. J. Streicher: Was that in 1997?

Richard: It was before that—I don't know, maybe 1996.

T. J. Streicher: When do you think this experience of going to another planet actually happened? Your recall was in 1997, but when did you actually go?

Richard: I think it happened in 1997, because I had those missing hours.

T. J. Streicher: How long did it take for your experience to sink in?

Richard: It sank in pretty quick.

T. J. Streicher: Did you feel that you needed the hypnotic regression, or did you feel you could have worked through this yourself?

Richard: I think I needed the regression.

T. J. Streicher: To relax you, or support you?

Richard: I am not sure. There is a change of consciousness; it's not like dreaming. If you're dreaming, you're unconscious. It's not like being awake either; it's like being in this twilight state of consciousness. Somehow in that state of mind I was able to access that information.

T. J. Streicher: But you knew that something had happened to you?

Richard: Yes.

T. J. Streicher: How much time elapsed from the actual experience to your recall of the experience?

Richard: Less than a year.

T. J. Streicher: Do you ever consider yourself a person of two worlds now?

Richard: Yes, I definitely do.

T. J. Streicher: Will you say a little bit more about that?

Richard: I did a series where I had one foot in one world and another foot in another world. I didn't speak openly about going to another planet, but I talked about the sense that sometimes we don't feel like this is totally where we belong and that there is someplace else where we do belong.

T. J. Streicher: Do you feel like you belong there sometimes?

Richard: Yes.

T. J. Streicher: Is there anything else you would like to say before we end the interview?

Richard: No, I think I've said it all.

T. J. Streicher: All right. I thank you very much, Richard. I really appreciate that.

Richard: You're welcome.

12

MISSION TO JUPITER, APRIL 27, 1973

Ingo Swann

Conducted July 15, 2010

Ingo Swann (1933–) is an American artist and an exceptionally successful subject in parapsychology experiments. As a child he spontaneously had numerous paranormal experiences, mostly of the OBE type, the study of which became a major passion as he matured. In 1970, he began acting as a parapsychology test subject in tightly controlled laboratory settings with numerous scientific researchers. Because of the success of most of these thousands of test trials, major media worldwide often referred to him as "the scientific psychic."

Between 1970 and 1973, at the American Society for Psychical Research (ASPR), Swann began suggesting experimental protocols to test for the existence of mind-dynamic processes that would enhance ESP perceptions. As a result, the Puthoff/Swann Psycho-energetics Remote-Viewing Project lasted for eighteen years. Swann has written several books on remote viewing and related topics, including *Natural ESP: Unlocking the Extrasensory Power of Your Mind* (1987) and *Penetration: The Question of Extraterrestrial and Human Telepathy* (1998). Moreover, most books and articles written after 1973 about parapsychology and *psi* (psychic or paranormal phenomena) matters

189

refer to Swann's work in some way. Many analysts of science and para-psychology generally concede that his work, and the high levels of official sponsorship it obtained, gradually influenced positive reevaluations of the validity of psi in human experience.

▼

Ingo Swann presents a different case because his experience came about as a result of a tightly controlled experiment at Stanford Research Institute (SRI) to help determine if remote-viewing capacities could extend to another planet. Jupiter was selected because two NASA spacecrafts (Pioneer 10 and 11) were shortly scheduled to fly by it, which would reveal new information about that gaseous giant that could be compared to Swann's remote-viewing perceptions. Swann's Jupiter probe experiment ultimately proved to be a success, but, more importantly, it also supported the concept that some aspect of human consciousness innately "houses" such capacities, which many have reported throughout history. Swann is included here because his experiences are important and relevant to the overall investigation, but the data summarized in the next chapter will be based only on the accounts of the other six interviewees.

▼

Ingo: I worked with Dr. Gertrude Schmeidler early, when I was volunteering to be a research guinea pig. She proposed an experiment, [before] which I did not know I could do any of these things. She put sealed thermistors in different locations in different rooms. She would tell me to make one of them colder or hotter, or do nothing. So that worked real well, but at the time parapsychology had never had a repeatable experiment, and that was one benchmark that we were bumping up against. Back in those times parapsychologists tried psychokinesis on something that was left up to the subject, not to the experimenter. But she was going to take that role over and tell me what to do to which thermistor. This was an elaborate experiment; all the thermistors were fed into the big computer, so there was really no guesswork. She succeeded at both benchmarks, and it was a repeatable experiment, dependent on the command of the experimenter, not the guinea pig. This is what made me famous, practically overnight. It was in 1971, and here is a report of the large media impact that the experiment had. At that time, parapsychology practically had no media impact at all. For instance, *Time* magazine, *The Smithsonian, Newsweek*—they were all reporting on her experiment. *The Washington Post* was still reporting on it in 1977.

T. J. Streicher: What do you think of the interview questions that I have been asking all the participants—could you answer these questions?

Ingo: No, I don't think so. You will have to create some new ones. Maybe you could create them as you go along, so you can give me the gist of it.

T. J. Streicher: You are reading the gist of it right now. Here is my first question. What planet did you feel you had visited?

Ingo: We didn't visit—we made an experimental excursion, a deliberate excursion, and we tried this as an experiment. We didn't just sort of have it in a dream or something like that. We found no people on Jupiter, so most of your questions are not appropriate to me. We're talking about people who had an experience and then came back. They can be asked a lot of things, but they didn't come back with anything in terms of answers to your questions. In this case we came back with data, information that proved to be correct.

T. J. Streicher: It says here there is an enormous mountain range. This manuscript is very detailed—did you do this?

Ingo: Yes, this is the session that was recorded at the time.

T. J. Streicher: I am trying to get a sense of how large Jupiter is.

Ingo: Big!

T. J. Streicher: It seems enormously flat.

Ingo: But I am on a surface.

T. J. Streicher: I don't want to project my own ideas into this, so I will display the experiment exactly how it is written.

Ingo: Yes.

T. J. Streicher: Reproduced here is the document of the Swann Jupiter Probe, experiment number 46, Stanford Research Institute, Palo Alto, California, conducted on April 27, 1973.

No big sharp noises for the next half hour, please.

6:03:25   There's a planet with stripes.

6:04:14   I hope it's Jupiter. I think it must have an extremely large hydrogen mantle. If a space probe made contact with that, it would be maybe 80,000–120,000 miles out from the planet surface.

6:06:00   So I'm approaching it on the tangent, where I can see it's a half moon, in other words half lit and half dark. If I move around to the lit side, it's distinctly yellow toward the right.

6:06:20   Very high in the atmosphere there are crystals; they glitter, so maybe the stripes are like bands of crystals, maybe like rings of Saturn, though not far out like that, very close within the atmosphere. (Unintelligible sentence) I bet you they'll reflect radio probes. Is that possible if you had a cloud of crystals that were assaulted by different radio waves? (Hal—That's right.)

6:08:00   Now I'll go down through. It feels really good there (laugh). I said that before, didn't I? Inside those cloud layers, those crystal layers, they look beautiful from the outside, but from the inside they look like rolling gas clouds—eerie yellow light, rainbows.

6:10:20   I get the impression, though I don't see, that it's liquid.

6:10:55   Then I came through the cloud cover. The surface looks like sand dunes. They're made of very large grade crystals so they slide. Tremendous winds sort of like maybe the prevailing winds of Earth but very close to the surface of Jupiter. From that view the horizon looks orange-ish or rose-colored, but overhead it's kind of greenish yellow.

6:12:35   If I look to the right, there is an enormous mountain range.

6:13:18   If I'm giving a description of where I've gone and where I am, it would be approximately where Alaska is, if the sun were directly overhead, which it is. The sun looks like it has a green corona, it seems smaller to me. (Hal—What color is the sun?) White.

6:14:45   I feel that there's a liquid atmosphere. Those mountains are really huge, but they still don't poke up through the crystal cloud cover. You know, I had a dream once something like this, where the cloud cover was a great arc, sweeping over the entire heaven. Those grains that make that sand orange are quite large. They have a polished surface and they look something like amber or like obsidian, but they're yellowish and not as heavy. The wind blows them; they slide along.

6:16:37   If I turn, the whole thing seems enormously flat. I mean, I get the feeling that if a man stood on those sands I think he would sink into them (laugh); maybe that's where that liquid feeling comes from.

6:18:10   I see something that looks like a tornado. Is there a thermal inversion here? I bet there is. I bet you that the surface of Jupiter will give a very high infrared count. The heat is held down.

6:19:55   I seem to be stuck; I'm not moving. I'll move more towards the equator. I get the impression that that must be a band of crystals similar to the outer ones, kind of bluish. They seem to be sort of in orbit, permanent orbit, down through another layer farther down which is like our clouds but moving fast. There's another area: liquid, like water. Looks like it's got icebergs in it, but they're not icebergs.

6:22:20   Tremendous winds. It's colder here, maybe it's because there's not a thermal inversion here.

6:23:25   I'm back. Okay. The atmosphere of Jupiter is very thick, I mean . . . (Ingo draws a picture . . . explains the drawing.) This is what appears to be a hydrogen mantle 100,000 miles off the surface. Those here are bands of crystals, kind of elements. They're pretty close to the surface. And beneath those are layers of clouds or what seem to be prevailing winds. Beneath that is the surface, which I saw was—well, it looked like shifting sands made out of some sort of slippery granulated stuff. And off in the distance, I guess, to the east was a very high mountain chain, 30,000 feet or so, quite large mountains. I feel these crystals will probably bounce radio waves. They're that type. Generally, that's all.

T. J. Streicher: Looks like there are icebergs on Jupiter?

Ingo: Yes, colder in some areas of the planet. These drawings were done during the session. Most of what I observed was not known about Jupiter. The mantle was extending about 100,000 miles above the surface. The mountains were not discovered—we did not have feedback on the mountains until rather recently. But now we know that Jupiter has a bigger core, as big as ten to twenty Earth masses. Here is a newspaper article about it. So it has a big core, a solid core; it is going to have tectonics, which means mountains, and caverns, and things.

T. J. Streicher: And geological shifts?

Ingo: Yes.

T. J. Streicher: This would bring more clarity concerning this planet, like how people think of the moon as a dead satellite. Some people think of Jupiter as a dead planet or satellite in the middle of nowhere.

Ingo: It's even bigger than I first thought, and it has a solid core.

T. J. Streicher: So who is to say that it couldn't be habitable?

Ingo: Me.

T. J. Streicher: Are you sticking to that?

Ingo: Yes, I'm good with that! If it were up to me, I think it is a pretty tough place out there. Do you remember I talked about gigantic icebergs? And about crystals? A few weeks ago I got this from a guy who works for Project Icarus, which is that group that searches for planets around distant stars. And this came as a surprise, because it turns out that those big icebergs that I saw as crystals—they say they are diamonds.

T. J. Streicher: Now we are going back to how the planets seem to be exploited by different organizations for their valuable resources.

Ingo: Well, it's not in the realm of possibility yet. But Project Icarus is one of the top five science projects on Earth today, and they say that those big icebergs are diamonds.

T. J. Streicher: I think I am more concerned about the humanistic element of all this, where this puts us as human beings, and what we have perceived as a lifeless universe for so long. Now it's looking like, with the increased knowledge we are getting through the ages, that there is the possibility of there being a more living universe.

Ingo: Well, you like to think in those big terms. I do, too, once in a while. But this was a scientifically organized experiment, this trip to Jupiter. Jupiter is a really tough place. I don't know if there could be life there or not—I didn't see any, or sense any. It's now admitted that it has concrete masses and other geological descriptions.

T. J. Streicher: Would you consider going back there?

Ingo: Why?

T. J. Streicher: To expand upon the original research.

Ingo: I don't care anymore. I don't know if I'm up to it, anyway. Remember, I was about forty years old at the time, and now I am approaching eighty. I don't know if my faculties still work or not.

T. J. Streicher: This is interesting, because I get some of the same comments from other people who have traveled to other places, such as Edgar Mitchell. When I asked him if he would ever consider going back to the moon—and I think you are both about the same age—he responded positively that he would indeed consider that opportunity. He was concerned, though, about his age and how he would relate to the experience at this time, but his experience, which he called a *samadhi* experience, as he returned to Earth from the moon, was so enlightening to him that it opened his mind up to the larger possibility of there being life elsewhere and the idea of a living cosmos, in the same way that that it did for John Glenn. So would you give more consideration to another experiment that could give greater detail?

Ingo: You're thinking of this as just a humanitarian thing, but this was a whole big deal, and there has to be a reason to go through a big deal like that. Who wants the information? *I* don't want it.

T. J. Streicher: There are a number of different governments that would want this information.

Ingo: I don't care about that.

T. J. Streicher: I'm not going there, but there are a number of different governments and entities that would want to make fortunes on all those natural resources out there.

Ingo: So, let them do that.

T. J. Streicher: Right, let them do that. But what I'm getting at is how we can raise consciousness by going within ourselves.

Ingo: Raise consciousness? Why?

T. J. Streicher: So we can stop killing each other.

Ingo: But why and how?

T. J. Streicher: This is how.

Ingo: This doesn't raise anybody's consciousness.

T. J. Streicher: Yes, it has, Ingo.

Ingo: No, it hasn't.

T. J. Streicher: Well, it has raised mine.

Ingo: Does this really raise consciousness for all these people? It might open the imagination, or change around a number of different reality boxes and things like that. But no, I am over with; I am done. I am too old, and I don't really care anymore.

T. J. Streicher: But what you don't know is that you have raised consciousness for a lot of people, like in academia, and how hard people are trying to understand this and be part of an anomalous experience that could raise their consciousness. Most of the people I have reported on have not only raised their consciousness but have also illuminated the possibility of there being other life in the universe. Weren't you somewhat stupefied by the fact that Jupiter might have a solid core?

Ingo: I don't think I was.

T. J. Streicher: By remote viewing the planet, you were able to change your own consciousness. Why couldn't that be available to other people? So that they could have hope of raising their own mental capacity or psyche to greater possibilities? That could really end conflict. It could bring us together and not keep us feeling like we are stuck.

Ingo: The only thing I liked doing in parapsychology were the experiments and research. I came to parapsychology, I did what I did, and I exited. Changing consciousness—if I contributed to that, that would be fine, but that is not an important thing to me anymore.

T. J. Streicher: But it's important to others.

Ingo: Well, let them find it then, let them change their own consciousness. I am going to die here within some expectable time, and I am not going to worry about the practical problems of the human species. I am past that.

T. J. Streicher: Well there is a reason you are sharing this with me.

Ingo: Probably because you are here.

T. J. Streicher: But you invited me here also.

Ingo: You asked if you could come.

T. J. Streicher: You could just as easily have said no. So there is a reason I am here.

Ingo: The reason for you being here and my reasons for talking with you seem to be two different things.

T. J. Streicher: Do you want me to just report on the scientific end of this?

Ingo: I don't care what you report on; it's your book.

T. J. Streicher: Okay, you are right. I am a humanistic psychologist. I am concerned about the species, and about all life.

Ingo: At my age, there is nothing I can do anymore.

T. J. Streicher: You have already done it.

Ingo: So, I did it, I did what I did, and I don't do it anymore.

T. J. Streicher: I think this could be considered a big thank you for what you have done. You went outside of consensus reality and beyond the dominant worldview.

Ingo: But look, this wasn't just me. This included all the people who worked with these projects, which means maybe five hundred people in all. It's not just me; without them this would never have happened.

T. J. Streicher: Who else went to other planets?

Ingo: I don't know, I would never have thought to go there if it weren't a challenge in an experimental situation promising good feedback. What do I care what's on Jupiter, really?

T. J. Streicher: That's the great thing about it: you didn't have projections about what you would see there. The fact is that almost a hundred percent of it has proved to be true. That's coming back, that says something that can be supported by facts. Now do you see the importance?

Ingo: Well, I did it; I don't have to prove anything.

T. J. Streicher: Well, my book is about thanking you for what you've done.

Ingo: That's nice of you, to thank me.

T. J. Streicher: I am not trying to be nice. I'm just trying to keep the circle moving and do something extraordinary. Maybe it was the right time and the right place in your life, because you said you weren't capable of doing that right now, but you did do this.

Ingo: We did it, all the people that worked on this. If I had a superstar ego, then I might be more agreeable to your attitude. I really liked doing the research and the experiments and that's how I got into it. Then came the big media explosion as the result of Dr. Schmeidler's experiment, which took place before the Jupiter probe, by the way. These days I try to live in total obscurity.

T. J. Streicher: And you continue to do that. After reading this I get the gist, without being egocentric, that you took a stand and created this with your answers.

Ingo: But this would have never come about without the assistance of many other people.

T. J. Streicher: You can say the same thing about how we come into this world. We really don't do anything alone, do we?

Ingo: Very little, I think. So, now you can ask your questions.

T. J. Streicher: What was the name of this planet that you remote viewed?

Ingo: We think it was Jupiter.

T. J. Streicher: What made you think it was Jupiter?

Ingo: Because that is where we intended to go. It gets a bit technical. Jupiter is a rather large planet, which you can see sometimes, but not all the time. So you have to find out where it is in relationship to the sun, and then you have to find out where Earth is in relationship to the sun. I forget where Jupiter was back then, but you look back to Earth and you see the sun and then you say, all right, Jupiter is on the other side of the sun, so you have to get past the sun to get to it. It's like in back of it, and then you wait until you can see it.

T. J. Streicher: Do you have any idea of how large it could be?

Ingo: It's big. I don't really know because I am not an astrophysicist, but it was big, possibly twenty times bigger than Earth.

T. J. Streicher: Did you experience any seasons on the planet?

Ingo: No, because Jupiter has big winds blowing around, so I don't think so.

T. J. Streicher: What did the sky look like?

Ingo: The sky was a brownish color and very beautiful. It's not black out there, and you could see other planets and stars. "Magnificent" would be an understatement.

T. J. Streicher: Any type of vegetation?

Ingo: No.

T. J. Streicher: Landscapes?

Ingo: Yes, mountains.

T. J. Streicher: Water?

Ingo: No.

T. J. Streicher: Resources?

Ingo: No.

T. J. Streicher: What about the crystal formations?

Ingo: Crystals of all kinds, that could be considered resources, but I did not think of it that way. Some of the crystals were as big as icebergs and they were floating in some kind of liquid that was not water.

T. J. Streicher: Do you recall the color of that liquid?

Ingo: Sort of clearish.

T. J. Streicher: Any noises or lights?

Ingo: Oh! Storms, wind, and a tornado, where I was.

T. J. Streicher: But no lights. Was there daylight?

Ingo: Remember, we are not using our eyeballs up there; we are using a spectrum of sensitivity that is bigger than our eyeballs can tell us, and we are utilizing an expanded spectrum of sensitivity. As a species we are sometimes limited to what we see with our eyes.

T. J. Streicher: Yes. Sometimes this can just blind us to what might be there because of all the conditioning going on in our lives, or what we are supposed to see.

Ingo: I don't. To me, it's like going beyond the veil, which can be scary for some people. I don't mind that analogy. I painted a big painting once that had a big veil covering it, and I think I threw it away too.

T. J. Streicher: And all the way through your books, the difficulties you encountered would have prevented others from proceeding, where as you persisted. It seems as though there were something that you needed to find out.

Ingo: Yes, I did; basically if I could succeed well at the experiment.

T. J. Streicher: And you also moved forward. Would you consider yourself a risk taker?

Ingo: Sometimes, yes.

T. J. Streicher: You realize the real advantage, too, of taking a risk?

Ingo: A considerate risk, yes, but I am not stupid about it.

T. J. Streicher: You have taken considerable risk and expanded your consciousness, while hoping others might do the same when feeling stuck in a particular way of thinking.

Ingo: Yes, I agree with that.

T. J. Streicher: I am a believer that we create our own reality.

Ingo: How about if I could be like myself, my real self? Everything comes down to oneself anyway, and you can't deal with yourself by comparing yourself to some other role model, because then that's a quirk.

T. J. Streicher: So are you implying that we are all unique?

Ingo: No, I am implying that we are what we are; each self is what each self is. The problem is that people cannot find their self because they are so busy making comparisons with other selves that they read about.

T. J. Streicher: Thank you for sharing that, because that helps me understand why you might take those risks and maybe find out more of your true self. How do you feel now about the Jupiter experiment?

Ingo: Oh, it was terrific back then, but there haven't been that many people paying any attention, and it was just forgotten about. It took about nine years for those two Pioneer spacecrafts to pass Jupiter, so I said, why don't we try to get there first and then compare what we find with what they find? But it took nine years for them to find what they found. The results that they found are all certified scientific documents.

T. J. Streicher: How do you think this experiment affected you?

Ingo: Not very much. When you get too far outside of other people's reality boxes, they don't even know what you are talking about, and they are probably not interested either.

T. J. Streicher: How interested were you in the Pioneer probe report, nine years later?

Ingo: Well, I thought what they found should be archived. But it did take them nine years to find the ring, for instance, which was one of the first things I had noted. But I was busy going off and doing other things. At first I wasn't paid that much, but a little later I got paid well. I was one of the few people who were actually paid for their psychic abilities. I usually worked under contract as a consultant, and I was my own manager.

T. J. Streicher: Do you feel there was any change in you?

Ingo: Not much, because comparative data were not available until nine years later. When it started coming in, there was almost a ten-year gap in getting any feedback at all.

T. J. Streicher: Can you describe what you were thinking and feeling at the time of your probing?

Ingo: Well, afterward I found out that notices were sent out to fifty scientists or so that this was going to take place. I didn't have that in mind at all at the time. There was nothing I could do about it, so the night before I went out with a friend and got terribly drunk. The next morning they came and I had to do it, with a considerable hangover. But I did it, and I was glad it was over with. Then I went home and went to bed.

T. J. Streicher: When you are remote viewing, are you sensing and feeling anything—like, were you awestruck when you saw the gigantic icebergs?

Ingo: No, not that way, you have to stay on task or something like that, but I try to stay open to other things also.

T. J. Streicher: What do you think was the most meaningful part of this?

Ingo: Well, for ten years we didn't know it had any meaning.

T. J. Streicher: But to you personally?

Ingo: I am an artist; it's like being lost in a painting. So when it was over with, then it was over with. The painting you are now looking at is called *Cosmic Intelligence,* and I like looking at it, even though it is my own work.

T. J. Streicher: I think you liked the Jupiter experiment too.

Ingo: Yes, but I did it with a huge hangover; I couldn't back out. So I found myself between a rock and a hard place. The only way through it was to do it, and I did it and that's all I can say about it. I didn't have any high-minded, spiritual, or la-di-da type of things attached to it. I just did it and there it is.

T. J. Streicher: Most of your findings were verified, so there is something in this that went beyond your normal consciousness.

Ingo: Yes, yes, okay.

T. J. Streicher: You even did it with a hangover; you didn't seem egocentric about it. Do you think this could have any bearing on connections with humanity?

Ingo: I don't know.

T. J. Streicher: Well, other human beings sent physical probes out there, and the media certainly got involved.

Ingo: It was "a scientifically observed paranormal experiment."

T. J. Streicher: I am thinking that, through this experiment, it has helped pull humanity together, and also helped people in extending themselves.

Ingo: I agree with that.

PART 3

▼

WHERE
THE EVIDENCE
LEADS US

13

FINDINGS

Signposts of Changing Consciousness

There are trillions upon trillions of ancient galaxies consisting of a trillion trillion trillion trillion aged solar systems that are likely ringed with planets—many probably quite like our own.

RHAWN JOSEPH, PH.D.

The initial finding of this study acknowledges the participants' sincerity, compassion, and willingness to share their thoughts, feelings, and experiences. The author was received in a courteous, respectful, and friendly manner by all the participants. All had a genuine interest in assisting with this study. They were all articulate and seemed to answer all questions candidly. (The findings discussed in this chapter refer to the six interviewees, not including Ingo Swann. Some of the material presented in the following tables was taken from follow-up interviews not included in this text.)

Another finding is that the quest for spiritual values and higher consciousness appeared evident in all the participants. This finding is similar to the reports of extra-planetary experiences summarized in the literature review in chapter 4, in which all eight reporters mentioned the spiritual significance of their experiences. Experiencer Klarer, for example, referred to "the light we are all made out of. . . . All of creation is light."[1] The participants in this study all appear to share such spiritual qualities as the willingness to work through their fear and not accept consensus reality as a predisposed truth. This corresponds also with Mack's postulation, quoted earlier, that "Perhaps these individuals . . . have a different consciousness, are more fearless—or willing to be out of control and move through their terror."[2]

Another important finding was that none of the participants reported their experience on another planet, moon, or star as an alien abduction. The alien abduction experience (AAE) is a different type of phenomenon, one that was reviewed in chapter 2. The AAE describes a person being taken by force or being kidnapped by extraterrestrial beings, whereas none of the participants in this study reported this type of activity as a part of their journeys to another planet, moon, or star. For example, Gary stated: "Later, one of my space visitors—one of my friends—took me there physically . . . aboard a ship, which picked me up here and flew me there." This finding also is consistent with the literature review of eight reports of experiences on other planets, in which none of the experiencers indicated that they were taken by force to another planet, but rather they were invited to visit.

The fourth finding is that there are many similarities between near-death experiences (NDEs), mentioned in chapter 3, and the experiences of people who have reported visits to other planets, moons, or stars. Like the NDE, these reported experiences have occurred throughout history and in most cultures. Most NDE experiences are eventually regarded as positive events, after the experiencer gradually adjusts to a paradigm shift. NDE researchers Ring (1980, 1984, 1992, 1999) and Moody (1975, 1977) found that NDE experiencers often reported a greater appreciation for life, a renewed sense of purpose, a greater confidence and flexibility in coping with personal status and material possessions, a greater compassion for others, a heightened sense of spiritual purpose, and a reduced fear of death. The findings in this study of people who reported experiences on other planets, stars, or moons are very similar. This is also in agreement with the statements seen in the literature review. For example, Vorilhon reported less fear of death: "Death should not be an occasion for sad meetings but on the contrary a joyful celebration, for it is the moment when the beloved one perhaps reaches the paradise of the eternals with the Elohim our creators."[3]

Another important finding is that all participants noted that they had been criticized for their beliefs in UFOs and ETs, but they also agreed that they tended not to be interested in what others thought about them. Most of the participants observed that they were quite discerning about whom they talked to concerning this topic, for fear of being criticized. In general, such a choice is especially likely when what is being reported is anomalous or outside consensus reality. This finding is consistent with the literature review reports of experiences on other planets, where all eight experiencers were criticized as hoaxers, liars, or spinners of imaginary stories. Nonetheless, the experiences appear to have had meaning for the experiencers.

The sixth finding was that none of the participants reported abuse of drugs or medications. Although there was some self-reported use of alcohol and medications, all participants insisted that they were not abusing such substances at the time of their experience. This finding is consistent with the literature, for none of the eight reports of people who visited other planets ever mentioned any problems with or usage of drugs or medications.

Perhaps the most interesting finding in this study was that of the common characteristics and similarities of the participants. Thematic analysis of the interviews revealed that twenty-five common themes were presented by the six participants. Several other themes were shared by the participants, though less commonly.

COMMON THEMES

The following are the twenty-five themes that all six participants shared in common.

1. All participants were capable of articulating a deep, rich, and meaningful narrative concerning their experience on other planets, moons, or stars, and the transformational effects evoked from that experience.

2. All participants reported that their experiences on other planets, moons, or stars were mostly positive and gave brief descriptions of what their experience was like, shown in table 1 below.

TABLE I. POSITIVE REPORTS

PARTICIPANT	DESCRIPTION
Richard	"I felt euphoric. I felt I couldn't believe it."
Marilynn	"Ecstatic. It is very similar to the experiences that the mystics might describe as ecstasy or samadhi in Hinduism. . . . It's the unconditional love that you feel, and the power, and it's almost a sense like I am home."
Edgar	"There is the epiphany in coming home. . . . I still don't have an answer from a cosmological sense as to what causes humans to have a peak experience. In ancient Sanskrit it is called a *samadhi* experience, and in the Buddhist tradition it is called a *satori*. . . . I only know it shifts your perspective."
Gary	"There was a sense of awe just from the reality of being there. . . . So it was a marvelous experience; I mean, it was just glorious."
Norma	"When communicating with these Beings . . . I have had only positive experiences . . . when I applied their guidance and some of the concepts they introduced to me, I began to find that they worked, and my life got better and better."
Alex	"[I was] living in a civilization that does not judge but only supports you, that cares for you, everybody working together for the betterment of the one. Coming here [to planet Earth] was a very big disappointment."

3. All participants indicated that they believe other intelligent life forms exist in our universe and that they are presently visiting the Earth. For example, Edgar stated: "Oh, I have no doubt about it. The fact is that we have been visited, and the whole UFO phenomenon—we have been visited."

4. All participants experienced seeing or being inside a spacecraft.

5. All participants indicated that they had seen landscapes, and each

described what the ground looked like at the place he or she visited. Therefore Richard said: "It was reddish brown dirt, and I was on top of a very high mesa, and I could see another mesa on the horizon. It seemed to me that it was sunset and the sky had purple with red and all that, and the temperature felt very moderate."

6. All participants reported a new attitude about themselves and the world they live in, caused by the experiences they had on other planets or moons. For example, Norma noted that she had come to be "grateful every day, by allowing and learning, by being a student, and by being open to receiving more ideas. I choose. I evaluate whether the new experiences are for me or not. If I like them, then I say, thank you. If I don't, there is no judgment. Everything that I have learned in twenty years from my experiences and communications with them has made my world better."

7. All participants described a change in consciousness. For instance, Edgar said: "To me raising consciousness means shifting the ethical structure of our thought, to be more concerned for the greater good, for the whole. And to accept our individual role in doing that."

8. All participants noted their desire to be of service to help humanity understand our connection with the cosmos. For instance, Marilynn stated: "Sometimes I say that God assigned me to be a reporter in other realms. My spirit began to travel through what I call 'star tunnels' but which are very similar to what science terms black holes. But when you mystically travel through these 'gateways' you enter into the sphere that I term the 'galactic heavens.' It is another dimensional reality of the universe, and within it is heaven. It encompasses everything we have that is knowledge-based here on Earth with everything that the galactic heavens contain in terms of knowledge."

9. All participants reported utilizing extrasensory perception (ESP), such as telepathy, during their experience.

10. All participants indicated that their gut feelings evoked intuitive information. Thus Norma said: "Having experienced these situations, I came to understand and realize that very deeply in my soul there are higher places to live, and in some ways it makes me yearn

to be in a community where everyone respects one another."

11. All participants reported that their experiences had given them an enhanced connection with humanity. For example, Norma stated: "I think it has made me lighter, made me appreciate life forms and the interconnectedness of all people and Beings. Therefore I would say that I believe it has made me a more loving person. It's made me a person who is now able to love and appreciate all because of their grace and everything that they command. If I took a piece of it here, I would have to be kinder, more compassionate, more loving to other people. because that's the way they are."

12. All participants reported that their concern with the material things of life changed as a result of this experience.

13. All participants noted that their experiences on other planets or moons had been meaningful experiences. For instance, Marilynn observed: "You feel that you are surrounded by God, in a sense. It's not that these beings are God; it's just that you are in such a higher place. . . . The unconditional love is palpable. . . . It's a beauty and power; it's energy they fill you with. They always have a mission for you, going in steps. There is something that they want you to do. You are always excited to see them again."

14. All participants noted that they are concerned about the welfare of planet Earth and humanity as a result of their experiences. For example, Edgar stated: "It is disturbing that the population continues unabated and refuses to sincerely adapt a consciousness that embraces renewable resources as a solution. Sustainability remains as a major thrust and focus of my thinking at this point."

15. All participants reported that their ability to help others had changed as a result of their experiences. Thus Marilynn said: "I now work more in a service capacity. For many years, I worked for the Catholic Church, so we did a lot with the homeless, the sick, and all sorts of things. But my energies are now on my family and the work of the Out-of-Body Travel Foundation, aimed at reducing spiritual hunger, but also working to restore that which has been lost—within our spirits."

16. All the participants reported that they had messages to share

concerning humankind. All voiced their concerns regarding the fragility of our planet Earth and everything that occupies it. They showed sensitivity and interest in sharing a sense of alarm concerning Earth changes, social unrest, and the possibility of nuclear war in the future. Table 2, below, includes brief statements concerning what the participants would like others to understand.

TABLE 2. MESSAGES FOR HUMANKIND

PARTICIPANT	MESSAGE
Richard	"Eventually the sun is going to get bigger, and the Earth is eventually going to be vaporized, so we need to be working toward a way to go somewhere else."
Marilynn	"[The extraterrestrials are] trying to very quietly lead us in our subconscious minds . . . to higher places and higher thinking. But it can be one or the other—total destruction or an age of peace—it could be that extreme."
Edgar	"It is not acceptable that we humans are warlike and are threatening our own species and our very own existence on this planet by multiplying the way we are. We are not on a sustainable path."
Gary	"It's going to get worse before it gets better, but when it does get better then they are going to need people like me to help the rest of the folks cope and adjust and move into something that might approach a golden age."
Norma	"Let's . . . get on with this. Let's now move into these higher worlds with these other Beings and start enjoying another way of life."
Alex	"I have a goal . . . to be an example of unconditional love on this planet and hold the energies for those around me. . . . [That] means accepting everyone for who they are and where they are in their development. That's it, it has nothing to do with kissing and love is a misused word— unconditional love is just accepting everybody."

17. All participants reported that they have no fear of death. For example, Richard said: "No, I have no fear of death. I think that since

that experience there has been less fear—I just don't fear death. I take it as just traveling through another dimension."

18. All participants reported having esoteric beliefs, in addition to beliefs in UFOs and ETs. See table 3 for a listing.

TABLE 3. ESOTERIC BELIEFS

PARTICIPANT	BELIEF
Richard	Reincarnation
Marilynn	Reincarnation, out-of-body travel, near-death experiences
Edgar	Quantum physics, especially the quantum hologram
Gary	Reincarnation
Norma	Reincarnation, out-of-body travel
Alex	Reincarnation

19. All participants reported possessing allegedly paranormal skills including telepathy. For example, Richard mentioned his use of telepathy in communicating with extraterrestrials. He also reported utilizing the kabbalah, tarot readings, and biblical interpretations in his job as a minister. See table 4 for a listing.

TABLE 4. PARANORMAL SKILLS

PARTICIPANT	SKILL
Richard	Telepathy, kabbalah, tarot readings
Marilynn	Telepathy, precognition, out-of-body travel
Edgar	Telepathy, black body radiation
Gary	Telepathy, remote viewing, precognition, esoteric psychology
Norma	Telepathy, precognition, telekinesis, remote viewing, channeling
Alex	Telepathy, remote viewing

20. All participants reported significant life changes as a result of their experience on another planet or moon. Table 7, found in the section "Important Life Changes" below, describes the changes that the participants were willing to report.

21. All participants acknowledged a desire to return to their other planet or moon.

22. All participants communicated with some other entity, human or nonhuman, during their travels. For instance, Richard said: "As I was there, I noticed this alien being that I seemingly had a relationship with since I was a child, with him visiting me at different points."

23. All participants observed that they had been criticized or subjected to derogatory remarks or behavior directed toward them for their belief in UFOs and ETs. Edgar stated: "I was never directly criticized, but I am sure that people disagree with me concerning this issue."

    Richard reported: "I had a bad experience about six or seven years ago, when . . . they were filming . . . a documentary . . . on abduction and that sort of thing. But what ended up happening . . . [was that] they were making fun of people like me, suggesting that we were a bunch of nut cases, and that there were few people who actually had seen this."

    Gary noted: "This goes back to the reincarnation take, too. Sometimes those steps take many, many lives, and they simply have to live them out till they reach a point where they are able to wake up their mind and begin to understand these larger issues."

    Norma stated: "I no longer enjoy talking with people who, I perceive, are at such a low level of awareness or consciousness. That doesn't excite me anymore. I will no longer play these games, and I don't even go there anymore. I just walk away. It drains me too much to be at that level."

    Alex reported: "My own mother had a hard time with it, but my whole family and neighborhood saw ships all the time. . . . What really astounds me is no one ever talked about it. . . . How can you see something that's just so different and not talk about it?"

24. All participants have strongly responded to people who thought their experience was a fantasy, an illusion, or the result of mental illness. See table 5.

TABLE 5.
PARTICIPANT RESPONSES TO OTHER'S DISBELIEF

PARTICIPANT	RESPONSE
Richard	"This has given me more empathy and compassion when talking to people who have had unusual experiences of one kind or another. This is also why I am guarded and don't put it out there that I am doing this."
Marilynn	"I usually tell them that it is perfectly reasonable for them to think that [someone who had this kind of experience was crazy], because if I hadn't had these experiences myself, I would probably think the same thing. . . . If you have had it, then you are in kind of a quandary, because the power of the experiences is so much that you cannot deny them, but you also know that, if you told some people, they would think you were insane. . . . There have been people who have written books about near-death experiences that were very popular and did not include their reincarnation experience, for fear of not being understood."
Edgar	"That type of response is nonsense."
Gary	"Well, that's all right. I don't get upset about that; they are not ready to learn these things, and there is nothing I could say to make them ready to learn them. They have to go on their own trip."
Norma	"I don't care, because I know my experiences are real. I have had these experiences for twenty years. I am beyond the debate of whether it is real or not, and personally, I don't want to have conversations with people anymore who are still trying to decide whether or not UFOs are even real. We are so far beyond that. That wastes my time."
Alex	"I usually make a joke out of it and make a light comment like, 'You could be from another planet too.' . . . The thing is, I don't go around telling everybody that information."

25. All participants reported their experiences on other planets, moons, or stars to be genuine and undeniable spiritual experiences. At the same time the participants were clear that they did not consider their experiences to be religious, as they did not correspond to the dogma of institutionalized religious groups. The spiritual core of their experiences seemed so overwhelming that the participants agreed they would never forget what had happened, and that it had changed their lives forever. For instance, Gary said: "This has been a very enlightening experience; it has opened doors into the entire universe [for me] that I did not know existed before. I believe the purpose in life for human beings is to move toward enlightenment, to become more and more aware, to know a larger and larger universe, and this is why we are here, to do this."

LESS COMMON THEMES

In addition to these common themes occurring with all of the six participants, several other themes emerged as common to a few participants.

1. Most of the participants reported contact with extraterrestrial beings. For example, Gary explained: "I have been involved with visitors from space for many, many years. Part of that involvement is they are educating me, so I am able to ask a lot of questions of them. I started asking questions about whether or not our own government here on Earth had any kind of secret space station on the planet Mars; at that point they told me yes, and that is when I started investigating this."

2. Most participants reported a belief in reincarnation.

3. Most participants continue to have experiences with extraterrestrials. Thus Norma reported: "Not too many people can channel and receive messages from higher intelligences who claim they are from another part of the universe. My skill is a teachable skill. My abilities to channel must be originating in an area

of my mind or brain that humans, in general, have not fully developed yet."

4. All of the participants in this study were able to supply detailed descriptions of the planet, star, or moon they reported visiting. Most recalled the name of the planet they had visited, while one, Richard, reported never being told what the name of the planet was (see table 6, below).

TABLE 6. NAMES OF PLANETS, MOONS, OR STARS ALLEGEDLY VISITED

PARTICIPANT	NAME
Richard	"I was never told."
Marilynn	Alpha Centauri
Edgar	Earth's moon
Gary	Mars
Norma	Alpha Centauri
Alex	Arcturus

5. Half of the participants reported dreaming of another planet before actually going there.

6. Half of the participants reported that they believed they had an extraterrestrial ancestry.

7. Half of the participants reported prophetic visions. For example, Alex stated: "My Guardian showed me: that the Earth is heading for what looks like swirling gray energy around the black hole. He tells me that Earth is going to hit this swirling gray mass of energy and she is going to flip, and when she flips she will begin her transformation. He said there are many Beings here to help. He showed me oceans of lava—mountain tops blowing off with lava flying through the air. He also showed me many ships coming to take people off."

IMPORTANT LIFE CHANGES

I began my research with the question, "Do people who report having experiences on other planets, moons, or stars describe important life changes as a result?" Indeed, what may well be the most striking finding in relation to this study is that the participants' reports of life changes are fascinating, thought-provoking, and often remarkable.

Just as the cosmos may be seeded with life, the extra-planetary experience is like a seed waiting to sprout. As an initial experience, it may seem very beautiful and complete within itself. But the nature of a seed is to grow. As it grows, you can see the manifestations of each stage as the plant develops, such as the gowth of stems and leaves and ultimately fruit or blossoms.

One of the tasks of this book is to describe some greater life changes associated with the extra-planetary experience that becomes visible in some respect for all who care to see. The sprout is in the seed. Let's take a look at the beauty that is ultimately revealed by observing the seed experience of an extra-planetary experiencer and the subsequent important life changes they produce.

Typical reactions to the experience include enhanced spiritual insight, an expanded sense of cosmic awareness, less fear of death, and an increased motivation to be of service to humanity. Also reported is the apparent expansion of psychic and intuitive abilities such as telepathy, precognition, clairvoyance, and an extended connection with all of creation. All of these features can be powerful catalysts for change.

As we observe the life changes that occur at the core of the extra-planetary experience, we primarily find enhanced spiritual insight due to an expanded sense of cosmic awareness. Not surprising, for these people claim to have experienced a phenomenal event of visiting another planet, moon, or star. The spiritual core of the extra-planetary experience is so remarkable and overwhelming that the experiencer is literally catapulted into another world of thinking and being. It may take years or even a lifetime before the experiencer is able, or not, to grasp the full meaning of what has happened to him or her. These spiritual experiences often have an emphasis on the expansion of consciousness. Many of my participants describe openings and connections to what may be considered the "other world," and they describe the entities they find there as the Beings of Light, Source Energy, Home, the Divine, or God.

These connections to the other world and other worldly beings often provoke the experiencer to a new paradigm about death and what those experiences can teach us about death. Somehow they teach us not to fear death. In fact, one of the most consistent findings to emerge from the extra-planetary experience research is just that—the experiencers claim that they do not fear death.

Another important life change is the increased motivation to be of service to humanity. This feature was typical of the people I interviewed. Most people felt compelled to be of service to their fellow human beings. I looked at this life change as a humble action that may have been learned through the process of integrating their experience.

Significant changes that the participants chose to report are listed in table 7. In addition, many more examples came up during the interviews. These other important life changes included a quest for personal meaning, an appreciation for life, a decreased fear of death, a concern and desire to help others, the personal realization of a higher spiritual reality, a new view of death, planetary visions and dreams, a commitment to changing humanity's relationship with the Earth, a wish to become more open and express love more often, and the intent to become less interested in what others think of them along with transcending their aggressive impulses.

TABLE 7. MOST IMPORTANT LIFE CHANGES

PARTICIPANT	RESPONSE
Richard	"Well, the main change that took place was that I did not fear [my experiences] anymore."
Marilynn	"My mystical experiences led me to study all religion and to become Catholic. . . . The extraterrestrial experience is a religious experience—unfortunately probably very hard for a person who may not have experienced it to place in this context. God is behind it all."

TABLE 7. MOST IMPORTANT LIFE CHANGES (continued)

PARTICIPANT	RESPONSE
Edgar	"'Wow, I am seeing things in a different way, and then trying to put that together into a story as to what it is.' I still don't have an answer. . . . I appreciate the complexities of the universe."
Gary	"I have a lot less anger inside of me than I used to have. I have less interest in some of the more traditional things in our world. . . . I have no patience with war at all. . . . It has been my conclusion after these experiences that almost all the people on our planet are living in fear and superstition."
Norma	"I now understand the value of [life]. I cherished the knowledge, as I brought the ideas back into my everyday life. I now consciously try to have a better life around me (with more grace). I value wisdom, Light, and things like that, that feed my soul."
Alex	"My goal has always been to be the best person I possibly can be. I have a different definition of what that is now and have the courage to live my Truth. The goal is to become an unconditional loving Being who can accept everyone for who they are, where they are, what they are doing. To do this we need to step out of the programs given us and follow our authentic truthful selves."

This finding is consistent with the effects of various exceptional human experiences described in chapter 3 and in the reports of experiencers' travels to other planets given in the literature review in chapter 4. For example, Angelucci concluded that his experience conflicted with the belief of those around him that "man here on his tiny planet is cut off from contact with those other worlds and fully content to vision himself grandiosely as the highest intelligence in the universe."[4] Angelucci thought differently and was humbled by his experience on another planet. Similarly, Marilynn stated: "It just affected everything. It changed the entire path my life was taking. . . . When I was in my early twenties I was in the news business. I was a radio news anchor and reporter. . . . But it felt like I was being called in a completely different direction. Sometimes I say that God assigned me to be a reporter in other realms."

Edgar said: "The changes are the result of the big picture effect. You see things differently, and of course there is the epiphany in coming home. . . . I appreciate now—from our modern Hubble telescope data—that the universe is much larger, much grander, and much more complex than we ever thought it was in the past. We are still ignorant. We think we are a pretty smart species, but I usually say we are just barely out of the trees."

Norma said: "I began to understand my unity with all life and all energy, including the universe and the cosmos. One of the things that started to develop rapidly within me was my experiencing no fear. . . . Little by little, by connecting with them over and over again, I began to feel a self-confidence growing within me, and I no longer saw the world anymore as something to fear. I began to see the interconnectedness of everything, and I began to realize the power I had to shape my own destiny."

▼

During the nearly ten years that I have studied the extra-planetary experience phenomenon, my work has grown and taken root in a much broader and deeper field of interest. At first the phenomenon just seemed like a strange or extraordinary type of event that happened to a select few individuals. But over the years many more people have come forward with their stories and resulting life changes, which made me question my own antiquity and place in the cosmos.

As extra-planetary experience research expands and more people get involved, it's important that the details of the resulting life changes are documented for our study and learning. My plan is to stay available and involved with this phenomenon in order to accomplish just that. My hopes are that you, the reader, have received a greater understanding of the opportunities for enlightenment and learning these extra-planetary travels have brought forth in the lives of the study participants.

14

COMPARISON WITH ALTERNATIVE EXPLANATIONS OF ALIEN EXPERIENCES

Although none of the participants in this study presented their extraplanetary experiences as alien abduction experiences, the alternative explanations for AAEs presented in chapter 2 offer a useful set of criteria with which to compare the interviewees' experiences.

1. **Fantasy proneness.** Fantasy-prone individuals, who often have difficulty distinguishing between fantasy and reality, can spend half or more of their day fantasizing. Spanos et al. (1993) found that the UFO/ET experiencers they studied did not score as more fantasy prone or suggestible than control groups.[1] However, this does not mean that none of the participants in this study were fantasy prone, as they were not tested for fantasy proneness. The main concern of the study was the possibility of the participants reporting important life changes as a result of their experiences on another planet, moon, or star. It is not impossible that some of them could have imagined the whole event; what is certain

is that all of them seemed sincere and clear about what they had experienced.

2. **Escape from self.** While McLeod et al. (1996) disagreed with the proposition that reports of abduction represented the reporters' attempts to psychologically "escape from self,"[2] it remains possible that certain UFO/ET experiencers were creating memories motivated by their desire to escape from self-awareness. Perhaps some of the participants in this study could similarly have suffered from trauma-related illnesses that would lead to such attempts.

3. **Sleep anomalies.** Sleep anomalies such as paralysis, nightmares, sudden awakenings, and dreams of aliens could be grounds for the reporting of UFO/ET experiences. While Spanos et al. (1993) found no direct link between sleep anomalies and UFO/ET experiencers,[3] their findings do not indicate complete absence of sleep anomalies in the current study. For example, Richard reported the occasional use of sleeping pills. This could indicate a potential sleep disorder, in the absence of a more comprehensive report of this activity.

4. **Hypnosis.** Hypnosis can play a major role in producing alien abduction experiences in people with dissociative identity disorders.[4] In this study, there were no reports of dissociative identity disorder, but some participants reported seeking and utilizing professionals such as hypnotherapists to help them cope with purported UFO/ET experiences. For example, Alex mentioned using a hypnotherapist several times, adding that "the information that he is retrieving has nothing to do with what I already know."

5. **Psychopathology.** Reported contact with aliens can be evidence of psychopathology, but all the participants in this study seemed to be highly functioning adults, involved in lives with various occupations and maintaining meaningful interpersonal relationships. All participants seemed intelligent, emotionally available, and articulate about their spirituality. All seemed capable of coping with their reality at a functional Global Severity Index (GSI)

level and all had GSI scores within the normal range.* This finding is consistent with the literature review regarding psychopathology and UFO/ET experiencers. Spanos et al. (1993) found no support for "psychopathology theory,"[5] and Rodegheir (1994) reported that psychological testing of UFO/ET experiencers did not indicate that their profiles were pathological.[6]

6. **Hoaxes.** It is possible that reports of alien contact could be deliberate attempts to deceive for monetary or psychosocial rewards. But these rewards do not characterize the life stories of the majority of experiencers who prefer anonymity, like the people in this study. All the participants of this study have been coping with their experiences for the majority of their lives. All the participants of this study continue to process the effects of their experiences throughout their process of disclosure. This process can be supported and encouraged by counseling professionals. This finding is similar to the results found in the literature review concerning hoaxes. For example, Zimmer (1985), who tested the cultural rejection hypothesis that UFO believers are socially marginal and cultural outsiders expressing their alienation by adopting deviant beliefs, found no support for this theory.[7]

7. **Temporal lobe involvement.** This study did not test for temporal lobe involvement, although this might have been a factor with some of the participants.

8. **Traumatic birth experience effects.** In this study, none of the participants mentioned problems connected with traumatic birth experience. This issue never came up during the ninety-minute interview sessions. A more detailed and comprehensive report would be needed to assess this type of anomaly.

9. **Attention-seeking behavior.** None of the participants appeared to be seeking attention, special status, or financial gain from reporting their experiences. They were generally ordinary people who seemed

---

*The GSI includes nine dimensions measuring somatization, obsessions/compulsions, interpersonal sensitivity, depression, anxiety, hostility, phobic anxiety, paranoid ideation, and psychoticism. Each measure reflects a somewhat different aspect of psychological distress.

to have had an extraordinary experience. Most of the participants in this study initially preferred to remain anonymous although several agreed to let their real names be used for this book. For example, when Richard was asked if he talked to people about his experiences, he stated: "No, not at all." This finding is similar to reports in the literature review regarding experiencers and attention-seeking behavior, such as Westrum's (1977) statement that only 13 percent of UFO/ET experiencers actually reported their experience.[8]

10. **Low intelligence effect.** This study found that all the participants were intelligent adults. Three of them reported obtaining doctorate degrees; one reported obtaining a master's degree; one reported a bachelor of science degree; and one reported having completed one year of college. These findings are consistent with the literature challenging the possibility that UFO/ET experiencers are not well educated. Spanos et al. (1993) concluded that their sample of forty-nine UFO experiencers was neither more nor less intelligent than a community comparison group or a student comparison group.[9]

11. **False memories.** Many scientists would be willing to declare that AAEs are false memories based on other experiences. For example, Loftus and Bernstein (2005) stated: "The alien abduction and satanic ritual abuse cases seem to parallel a process that has been studied under the rubric of what might be called memory planting."[10] In this study, however, there were no reports of alien abduction or satanic ritual abuse. The participants in this study who developed relationships with purported extraterrestrial beings did not claim abuse by these beings. It remains possible, nonetheless, that some of these participants could have "planted memories" that caused them to fall sway to suggestions by hypnotherapists or other influential people.

CONCLUSION

Throughout history and in all cultures there have been reports of people seeing strange objects in the sky. Others have commented that, if there actually were UFOs, they would see them too. But is this a fair statement? One aspect that needs to be considered in this respect is what is known as *inattentional blindness,* a term that means the "failure to notice and remember perceptible stimuli in the visual background while the focus of attention is elsewhere."[1] The fact that humans can be blind to unexplained phenomena has been demonstrated in research studies. For example, lifeguards are so conditioned to observe people struggling on the surface of the water that they sometimes do not see people lying unconscious on the bottom of the pool. It is possible that our brains may not be capable of handling something not understood or outside of our consensus reality.

There have always been people who have seen things that others have not. Early records of the first encounters of the original natives of the Americas with foreigners note that many of them did not know what they were seeing when they first observed the huge European warships approaching their landmass.[2] Some of these gigantic European ships, such as the Spanish galleons, weighed four hundred tons, were equipped with forty cannons, were three stories in height, and carried up to twelve horses, which were also alien to the natives and evoked considerable fear and panic.[3] For many natives, the huge ships may have been viewed as an unimaginable sight, so unimaginable that they might have appeared as a moving mountain, a sea serpent, or maybe nothing comprehensible at all, as these peoples were familiar only with dugout canoes at the time. In addition, people have the tendency to try to explain their experiences from their own personal worldviews. Gene Stuart (1981) has described an early report of Cortez's fleet approaching the coast of Mexico.

> The crippled man was a common man and loyal, who came from the Forest of the afterworld near the Gulf Coast. There he had seen a miracle so inexplicable he walked all the way to the highlands and on to the city in spite of the fact he had no toes. He told Moctezuma he had watched "a mountain range or small mountain floating in the midst of the water, and moving here and there without touching the shore. My lord, we have never seen the like of this, although we guard the coast and are always on watch."[4]

Another example could be the sighting of the United States space shuttle. How many people in remote parts of the world would actually know what they were seeing if they viewed this spacecraft in the sky for the first time?

A Native American elder woman recently described to this author a UFO experience that resembled an "island coming down." She was very articulate about what she had seen and meant it quite literally. It would be hard to know how a clinically oriented Western psychotherapist might regard this description. Although it might sound absurd from the conventional point of view, this author felt honored that she was willing to share her experience.

For most people in the Western world, UFOs and extraterrestrials do not exist except in the minds of the presumably deluded. Members of this skeptical population prefer to think that these types of accounts are believed only by uneducated, young, foolish, and gullible people who may also believe in Bigfoot and the Loch Ness monster.

People who report experiences on other planets provide a rare, complex, and usually insufficiently articulated narrative. The problem of articulation may result from the ways these experiences diverge from Western culture's dominant worldview. Another reason may be the propensity for the mental health practitioner to pathologize this type of experience, perhaps due to the unfamiliarity of these phenomena: people make judgments by means of their own worldview, and most psychiatrists and psychologists are no exception. A misdiagnosis can lead to potential harm for the experiencer, and the resulting depression or anxiety may be considered iatrogenic in nature (that is, induced inadvertently by a physician or surgeon or by medical treatment or diagnostic procedures).

Despite the general skepticism, those who believe in and devote time and money to the study of UFOs and extraterrestrials choose to call these phenomena "matters of literal fact." The intention here is not to try to resolve these issues. Choosing to be a believer, a doubter, or an agnostic is an individual matter.

While such experiences do not fit into Westerners' consensus reality or the dominant Newtonian/Cartesian worldview, many accounts about them appear to be compelling if not convincing. It is, therefore, important that researchers continue to explore the possibility of the existence and visitation of extraterrestrial intelligent life. The current focus, on the other hand, is on what these people are experiencing and particularly the impact of the experiences on the person's life. Is this some type of delusional phenomenon, or might these reports reflect veridical evidence? The evidence may be termed impressive but not necessarily persuasive. In any case, nobody can persuade all the doubters.

There is considerable speculation concerning intelligent extraterrestrial life and experiences on other planets, moons, and stars. It is important to remember that many scientific "facts" in the past, such as the Earth being the center of the universe, have later been proved to be false. Some hundreds of years ago, most scientists thought that this galaxy constituted the entire universe. We know now that it is one of more than 400 billion galaxies in the universe, and that the number may still be growing.[5] As Fred Guterl, of *Newsweek International,* puts it, "The question now is how many of those 100 billion potential Earths can we reasonably expect to have harbored H_2O and served as a cradle of life, intelligent or not?"[6] One may recall the words of former president John F. Kennedy: "Space achievement . . . in many ways may hold the key to our future on Earth" (May 8, 1961), as having meaning for us all.

This book has presented a historical perspective concerning extra-terrestrial reports in the literature, along with a qualitative research study of seven people who have reported experiences on another planet, moon, or star. Most of the participants claimed they experienced contact with extraterrestrial intelligent life.

Many of the participants revealed their love for humanity and their appreciation for spirituality, such as realizing we are not just human beings having a spiritual experience but spiritual beings having a human experience. Could we be moving into a time when we will know that the physical life is only a part of the whole life, and maybe not even the most important part? Is it possible that individuals who report experiences on other planets, moons, or stars may be a catalyst for human evolution? While the scientific community remains skeptical, many people are absolutely certain these experiences are real.

Just as the history of science is a history of scientific revolutions, the history of human beings will be a history of human revolutions, where we will no longer accept limitations on who we are. Our view of ourselves and our place in the cosmos will also change. Instead of experiencing ourselves as alone and disconnected in a lifeless cosmos, we may come to realize that not only is there abundant life in the cosmos, but that our consciousness can exist beyond the brain. We may also realize that when our bodies die our consciousness may continue in some form. With new realizations of consciousness, soul, spirit, and new meaning to our lives, we may be reminded that we are a significant part of everything. We become a participant in the full spectrum of being human. The next revolution has already begun.

PARTICIPANT QUESTIONNAIRE

In this appendix I've reproduced the standard questionnaire I used in my studies, shown below.

▼

Have you had an experience of visiting another planet? Will you share your experience with me confidentially as a part of a research study?

I am conducting a doctoral research study of experiences one may have had during travels to another planet and possible changes caused from these experiences. I am interested in learning about your experiences. I have particular interest in how those experiences may have changed your life. If you have had such experiences and are interested, please fill out the attached information questionnaire and consent forms. This questionnaire may require approximately 15 to 30 minutes to complete.

THOMAS J. STREICHER, STUDENT RESEARCHER
SAYBROOK GRADUATE AND RESEARCH CENTER
SAN FRANCISCO, CALIFORNIA

Name: _____

(Your real name will not be used in this study; you will be given a
code name to assure your anonymity.)

Age: _____   ❏ Male   ❏ Female

Occupation: _____

Race/Ethnicity: ❏ African-American   ❏ Latino/Hispanic

❏ White, non Latino/Hispanic   ❏ Asian (Specify): _____

Other: _____

Education: ❏ High School   ❏ College   ❏ Graduate School
             ❏ Doctorate

Religion (if any): _____

Spiritual Orientation: ❏ None   ❏ Belief in something greater than
                                       oneself

Phone Number: _____

E-mail: _____

Address: _____

_____

1. What are your earliest memories of experiences on another planet?

❏ Profound   ❏ Unfavorable   ❏ Indifferent

Other: _____

2. Did you ever dream of going to another planet before actually
   going to another planet?

❏ Yes   ❏ No   ❏ Indifferent

Other: _____

3. How did you travel to another planet?

❑ Spacecraft   ❑ Astral Projection   ❑ Meditation   ❑ Dream

Other: _____

4. What did you see on this other planet? Please check all that apply.

❑ Landscapes   ❑ Other Beings   ❑ Buildings   ❑ Vehicles

Other: _____

5. Would you like to go back to this planet?

❑ Yes   ❑ No   ❑ Indifferent

Other: _____

6. Was your experience   ❑ Positive   ❑ Negative

7. Do you ever feel like your gut feelings are trying to tell you something?

❑ Yes   ❑ No   ❑ Indifferent

8. What, if any, changes occurred from this experience? How would you describe your change?

_____

_____

9. Would you consider this to be a religious/spiritual experience?

❑ Yes   ❑ No   ❑ Indifferent

10. What do you know about the paranormal?

_____

_____

_____

11. Do you feel you possess paranormal skills such as:

❏ Telepathy ❏ Precognition ❏ Telekinesis ❏ Remote Viewing

Other: _____

12. Did you communicate with others during your travels?

_____

_____

_____

_____

13. Is there anything else you would like to add or comment about?

_____

_____

_____

_____

Thank you for completing this questionnaire. Your information is much appreciated and will be a valuable part of this research.

▼

SYNOPSIS OF PSYCHOPATHOLOGY TEST RESULTS

This appendix summarizes the major features of the SCL-90-R or the Symptom Checklist-90-R developed by Leonard R. Derogatis, Ph.D. (1994). This self-report measure of psychopathology was designed to reflect psychological symptom patterns of psychiatric and medical patients. The scores of the nine primary symptom dimensions and three global indices were derived from the SCL-90-R results of the interviewees (except for Ingo Swann). The nine primary symptom dimensions and three global indices are explained below.

THE PRIMARY SYMPTOM DIMENSIONS

1. **Somatization (SOM).** *Essence:* The somatization dimension reflects distress arising from perceptions of bodily dysfunction. Complaints focus on cardiovascular, gastrointestinal, respiratory, and other systems with strong autonomic mediation. Pain and discomfort of the gross musculature and additional somatic equivalents of anxiety are also components of somatization.

2. **Obsessive-Compulsive (O-C).** *Essence:* The obsessive-compulsive dimension includes symptoms that are often identified with the

standard clinical syndrome of the same name. This measure focuses on thoughts, impulses, and actions that are experienced as unremitting and irresistible and that are of an unwanted nature. Behavior and experiences of a more general cognitive performance deficit are also included in this measure.

3. **Interpersonal Sensitivity (I-S).** *Essence:* The interpersonal sensitivity dimension focuses on feelings of inadequacy and inferiority, particularly in comparison with other people. Self-deprecation, self-doubt, and marked discomfort during interpersonal interactions are characteristic manifestations of this syndrome. In addition, individuals with high scores on I-S report acute self-consciousness and negative expectations concerning interpersonal behavior and others' perceptions of them.

4. **Depression (DEP).** *Essence:* The symptoms of the depression dimension reflect a representative range of the manifestations of clinical depression. Symptoms of dysphoric mood and affect are represented as are signs of withdrawal of life interest, lack of motivation, and loss of vital energy. In addition, feelings of hopelessness, thoughts of suicide, and other cognitive and somatic correlates of depression are included.

5. **Anxiety (ANX).** *Essence:* General signs of anxiety such as nervousness, tension, and trembling are included in the definition as are panic attacks and feelings of terror, apprehension, and dread. Some somatic correlates of anxiety are also included as dimensional components.

6. **Hostility (HOS).** *Essence:* The hostility dimension reflects thoughts, feelings, or actions that are characteristic of the negative affect state of anger. The selection of items includes all three modes of expression and reflects qualities such as aggression, irritability, rage, and resentment.

7. **Phobic Anxiety (PHOB).** *Essence:* Phobic anxiety is defined as a persistent fear response—to a specific person, place, object, or situation—that is irrational, disproportionate to the stimulus, and leads to avoidance or escape behavior. The items of this dimension focus on the more pathognomonic and disruptive manifestations

of phobic behavior. Phobic anxiety is very similar in definition to "agoraphobia," which is also called "phobic-anxiety-depersonalization syndrome."

8. **Paranoid Ideation (PAR).** *Essence:* The paranoid ideation dimension represents paranoid behavior fundamentally as a disordered mode of thinking. The cardinal characteristics of projective thought, hostility, suspiciousness, grandiosity, centrality, fear of loss of autonomy, and delusions are viewed as primary reflections of this disorder. Item selection was oriented toward representing this conceptualization.

9. **Psychoticism (PSY).** *Essence:* The psychoticism dimension was designed to represent the construct as a continuous range of human experience. Items indicative of a withdrawn, isolated, schizoid lifestyle were included as were first-rank symptoms of schizophrenia such as hallucinations and thought control. The psychoticism dimension provides for a graduated continuum from mild interpersonal alienation to dramatic psychosis. In this respect, the present definition owes much to the work of Eysenck and Eysenck (1968).

THE THREE GLOBAL INDICES

There are three global indices of distress associated with the SCL-90-R. The function of each of these global measures is to communicate in a single score the level of the individual's distress. Each measure reflects a somewhat different aspect of psychological distress.[1] When used configurally, these indices provide data that are very helpful in accurately assessing the clinical picture.

1. **The Global Severity Index (GSI).** *Essence:* The global severity index is the best single indicator of the current level or depth of a disorder. It combines information concerning the number of symptoms reported with the *intensity* of perceived distress. The GSI should be used in most instances where a single summary measure is called for.

2. **The Positive Symptom Distress Index (PSDI).** *Essence:* The posi-

tive symptom distress index functions as a measure of response style by indicating whether the respondent was augmenting or attenuating symptomatic distress. That is, the PSDI reflects the *average level* of distress reported for the symptoms that were endorsed. As such, it can be interpreted as a measure of symptom intensity.

3. **The Positive Symptom Total (PST).** *Essence:* The positive symptom total is simply a reflection of the *number of symptoms* endorsed by the respondent, regardless of the level of distress reported. It can be interpreted as a measure of symptom breadth.

RESULTS OF THE SCL-90-R FROM THE SIX INTERVIEWEES

The Global Severity Index (GSI) was utilized because it is the best single indicator of the current level or depth of a disorder. A score of 63 or higher is considered a possible risk or case.[2] The six interviewees (Ingo Swann was not included) discussed in this book scored in the normal range and all had scores lower than 63.

GLOSSARY

Note to Reader: I've included these terms because they are specialized, and I want you to identify with the exact meaning I've provided rather than the lay understanding you may already attach to them. To reach out to such a wide audience is a daunting task—there is always the matter of interpretation as well as disagreements about the exact definition of words. Because of this, I have utilized the *APA Dictionary of Psychology* in an attempt to provide the clearest and most uniform understanding of the terms I use in this book.

Assimilation: According to the *American Psychological Association Dictionary of Psychology,* "In Jean Piaget's theory of cognitive development, the process of incorporating information into already existing cognitive structures without modifying those structures."[1]

Alien Abduction: According to Dr. John Edward Mack, the alien abduction phenomenon can be defined as—but not limited to—the alleged experience of being taken by humanoid or nonhuman beings, in most cases against one's will, into some type of enclosure where a variety of procedures and communications occur.[2] Researchers such as Hopkins et al. (1992) have commented that the experience may also be associated with waking up with a feeling of being paralyzed, with a sense of a strange figure or figures present, and also with unaccounted-for periods of time.

Clairvoyance: The "acquisition of information about a place, event, or object without sensory mediation. Unlike telepathy, clairvoyance does not depend upon direct contact with another person."[3]

Consciousness: According to the *American Psychological Association Dictionary of Psychology,* "The phenomena that humans report experiencing, including mental contents ranging from sensory and somatic perception to mental images, reportable ideas, inner speech, intentions to act, recalled memories, semantics, dreams, hallucinations, emotional feelings, 'fringe' feelings (e.g., a sense of knowing), and aspects of cognitive and motor control. Operationally, these contents of consciousness are generally assessed by the ability to report an event accurately."[4]

Extra-Planetary Experience (XPE): A reported experience by individuals claiming that they have visited another planet, star, or moon. The experience may have taken place while the experiencer claimed to have been in the physical body or while separated from the body as in an out-of-body experience. Typical reactions to the experience include an expanded sense of cosmic awareness, less fear of death, increased motivation to be of service to humanity, and enhanced spiritual insight. I invented the term Extra-Planetary Experience (XPE) to help define and further explore this extraordinary phenomenon.

Extrasensory Perception (ESP): The purported ability to receive information by non-sensory means, commonly referred to as telepathy, precognition, remote viewing, or clairvoyance. "The criterion for judging whether an experience probably involves ESP is simple. It must be one that brings information new to the person and that brings it without sensory mediation."[5]

Extraterrestrial: Originating, existing, or occurring outside the Earth or its atmosphere.

Extraterrestrial Contactee: A person who claims to be or to have been in contact with extraterrestrial beings.

Fantasy-Proneness: The ability to create imaginative narratives, often with an inability to distinguish truth from fiction. "Such persons often have difficulty in distinguishing between fantasy and reality, and tend to keep their fantasy worlds as closely guarded secrets."[6]

Inattentional Blindness: According to the *American Psychological Association Dictionary of Psychology,* "Failure to notice and remember otherwise perceptible stimuli in the visual background while the focus of attention is elsewhere. Research into inattentional blindness has led some to conclude that there is no conscious perception of the world without attention."[7]

Intuition: According to the *American Psychological Association Dictionary of Psychology,* "Immediate insight or perception as contrasted with conscious reasoning or reflection. Intuitions have been characterized alternatively as quasi-mystical experiences or as the products of instinct, feeling, minimal sense impressions, or unconscious forces."[8]

Out-of-Body Experience: According to the *American Psychological Association Dictionary of Psychology,* "A dissociative experience in which the individual imagines that his or her mind, soul, or spirit has left the body and is acting or perceiving independently. Such experiences are often reported by those who have recovered from the point of death . . . they have also been reported by those using hallucinogens or under hypnosis. Certain occult or spiritualistic practices may also attempt to induce such experiences."[9]

Remote Viewing: According to C. Swanson, in *The Synchronized Universe: New Science of the Paranormal,* "The ability to see and sense things at a distance or at other times through paranormal means. In the present context, it often involves specific procedures and protocols to assist in the process."[10]

Resonance: Resonance is a key to effective witnessing. Merely listening to the experiencer is not enough. Also referred to as *sympathetic resonance,* in which the experiencer's emotions must resonate as true to the listener. The listener makes note of the presence of appropriate emotions that ring true to the situation, and the response of their own empathy is vital. When resonance occurs the experiencer has truly been heard, and the sincerity resonates between experiencer and listener as with two tuning forks.

Scientific Revolutions: A term used by many scientists such as Joseph (2001, p. 7), Swanson (2003, p. 3), and Kuhn (1970) to explain that present scientific theories may be incomplete or outmoded and that mounting new contradictory evidence has accumulated to the point of tipping the scales toward new paradigms. This term also suggests that the history of science is a series of scientific revolutions.

Semistructured Interview: Sometimes referred to as "patterned interview." It "is a type of interview, often used in personnel selection, that is designed to cover certain specific areas (e.g., work history, education, home situation, etc.) but at the same time give the interviewer the chance to steer the dialogue into side channels and ask questions on points that need to be clarified" (VandenBos 2007, p. 678).

Spirituality: According to the *American Psychological Association Dictionary of Psychology,* "A concern for or sensitivity to the things of the spirit or soul, especially as opposed to material things."[11]

Telepathy: The purported process by which information is conveyed from one individual to another by means other than the known senses. Telepathic communication is presumed to be direct communication from one mind to the other without the intervention of any known physical form of energy transmission.[12]

Teleportation: According to C. Swanson, in *The Synchronized Universe: New Science of the Paranormal:* "The act of transporting objects or beings from one place to another, without the object seeming to exist in intermediate locations. Walls and structures are no obstacle to this process, which occurs almost instantaneously. The object often seems to fade out or instantly appear somewhere else."[13]

Worldview: A psychological organizing system that comprises a mental structure of assumptions about the way things are, or must be, and functions as if it were the very foundation of the psyche.[14] The *American Psychological Association Dictionary of Psychology* notes that it is from the German word *Weltanschauung,* meaning "any fundamental understanding of the universe, and of humankind's place within it, held by a person, a culture, or a subculture."[15]

Notes

INTRODUCTION

1. Osman, *Space History.*
2. Mitchell, "Exploring Contact with the Cosmos."
3. Lewels, *The God Hypothesis,* 7.
4. Harpur, *The Philosopher's Secret Fire,* 100.
5. Time/CNN, "Poll: U.S. Hiding Knowledge of Aliens."
6. Dolan, *UFOs and the National Security State,* 17.
7. Friedman, *Top Secret/Majic,* 1.
8. Lewels, *The God Hypothesis.*
9. Kuhn, *The Structure of Scientific Revolutions,* 10.
10. Arp, "What Has Science Come To?" 450.
11. Radin, "The Enduring Enigma of the UFO," 27.
12. Jung, *Flying Saucers,* 146–47.
13. Bair, *Jung,* 568.
14. Jung, *Flying Saucers,* 146–47.
15. Angeluccis, *The Secret of the Saucers.*
16. Jung, *Flying Saucers.*
17. Ibid., 134.
18. Personal communication, J. E. Mack, May 16, 2004.
19. Mack, *Abduction,* 11.
20. Ibid., 45.
21. Mack, "Why Worldviews Matter."

CHAPTER I. ANCIENT TRADITIONS AND MODERN SCIENCE

1. Cremo, *Human Devolution,* 384.

2. Kramer, *History Begins at Sumer,* 31.

3. Roux, *Ancient Iraq,* 85.

4. Horn, *Humanity's Extraterrestrial Origins.*

5. Prabhupada, *Bhagavad-Gita,* 19–20.

6. Ibid., 57.

7. Picknett and Prince, *The Stargate Conspiracy.*

8. Faulkner, *The Ancient Egyptian Pyramid Texts,* 886.

9. Tomas, *We Are Not the First,* 117.

10. Downing, *The Bible and Flying Saucers,* 180.

11. Krippner, "The Epistemology and Technologies of Shamanic States of Consciousness."

12. Wilber, *Up From Eden.*

13. Eliade, *Shamanism.*

14. Harpur, *The Philosopher's Secret Fire,* 245.

15. Sarangerel, *Chosen by the Spirits.*

16. Fox, *The Coming of the Cosmic Christ.*

17. Goodman, *Lakota Star Knowledge.*

18. Black Elk and Lyon, *Black Elk,* 32.

19. Clark and Coleman, *The Unidentified.*

20. Temple, *The Sirius Mystery.*

21. Benest and Duvent, "Is Sirius a Triple Star?"

22. Scranton, *The Science of the Dogon,* 193.

23. Hoyle and Wickramasinghe, *Astronomical Origins of Life.*

24. Joseph, Schild, and Wickramasinghe, *Life on Earth Came from Other Planets,* 506–7.

25. Joseph, *Astrobiology, the Origin of Life and Death of Darwinism,* 145.

26. Hoover, *Instruments, Methods, and Missions for Astrobiology,* xi.

27. Hoover, *Instruments, Methods, and Missions for Astrobiology,* 2nd edition.

28. Joseph, *Astrobiology,* 115.

CHAPTER 2. ALIEN ABDUCTION EXPERIENCES

1. Mack, *Abduction,* 398.

2. Mack, "The Alien Abduction Phenomenon," 11.

3. Hopkins, Jacobs, and Westrum, *Unusual Personal Experiences.*

4. Bloecher, Clamar, and Hopkins, "Summary Report on the Psychological Testing of Nine Individuals Reporting UFO Abduction Experiences," and Parnall and Sprinkle, "Personality Characteristics of Persons Who Claim UFO Experiences."

5. Mack, *Abduction*.

6. Wilson and Barber, "The Fantasy-Prone Personality."

7. Bartholomew, Basterfield, and Howard, "UFO Abductees and Contactees."

8. Ring and Rosing, "The Omega Project."

9. Spanos et al., "Close Encounters."

10. Wilson and Barber, "The Fantasy-Prone Personality."

11. Newman and Baumeister, "Toward an Explanation of the UFO Abduction Phenomenon," 123.

12. McLeod, Corbisier, and Mack, "A More Parsimonious Explanation for UFO Abduction," 156.

13. McLeod, Corbisier, and Mack, "A More Parsimonious Explanation for UFO Abduction."

14. Spanos et al., "Close Encounters."

15. Ganaway, "Historical Versus Narrative Truth."

16. Spanos et al., "Close Encounters."

17. Bloecher, Clamar, and Hopkins. "Summary Report on the Psychological Testing of Nine Individuals Reporting UFO Abduction Experiences"; Mack, *Abduction;* Parnell, "Measured Personality Characteristics of Persons Who Claim UFO Experiences"; Parnell and Sprinkle, "Personality Characteristics of Persons Who Claim UFO Experiences"; and Ring and Rosing, "The Omega Project."

18. Spanos et al., "Close Encounters."

19. Rodeghier, "Psychosocial Characteristics of Abductees."

20. Zimmer, "Belief in UFOs as Alternative Reality."

21. Spanos et al., "Close Encounters."

22. McLeod, Corbisier, and Mack. "A More Parsimonious Explanation for UFO Abduction"; and Newman and Baumeister, "Toward an Explanation of the UFO Abduction Phenomenon."

23. Lawson, "Perinatal Imagery in UFO Abduction Reports."

24. Mack, *Abduction;* Jacobs, *The Threat;* Vallee, *Dimensions;* and Hopkins, *Intruders*.

25. Westrum, "Social Intelligence about Anomalies."

26. Newman and Baumeister, "Toward an Explanation of the UFO Abduction Phenomenon," 104.

27. Spanos et al., "Close Encounters."

28. Zachary, *Shipley's Institute of Living Scale.*

29. Loftus and Bernstein, "Rich False Memories."

30. Loftus and Pickrell, "The Formation of False Memories."

31. Loftus, "Creating False Memories."

32. Van der Kolk, "The Compulsion to Repeat the Trauma."

33. McLeod, Carbisier, and Mack. "A More Parsimonious Explanation for UFO Abduction."

34. Mack, *Abduction,* 407.

35. Appelle, Lynn, and Newman, "Alien Abduction Experiences," 276; cited in Seppa, "Wisdom," 9.

CHAPTER 3. OTHER REALITY-EXPANDING EXPERIENCES

1. Moody and Perry, *Coming Back,* 11.

2. VandenBos, *The American Psychological Association Dictionary of Psychology.*

3. Ring, *The Omega Project.*

4. Ibid.

5. Mack, *Abduction,* 17.

6. Targ, *Limitless Mind,* 77.

7. Swann, *Penetration,* 19–23.

8. Targ and Puthoff, *Mind-Reach.*

9. Swann, *Penetration.*

10. Targ and Puthoff, *Mind-Reach,* 212.

11. Brown, *Cosmic Voyage,* 25.

12. White, "The Human Connection Project"; White, "Dissociation, Narrative, and Exceptional Human Experiences."

13. White, "Dissociation, Narrative, and Exceptional Human Experiences," 4.

14. Freud, *The Interpretation of Dreams;* Jung, *Man and His Symbols.*

15. Tart, *Open Mind, Discriminating Mind,* 200.

16. Jung, *Memories, Dreams, Reflections.*

17. Ibid., 323.

18. Krippner, Bogzaran, and Carvalho, *Extraordinary Dreams and How to Work with Them,* 5.

19. Mack, *Abduction; Passport to the Cosmos.*

20. Harpur, *The Philosopher's Secret Fire;* Larkins, *Talking to Extraterrestrials.*

21. Angelucci, *The Secret of the Saucers*; Adamski, *Inside the Space Ships*; Vorilhon, *Space Aliens Took Me to Their Planet*; and Larkins, *Talking to Extraterrestrials*.

CHAPTER 4. HISTORICAL REPORTS OF EXPERIENCES ON OTHER PLANETS

1. Angelucci, *The Secret of the Saucers*.
2. Ibid., 8–9.
3. Ibid., 13.
4. Ibid., 97.
5. Ibid., 115.
6. Jung, *Flying Saucers*, 112.
7. Adamski, *Flying Saucers Have Landed*.
8. Adamski, *Inside the Space Ships*.
9. Zinsstag and Good, *George Adamski*, 10.
10. Ibid., 1.
11. Ibid., 69.
12. Ibid., 147–58.
13. Klarer, *Beyond the Light Barrier*, 17.
14. Ibid., 26.
15. Ibid., 47.
16. Ibid., 52.
17. Ibid., 87
18. Ibid., 108.
19. Ibid., 157.
20. Ibid., 164.
21. Ibid., 191.
22. Vorilhon, *Space Aliens Took Me to Their Planet*, 20.
23. Ibid., 237–38.
24. Hubbard, *Visitors from Lanulos*, 17.
25. Ibid.
26. Ibid., 43
27. Ibid.
28. Desmarquet, *Abduction to the 9th Planet*, 1–2.
29. Ibid., 62.
30. Ibid.
31. Rampa, *My Visit to Venus*, 46–47.

32. Ibid., 51.

33. Brauen, *Dreamworld Tibet,* 93.

34. Ibid., 93.

35. Kinder, *Light Years.*

36. Moosbrugger, *And Yet . . . They Fly.*

37. Billy Meier, personal communication, September 24, 2003.

38. Deardorff, *Celestial Teachings.*

39. *Talmud of Jmmanuel,* 1:88, 28:59.

40. Korff, *The Billy Meier Story.*

41. Kinder, *Light Years.*

CHAPTER 5. LIFTING THE CURTAIN

1. Braud and Anderson, *Transpersonal Research Methods for the Social Sciences.*

2. Mertens, *Research Methods in Education and Psychology.*

3. Boyatzis, *Transforming Qualitative Information.*

CHAPTER 13. FINDINGS: SIGNPOSTS OF CHANGING CONSCIOUSNESS

1. Klarer, *Beyond the Light Barrier,* 191.

2. Mack, *Abduction,* 45.

3. Vorilhon, *Space Aliens Took Me to Their Planet,* 286.

4. Angelucci, *The Secret of the Saucers,* 115.

CHAPTER 14. COMPARISON WITH ALTERNATIVE EXPLANATIONS OF ALIEN EXPERIENCES

1. Spanos et al., "Close Encounters."

2. McLeod, Carbisier, and Mack. "A More Parsimonious Explanation for UFO Abduction."

3. Spanos et al., "Close Encounters."

4. Ganaway, "Historical Versus Narrative Truth."

5. Spanos et al., "Close Encounters."

6. Rodegheir, "Psychosocial Characteristics of Abductees," 296–303.

7. Zimmer, "Belief in UFOs as Alternative Reality."

8. Westrum, "Social Intelligence about Anomalies."

9. Spanos et al., "Close Encounters."

10. Loftus and Bernstein, "Rich False Memories," 102.

CONCLUSION

1. VandenBos, *The American Psychological Association Dictionary of Psychology.*
2. Stuart, *The Mighty Aztecs.*
3. Levy, *Conquistador.*
4. Stuart, *The Mighty Aztecs,* 152.
5. Krauss and Scherrer, "The End of Cosmology?"
6. Guterl, "What You Need to Know."

APPENDIX B. SYNOPSIS OF PSYCHOPATHOLOGY TEST RESULTS

1. Derogatis, Yevzeroff, and Wittelsberger, "Social Class, Psychological Disorders, and the Nature of the Psychopathologic Indicator."
2. Derogitis, *SCL-90-R Administration, Scoring, and Procedures Manual.*

GLOSSARY

1. VandenBos, *The American Psychological Association Dictionary of Psychology,* 76.
2. Mack, *Abduction; Passport to the Cosmos.*
3. Broughton, *Parapsychology,* 34.
4. VandenBos, *The American Psychological Association Dictionary of Psychology,* 218.
5. Rhine, *ESP in Life and Lab,* 39.
6. Bartholomew, Basterfield, and Howard. "UFO Abductees and Contactees," 217.
7. VandenBos, *The American Psychological Association Dictionary of Psychology,* 472.
8. Ibid., 499.
9. Ibid., 661.
10. Swanson, *The Synchronized Universe,* 15.
11. VandenBos, *The American Psychological Association Dictionary of Psychology,* 884.
12. Broughton, *Parapsychology.*
13. Swanson, *The Synchronized Universe,* 115.
14. Mack, *Passport to the Cosmos.*
15. VandenBos, *The American Psychological Association Dictionary of Psychology,* 996.

BIBLIOGRAPHY

Adamski, George. "Book Two." In *Flying Saucers Have Landed,* edited by D. Leslie and G. Adamski. New York: British Book Centre, 1953.

———. *Inside the Space Ships.* New York: Abelard-Schuman, 1955.

———. *My Trip to the Twelve Councilors' Meetings That Took Place on Saturn—March 27 & 30, 1962.* Vista, Calif.: Science of Life Booklet, New Age, 1962.

American Psychological Association. *Publication Manual of the American Psychological Association.* 5th ed. Washington, D.C.: American Psychological Association, 2002.

Anderson, R. "Intuitive Inquiry: Interpreting Objective and Subjective Data." *Revision: Journal of Consciousness and Transformation* 22, no. 4 (2002): 31–39.

Angelucci, Orfeo. *The Secret of the Saucers.* Amherst, Wis.: Amherst Press, 1955.

Appelle, S., S. J. Lynn, and L. Newman. "Alien Abduction Experiences." In *Varieties of Anomalous Experience: Examining the Scientific Evidence,* edited by E. Cardena, S. J. Lynn, and S. Krippner. Washington, D.C.: American Psychological Association, 2000.

Arp, H. "What Has Science Come To?" *Journal of Scientific Exploration* 14, no. 3 (2000): 447–54.

Bair, Deirdre. *Jung: A Biography.* New York: Little, Brown, 2003.

Bartholomew, R., K. Basterfield, and G. Howard. "UFO Abductees and Contactees: Psychopathology or Fantasy Proneness?" *Professional Psychotherapy: Research and Practice* 22 (1991): 215–22.

Becker, Carl. *Paranormal Experience and Survival of Death.* Albany: State University of New York Press, 1993.

Bem, D., and C. Honorton. "Does Psi Exist? Replicable Evidence for an

Anomalous Process of Information Transfer." *Psychological Bulletin* 115 (1994): 4–15.

Benest, D., and J. L. Duvent. "Is Sirius a Triple Star?" *Astronomy and Astrophysics* 299 (1995): 621–28.

Binder, Otto. *Flying Saucers Are Watching Us*. New York: Belmont, 1968.

Black Elk, Wallace, and William S. Lyon. *Black Elk: The Sacred Ways of a Lakota*. New York: Harper Collins, 1991.

Bloecher, T., A. Clamar, and B. Hopkins. "Summary Report on the Psychological Testing of Nine Individuals Reporting UFO Abduction Experiences." In *Final Report on the Psychological Testing of UFO "Abductees."* Mt. Rainier, Md.: Fund for UFO Research, 1985.

Boyatzis, Richard E. *Transforming Qualitative Information: Thematic Analysis and Code Development*. Thousand Oaks, Calif.: Sage, 1998.

Boylan, Richard J., and Lee K. Boylan. *Close Extraterrestrial Encounters*. Columbus, N.C.: Granite, 1993.

Braud, William, and Rosemarie Anderson. *Transpersonal Research Methods for the Social Sciences: Honoring Human Experience*. Thousand Oaks, Calif.: Sage, 1998.

Brauen, Martin. *Dreamworld Tibet: Western Illusions*. Trumbell, Conn.: Weatherhill, 2004. First published in 2000.

Brockway, Robert. *Young Carl Jung*. Wilmette, Ill.: Chiron, 1996.

Broughton, Richard S. *Parapsychology: The Controversial Science*. New York: Ballantine, 1991.

Brown, Courtney. *Cosmic Voyage: A Scientific Discovery of Extraterrestrials Visiting Earth*. New York: Penguin, 1996.

Campbell, Joseph. *The Hero with a Thousand Faces*. Princeton, N.J.: Princeton University Press, 1949.

Cardena, E., S. Lynn, and S. Krippner, eds. *Varieties of Anomalous Experience: Examining the Scientific Evidence*. Washington, D.C.: American Psychological Association, 2000.

Carlsberg, Kim. *Beyond My Wildest Dreams: Diary of a UFO Abductee/A True Story*. Santa Fe, N.M.: Bear and Company, 1995.

Clark, Jerome, and Loren Coleman. *The Unidentified: Notes toward Solving the UFO Mystery*. New York: Warner, 1975.

Cohane, John. *Paradox: The Case for the Extraterrestrial Origin of Man*. New York: Crown, 1977.

Collyns, Robin. *Did Spacemen Colonize the Earth?* Chicago, Ill.: Henry Regnery, 1976.

Crandall, Lee. *The Venusians*. Los Angeles: New Age, 1955.

Cremo, Michael A. *Human Devolution: A Vedic Alternative to Darwin's Theory.* Los Angeles: Bhaktivedanta, 2003.

Cremo, Michael A., and Richard L. Thompson. *The Hidden Story of the Human Race.* Badger, Calif.: Govardhan Hill, 1994.

Davies, Paul. *The 5th Miracle: The Search for the Origin and Meaning of Life.* New York: Orion, 1990.

———. "The Harmony of the Spheres." *Time* 147 (1996): 58–61.

De Mille, Richard. *The Don Juan Papers: Further Castañeda Controversies.* Lincoln, Nebr.: iUniverse, 2001.

Deardorff, James. *Celestial Teachings.* Tigard, Ore.: Wild Flower, 1990.

Denzin, N. K., and Y. S. Lincoln, eds. *Handbook of Qualitative Research.* Thousand Oaks, Calif.: Sage, 1994.

Denzler, Brenda. *The Lure of the Edge: Scientific Passions, Religious Beliefs, and the Pursuit of UFOs.* Berkeley: University of California Press, 2001.

Derogatis, Leonard. R. *SCL-90-R Administration, Scoring, and Procedures Manual.* 3rd ed. Minneapolis, Minn.: Pearson, 1994.

Derogatis, L. R., H. Yevzeroff, and B. Wittelsberger. "Social Class, Psychological Disorders, and the Nature of the Psychopathologic Indicator." *Journal of Consulting and Clinical Psychology* 43 (1975): 183–91.

Desmarquet, Michel. *Abduction to the 9th Planet.* Melbourne: Arafura, 1993.

Dolan, Richard. *UFOs and the National Security State.* Rochester, N.Y.: Keyhole, 2000.

Downing, Barry H. *The Bible and Flying Saucers.* New York: Marlowe, 1997.

Eliade, Mircea. *Shamanism: Archaic Techniques of Ecstasy.* Princeton, N.J.: Princeton University Press, 1964.

Faulkner, R. O. *The Ancient Egyptian Pyramid Texts.* Oxford, UK: Oxford University Press, 1969.

Ferris, T. "Seeking New Earths." *National Geographic,* December 2009, 91–93.

Fiore, Edith. *Encounters: A Psychologist Reveals Case Studies of Abduction by Extraterrestrials.* New York: Ballantine, 1989.

Flourney, Theodore. *From India to the Planet Mars.* Princeton, N.J.: Princeton University Press, 1994.

Fox, Matthew. *The Coming of the Cosmic Christ.* New York: Harper Collins, 1988.

Freud, Sigmund. *The Interpretation of Dreams.* Ware, Hertfordshire, UK: Wordsworth Editions, 1997. First published in 1900.

Friedman, Stanton. *Top Secret/Majic: Operation Majestic-12 and the United States Government's UFO Cover-up.* New York: Marlowe, 2005.

Ganaway, G. K. "Historical Versus Narrative Truth: Clarifying the Role of

Exogenous Trauma in the Etiology of MPD and Its Variants." *Dissociation* 2 (1989): 205–20.

Ghose, Aurobindo. *The Life Divine*. Pondicherry, India: Sri Aurobindo Ashram Press, 1949.

Gibbons, Gavin. *They Rode in Spaceships*. New York: Citadel, 1957.

Gladwell, Malcolm. *Blink: The Power of Thinking without Thinking*. New York: Little, Brown, 2005.

Godwin, Malcolm. *Angels: An Endangered Species*. New York: Simon and Schuster, 1990.

Good, Timothy. *Alien Contact: Top-Secret UFO Files Revealed*. New York: William Morrow, 1993.

Goodman, Ronald. *Lakota Star Knowledge: Studies in Lakota Stellar Theology*. Mission, S.D.: Sinte Gleska University Mission, 1992.

Grinspoon, L., and A. D. Persky. "Psychiatry and UFO Reports." In *UFOs: A Scientific Debate*, edited by C. Sagan and T. Page. Ithaca, N.Y.: Cornell University Press, 1972.

Grof, Stanislav. *The Holotropic Mind: The Three Levels of Human Consciousness and How They Shape Our Lives*. New York: Harper Collins, 1993.

Guterl, F. "What You Need to Know: Aliens Exist." *Newsweek*, August 24, 2009, 50–51.

Hall, R. "Escaping the Self or Escaping the Anomaly?" *Psychological Inquiry* 7 (1996): 143–48.

Harpur, Patrick. *Daimonic Reality: Understanding Otherworld Encounters*. New York: Random House, 1994.

———. *The Philosopher's Secret Fire: A History of the Imagination*. Chicago: Ivan R. Dee, 2002.

Hoagland, Richard C., and Mike Bara. *Dark Mission: The Secret History of the National Aeronautics and Space Administration*. Los Angeles: Feral House Books, 2007.

Hoover, R. B., ed. *Instruments, Methods, and Missions for Astrobiology*. Bellingham, Wash.: International Society for Optical Engineering, 1998.

———, ed. *Instruments, Methods, and Missions for Astrobiology*. 2nd ed. Bellingham, Wash.: International Society for Optical Engineering, 2000.

Hopkins, Budd. *Intruders: The Incredible Visitations at Copley Woods*. New York: Random House, 1987.

Hopkins, Budd, David M. Jacobs, and Ron Westrum. *Unusual Personal Experiences: An Analysis of the Data from Three National Surveys Conducted by the Roper Organization*. Las Vegas: Bigelow Holding, 1992.

Horn, Arthur D., and Lynette M. Horn. *Humanity's Extraterrestrial Origins:*

ET Influences on Humankind's Biological and Cultural Evolution. Lake Montezuma, Ariz.: A. and L. Horn, 1994.

Hoyle, Fred, and Wickramasinghe, Nalin C. *Astronomical Origins of Life: Steps Towards Panspermia.* Norwell, Mass.: Klewer Academic Publishers, 2000.

Hubbard, Harold. *Visitors from Lanulos.* New York: Vantage, 1971.

Huxley, Aldous. *The Perennial Philosophy.* London: Chatte and Windus, 1946.

Jacobs, David. "A Brief History of Abduction Research." *Journal of Scientific Exploration* 23, no. 1 (2009): 69–77.

———. *The Threat.* New York: Simon and Schuster, 1998.

James, William. *The Meaning of Truth.* New York: Prometheus Books, 1997. First published in 1911.

———. *The Principles of Psychology.* New York: H. Holt, 1929.

———. *Varieties of Religious Experience.* New York: Macmillan, 1997. First published in 1902.

Jones, E. "Misidentified Flying Objects? A Critique." *Journal of Near-death Studies* 12, no. 4 (1994): 267–72.

Joseph Rhawn. *Astrobiology, the Origin of Life, and the Death of Darwinism: Evolutionary Metamorphosis.* 2nd ed. San José: University Press of California, 2001.

Joseph, Rhawn, Rudolf Schild, and Chandra Wickramasinghe. *Life on Earth Came from Other Planets: The Origins & Evolution of Life.* Cambridge, Mass.: Cosmology Science Publishers, 2010.

Julien, Eric. *The Science of Extraterrestrials: UFOs Explained at Last.* Fort Oglethorpe, Ga.: Allies, 2006.

Jung, Carl J. *Flying Saucers: A Modern Myth of Things Seen in the Skies.* London: Routledge and Kegan Paul, 1959.

———. *Man and His Symbols.* Garden City, N.Y.: Doubleday, 1964.

———. *Memories, Dreams, Reflections.* London: Pantheon, 1965.

———. "On Synchronicity." In *The Portable Jung,* edited by J. Campbell. New York: Penguin, 1971.

———. "Psychological Types." In *The Portable Jung,* edited by J. Campbell. New York: Penguin, 1971.

———. "The Spiritual Problem of Modern Man." In *The Portable Jung,* edited by J. Campbell. New York: Penguin, 1971.

———. "The Transcendent Function." In *The Portable Jung,* edited by J. Campbell. New York: Penguin, 1971.

Kinder, Gary. *Light Years.* New York: Atlantic Monthly Press, 1987.

Kitei, Lynne D. *The Phoenix Lights.* Charlottesville, Va.: Hampton Roads, 2004.

Klarer, Elizabeth. *Beyond the Light Barrier.* Aylesbury, UK: Howard Timms, 1980.

Klimo, Jon. *Channeling: Investigations on Receiving Information from Paranormal Sources.* Los Angeles: Jeremy P. Tarcher, 1987.

Korff, Kal. *The Billy Meier Story: Spaceships of the Pleiades.* New York: Prometheus Books, 1995.

Kramer, Samuel N. *History Begins at Sumer.* Garden City, N.Y.: Doubleday, 1959.

Krauss, L., and R. Scherrer. "The End of Cosmology?" *Scientific American* (March 2008): 46–53.

Krippner, S. "The Epistemology and Technologies of Shamanic States of Consciousness." *Journal of Consciousness Studies* 7, no. 11 (2000): 93–118.

Krippner, Stanley, Fariba Bogzaran, and Andre P. de Carvalho. *Extraordinary Dreams and How to Work with Them.* Albany: State University of New York Press, 2002.

Kuhn, Thomas S. *The Structure of Scientific Revolutions.* Chicago: University of Chicago Press, 1970.

Kvale, Steinar. *Interviews: An Introduction to Qualitative Research Interviewing.* Thousand Oaks, Calif.: Sage, 1996.

Larkins, Lisette. *Talking to Extraterrestrials: Communicating with Enlightened Beings.* Charlottesville, Va.: Hampton Roads, 2002.

Lawson, A. "Perinatal Imagery in UFO Abduction Reports." *Journal of Psychohistory* 12 (1984): 211–39.

Levy, Buddy. *Conquistador: Hernan Cortes, King Montezuma, and the Last Stand of the Aztecs.* New York: Bantam, 2009.

Lewels, Joe. *The God Hypothesis: Extraterrestrial Life and Its Implications for Science and Religion.* Mill Spring, N.C.: Blue Water, 1997.

Loftus, E. F. "Creating False Memories." *Scientific American* 277, no. 3 (1997): 70–75.

Loftus, E. F., and D. M. Bernstein. "Rich False Memories: The Royal Road to Success." In *Experimental Cognitive Psychology and Its Applications,* edited by A. F. Healy. Washington, D.C.: American Psychological Association, 2005.

Loftus, E. F., and J. E. Pickrell. "The Formation of False Memories." *Psychiatric Annals* 25 (1995): 720–25.

Mack, John E. *Abduction: Human Encounters with Aliens.* New York: Charles Scribner's Sons, 1994.

———. "The Alien Abduction Phenomenon." *Noetic Sciences Review* 23 (1992).

———. *Passport to the Cosmos: Human Transformation and Alien Encounters.* New York: Crown, 1999.

————. "Why Worldviews Matter." In *Mind Before Matter: Visions of a New Science of Consciousness,* edited by T. Pfeifer and J. E. Mack. Winchester, U.K.: O Books, 2007.

Mandelker, Scott. *From Elsewhere: Being ET in America.* New York: Deli, 1995.

Maslow, A. H. *The Farther Reaches of Human Nature.* Middlesex, U.K.: Penguin, 1971.

————. *Religions, Values and Peak Experiences.* New York: Penguin, 1970.

————. *Toward a Psychology of Being.* New York: John Wiley and Sons, 1999.

Matlock, J. G. "Past Life Memory Case Studies." In *Advances in Parapsychological Research 6,* edited by S. Krippner. Jefferson, N.C.: McFarland, 1990.

McIvor, S. "UFO (Flying Saucer) Groups: A Look at British Membership." *Zetetic Scholar* 11–12 (August 1987): 39–57.

McLeod, C., B. Corbisier, and J. Mack. "A More Parsimonious Explanation for UFO Abduction." *Psychological Inquiry* 7, no. 2 (1996): 156–68.

McMoneagle, Joseph. *The Stargate Chronicles: Memoirs of a Psychic Spy.* Charlottesville, Va.: Hampton Roads, 2002.

Mertens, Donna. *Research Methods in Education and Psychology: Integrating Diversity with Quantitative and Qualitative Approaches.* Thousand Oaks, Calif.: Sage, 1998.

Merton, Thomas. *The Seven Storey Mountain.* New York: Harcourt, Brace, 1948.

Milanovich, Norma J., and Shirley D. McCune. *The Light Shall Set You Free.* Scottsdale, Ariz.: Athena, 1996.

Mitchell, E. "Exploring Contact with the Cosmos. A Native American/Western Science Conference and Dialogue on Extraordinary Experiences." Conference sponsored by PEER (Program for Extraordinary Experience Research), Cambridge and Newtonville, Mass., May 8–9, 1998.

Moody, Raymond. A. *Life after Life.* Covington, Ga.: Mockingbird, 1975.

————. *Reflections on Life after Life.* St. Simon's Island, Ga.: Mockingbird, 1977.

————. *Coming Back: A Psychiatrist Explores Past-life Journeys.* New York: Bantam, 1991.

————. *The Light Beyond.* New York: Bantam, 1988.

Moosbrugger, Guido. *And Yet . . . They Fly.* Tulsa, Okla.: Steelmark, 2001.

Morgan, R. F., ed. *The Iatrogenics Handbook: A Critical Look at Research and Practice in the Helping Professions.* San Francisco: Morgan Foundation, 1983.

Newman, L., and R. Baumeister. "Toward an Explanation of the UFO Abduction Phenomenon: Hypnotic Elaboration, Extraterrestrial Sadomasochism, and Spurious Memories." *Psychological Inquiry* 7, no. 2 (1996): 99–126.

Osman, Tony. *Space History.* New York: St. Martin's Press, 1983.

Parnall, J. "Measured Personality Characteristics of Persons Who Claim UFO Experiences." *Psychotherapy in Private Practice* 6 (1988): 159–65.

Parnell, J., and R. L. Sprinkle. "Personality Characteristics of Persons Who Claim UFO Experiences." *Journal of UFO Studies* 2 (1990): 45–58.

Picknett, Lynn, and Clive Prince. *The Stargate Conspiracy: The Truth about Extraterrestrial Life and Mysteries of Ancient Egypt.* New York: Berkeley, 1999.

Prabhupada, A. C. B., ed. and trans. *Bhagavad-Gita.* New York: Collier Books, 1972.

———, ed. and trans. *Srimad Bhagavatam.* New York: Bhaktivedanta Book Trust, 1972.

Pritchard, A., D. Pritchard, J. Mack, P. Kasey, and C. Yapp, eds. *Alien Discussions: Proceedings of the Abduction Study Conference Held at MIT.* Cambridge, Mass.: North Cambridge Press, 1994.

Pursglove, P. D., ed. *Zen in the Art of Close Encounters: Crazy Wisdom and UFOs.* Berkeley, Calif.: New Being Project, 1995.

Puthoff, H. "CIA-initiated Remote Viewing Program at Stanford Research Institute." *Journal of Scientific Exploration* 10 (1996): 63–76.

Quiros, C. "Exo-psychology Research: A Phenomenological Study of People Who Believe Themselves to Be Alien-human Hybrids." *Dissertation Abstracts International* 61, no. 9-B (2001): 4963.

Radin, Dean. *The Conscious Universe: The Scientific Truth of Psychic Phenomena.* New York: Harper Collins, 1997.

———. "The Enduring Enigma of the UFO." *Shift: At the Frontiers of Consciousness* (Winter 2008–2009): 22–27.

Rampa, Lobsang. *My Visit to Venus.* Clarksburg, W.Va.: Saucerian Books, 1966.

———. *The Third Eye: The Autobiography of a Tibetan Lama.* London: Martin Secker and Warburg, 1958.

Randles, Jenny. *Star Children: The True Story of Alien Offspring among Us.* New York: Sterling, 1995.

Raschke, C. "UFOs: Ultraterrestrial Agents of Cultural Deconstruction." *Archaeus: Cyberbiological Studies of the Imaginal Component in the UFO Contact Experience* 5 (1989): 21–32.

Rashid, I., E. A. Meier, J. H. Ziegler, and B. L. Greene, trans. *The Talmud of Jmmanuel.* Tigard, Ore.: Wild Flower, 1992.

Red Star, Nancy. *Legends of the Star Ancestors: Stories of Extraterrestrial Contact from Wisdomkeepers around the World.* Rochester, Vt.: Bear and Company, 2002.

Rhine, Louisa. E. *ESP in Life and Lab: Tracing Hidden Channels.* New York: Macmillan, 1967.

Rilke, Rainer M. *Letters to a Young Poet*. Novato, Calif.: New World Library, 2000. First published in 1929.

Ring, Kenneth. *Heading towards Omega: In Search of the Meaning of the Near-Death Experience*. New York: Morrow, 1984.

———. *Life at Death: A Scientific Investigation of the Near-Death Experience*. New York: Morrow, 1980.

———. *The Omega Project: Near-Death Experiences, UFO Encounters, and Mind at Large*. New York: Morrow, 1992.

Ring, K., and S. Cooper. *Mindsight: Near-Death and Out-of-Body Experiences in the Blind*. Palo Alto, Calif.: William James Center of Transpersonal Psychology, 1999.

Ring, K., and C. Rosing. "The Omega Project: A Psychological Survey of Persons Reporting Abductions and Other UFO Encounters." *Journal of UFO Studies* 2 (1990): 59–98.

Rodeghier, M. "Psychosocial Characteristics of Abductees." In *Alien Discussions: Proceedings of the Abduction Study Conference Held at MIT*, edited by Pritchard, A., D. E. Pritchard, J. E. Mack, P. Kasey, and C. Yapp. Cambridge, Mass.: North Cambridge Press, 1994.

Rodegheir, M., J. Goodpastor, and S. Blatterbauer. "Psychosocial Characteristics of Abductees: Results from the CUFOS Abduction Project." *Journal of UFO Studies* 3 (1991): 59–90.

Roux, Georges. *Ancient Iraq*. New York: Penguin, 1992.

Rubin, Herbert J., and Irene S. Rubin. *Qualitative Interviewing: The Art of Hearing Data*. Thousand Oaks, Calif.: Sage, 1995.

Sagan, Carl. *The Cosmic Connection: An Extraterrestrial Perspective*. New York: Doubleday, 1973.

Salla, Michael E. *Exopolitics: Political Implications of the Extraterrestrial Presence*. Temple, Ariz.: Dandelion Books, 2004.

Sarangerel. *Chosen by the Spirits: Following Your Shamanic Calling*. Rochester, Vt.: Destiny, 2001.

Scranton, Laird. *The Science of the Dogon: Decoding the African Mystery Tradition*. Rochester, Vt.: Inner Traditions, 2006.

Seppa, N. "Wisdom: A Quality That May Defy Age." *The APA Monitor* 28, no. 2 (1997): 1–9.

Shapiro, Robert. *Ultimate UFO Series: Andromeda*. Flagstaff, Ariz.: Light Technology, 2004.

Shermer, Michael. *Why People Believe Weird Things*. New York: W. H. Freeman, 1997.

Sitchin, Zecharia. *The Lost Book of Enki: Memoirs and Prophecies* of *an Extraterrestrial God*. Rochester, Vt.: Bear and Company, 2002.

———. *The Stairway to Heaven*. New York: Avon, 1980.

———. *The 12th Planet*. New York: Avon, 1976.

Sogyal Rinpoche. *The Tibetan Book of Living and Dying*. San Francisco: Harper Collins, 1992.

Spanos, N., P. Cross, K. Dickson, and S. Du Breuil. "Close Encounters: An Examination of UFO Experiences." *Journal of Personality and Social Psychotherapy* 102 (1993): 624–32.

Sprinkle, Leo. *Soul Samples: Personal Explorations in Reincarnation and UFO Experiences*. Columbus, N.C.: Granite, 1999.

Star Wisdom Conference. "Exploring Contact with the Cosmos. A Native American/Western Science Conference and Dialogue on Extraordinary Experiences." Conference sponsored by PEER (Program for Extraordinary Experience Research), Cambridge and Newtonville, Mass., May 8–9, 1998.

Stevenson, I. "Characteristics of Cases of the Reincarnation Type among the Igbo of Nigeria." *Journal of Asian and African Studies* 21 (1986): 204–16.

———. *Children Who Remember Previous Lives: A Question of Reincarnation*. Charlottesville: University Press of Virginia, 1987.

———. "The Evidence for Survival from Claimed Memories of Former Incarnations. Part 1. Review of the Data." *Journal of the American Society for Psychical Research* 54 (1960): 51–71.

———. *Twenty Cases Suggestive of Reincarnation*. 2nd ed. Charlottesville: University Press of Virginia, 1974.

———. *When Reincarnation and Biology Intersect*. Westport, Conn.: Greenwood-Praeger, 1997.

Stewart, R. *Creation Myth*. Longmead, UK: Element Books, 1989.

Stone-Carmen, J. "A Descriptive Study of People Reporting Abduction by Unidentified Flying Objects (UFOs)." In *Alien Discussions: Proceedings of the Abduction Study Conference Held at MIT*, edited by A. Pritchard, D. E. Pritchard, J. E. Mack, P. Kasey, and C. Yapp. Cambridge, Mass.: North Cambridge Press, 1994.

Stonely, Jack. *CETI: Communication with Extra-Terrestrial Intelligence*. New York: Warner Books, 1976.

Stuart, Gene S. *The Mighty Aztecs*. Washington, D.C.: National Geographic Society, 1981.

Swann, Ingo. *Everybody's Guide to Natural ESP: Unlocking the Extrasensory Power of Your Mind*. Los Angeles: Jeremy P. Tarcher, 1991.

———. *To Kiss Earth Good-Bye*. New York: Hawthorne Books, 1975.

———. *Penetration: The Question of Extraterrestrial and Human Telepathy*. Rapid City, S.D.: Ingo Swann Books, 1998.

Swanson, Claude. *The Synchronized Universe: New Science of the Paranormal*. Tucson, Ariz.: Poseidia, 2003.

Targ, Russell. *Limitless Mind: A Guide to Remote Viewing and Transformation of Consciousness*. Novato, Calif.: New World Library, 1996.

Targ, Russell, and Harold Puthoff. *Mind-Reach: Scientists Look at Psychic Ability*. New York: Delacorte/Eleanor Friede, 1977.

Tart, Charles. *Open Mind, Discriminating Mind: Reflections on Human Possibilities*. New York: Harper and Row, 1989.

———. *PSI: Scientific Studies of the Psychic Realm*. New York: Dutton, 1997.

———. "Psychics' Fears of Psychic Powers." *The Journal of the American Society for Psychical Research* 80 (1986): 279–92.

Tart, C. T., and C. M. Labore. "Attitude toward Strongly Functioning Psi: A Preliminary Survey." *The Journal of the American Society for Psychical Research* 80 (1986): 163–73.

Temple, Robert. *The Sirius Mystery*. Rochester, Vt.: Destiny, 1976.

Thompson, Richard. *Alien Identities: Ancient Insights into Modern UFO Phenomena*. San Diego, Calif.: Govardhan Hill, 1993.

———. *Angels and Aliens: UFOs and Mythic Imagination*. New York: Random House, 1991.

Time/CNN. "Poll: U.S. Hiding Knowledge of Aliens." CNN Interactive Poll Posted on the World Wide Web, June 15, 1997. www.cnn.com/us/9706/15/ufo.poll/index.html (accessed September 26, 1999).

Tomas, Andrew. *We Are Not the First*. New York: Bantam, 1973.

Vallee, Jacques. *UFOs in Space: Anatomy of a Phenomenon*. New York: Ballantine, 1990.

———. *Dimensions: A Casebook of Alien Contact*. New York: Contemporary, 1988.

———. *Forbidden Science: Journals 1970–1979*. Vol. 2. San Francisco: Documatica Research, 2008.

Van der Kolk, B. "The Compulsion to Repeat the Trauma: Re-Enactment, Revictimization, and Masochism." *Psychiatric Clinics of North America* 12, no. 2 (1989): 389–411.

VandenBos, G. R., ed. *The APA Dictionary of Psychology*. Washington, D.C.: American Psychological Association, 2007.

Von Ward, Paul. *Gods, Genes, and Consciousness: Nonhuman Intervention in Human History*. Charlottesville, Va.: Hampton Roads, 2004.

Vorilhon, Claude. *Space Aliens Took Me to Their Planet: The Most Important Revelation in the History of Mankind.* Waduz, Lichtenstein: Fondation pour l'accueil des Elohim, 1978.

Walsh, R., and F. Vaughan, eds. *Paths beyond Ego: The Transpersonal Vision.* Los Angeles: Jeremy F. Tarcher/Perigee, 1993.

Wambach, Helen. *Life before Life.* New York: Bantam, 1979.

Wendt, Herbert. *From Ape to Adam: The Search for the Evolution of Man.* New York: Random House, 1973.

Westrum, R. "Social Intelligence about Anomalies: The Case of UFOs." *Social Studies of Science* 7, no. 3 (1977): 271–302.

White, R. A. "Dissociation, Narrative, and Exceptional Human Experiences." In *Broken Images, Broken Selves: Dissociative Narratives in Clinical Practice,* edited by S. Krippner and S. M. Powers. Washington, D.C.: Brunner/Mazel, 2007.

———. "Exceptional Human Experiences and the Experiential Paradigm." *ReVision* 18 (1995): 18–25.

———. "The Human Connection Project: Educating through Planetary Consciousness." *Exceptional Human Experiences* 11, no. 1 (1993): 52–55.

Wilber, Ken. *Up from Eden: A Transpersonal View of Human Evolution.* Garden City, N.Y.: Doubleday, 1981.

Wilson, Clifford. *UFOs and Their Mission Impossible.* New York: Signet, 1974.

Wilson, S. C., and T. X. Barber. "The Fantasy-Prone Personality: Implications for Understanding Imagery, Hypnosis, and Parapsychological Phenomena." In *Imagery: Current Theory, Research, and Application,* edited by A. A. Sheikh. New York: Wiley, 1983.

Wolman, B., ed. *Handbook of Parapsychology.* New York: Van Nostrand Reinhold, 1977.

Wood, Ryan. S. *Majic Eyes Only: Earth's Encounters with Extraterrestrial Technology.* Broomfield, Calif.: Wood Enterprises, 2005.

Woolger, Roger. J. *Other Lives, Other Selves: A Jungian Psychotherapist Discovers Past Lives.* New York: Doubleday, 1987.

Yogananda, Paramahansa. *Autobiography of a Yogi.* Los Angeles: Self-Realization Fellowship, 1971.

Zachery, R. A. *Shipley's Institute of Living Scale.* Rev. ed. Los Angeles: Western Psychological Services, 1986.

Zimmer, T. "Belief in UFOs as Alternative Reality: Cultural Rejection or Disturbed Psyche?" *Deviant Behavior* 6, no. 4 (1985): 405–19.

Zinsstag, Lou, and Timothy Good. *George Adamski: The Untold Story.* Kent, UK: Ceti, 1983.

ABOUT THE AUTHOR

Thomas James Streicher, Ph.D. in psychology from Saybrook University, San Francisco, received his master's degree from the Institute of Transpersonal Psychology in Palo Alto, Calif., and his bachelor's in psychology from California State University, Sacramento. He is currently the founder and director of the nonprofit public benefit corporation Divine Spark, Inc. (2002). Divine Spark provides support and guidance for those in need, to activate the divine spark within each of them (www.divinespark.us).

Thomas is also involved with the Native Americans living on the Pine Ridge Indian Reservation in South Dakota, where he has delivered thousands of pounds of food and clothing as well as providing sewing machines, and has constructed two commercial-grade greenhouses. In support of this work, he created the Lakota Quilts website that features seven Lakota women and their original quilt work (www.lakotaquilts.com).

Since 1994, Thomas has been an active volunteer for substance abuse centers, drug recovery centers, Head Start preschool programs, AIDS foundation, spiritual guidance programs, and twelve-step programs, as well as giving community presentations to educate and raise consciousness. Thomas is a concerned human-rights activist dedicated to serving homeless and in-need people. For the intense drive he feels toward his volunteer work, Thomas credits his deep sense of spirituality, which is nondenominational and derives from the bond that he feels with his fellow creatures and connection with Nature.

Please visit his personal website at

www.thomasstreicher.com

Index

BOOKS OF RELATED INTEREST

The Secret History of Extraterrestrials
Advanced Technology and the Coming New Race
by Len Kasten

Inner Paths to Outer Space
Journeys to Alien Worlds through Psychedelics
and Other Spiritual Technologies
*by Rick Strassman, M.D., Slawek Wojtowicz, M.D.,
Luis Eduardo Luna, Ph.D., and Ede Frecska, M.D.*

Grey Aliens and the Harvesting of Souls
The Conspiracy to Genetically Tamper with Humanity
by Nigel Kerner

The Return of the Rebel Angels
The Urantia Mysteries and the Coming of the Light
by Timothy Wyllie

Science and the Near-Death Experience
How Consciousness Survives Death
by Chris Carter

Lost Knowledge of the Ancients
A Graham Hancock Reader
Edited by Glenn Kreisberg

Forbidden History
Prehistoric Technologies, Extraterrestrial Intervention,
and the Suppressed Origins of Civilization
Edited by J. Douglas Kenyon

Forbidden Science
From Ancient Technologies to Free Energy
Edited by J. Douglas Kenyon

INNER TRADITIONS • BEAR & COMPANY
P.O. Box 388
Rochester, VT 05767
1-800-246-8648
www.InnerTraditions.com

Or contact your local bookseller